EDUCATION IN THE BEST INT OF THE CHILD

A Children's Rights Perspective on Closing the Achievement Gap

A large body of research in disciplines from sociology and policy studies to neuroscience and educational psychology has confirmed that socioeconomic status remains the most powerful influence on children's educational outcomes. Socially disadvantaged children around the world suffer disproportionately from lower levels of educational achievement, which in turn leads to unfavourable long-term outcomes in employment and health. *Education in the Best Interests of the Child* addresses this persistent problem, which violates not only the principle of equal educational opportunity, but also the broader principle of the best interests of the child as called for in the U.N. Convention on the Rights of the Child.

Building on their previous book on children's rights, *Empowering Children*, Brian Howe and Katherine Covell identify types of reform that can significantly close the educational achievement gap. Their findings make an important argument for stronger and more comprehensive action to equalize educational opportunities for disadvantaged children.

R. BRIAN HOWE is a professor in the Department of Political Science and director of the Children's Rights Centre at Cape Breton University.

KATHERINE COVELL is a professor in the Department of Psychology and executive director of the Children's Rights Centre at Cape Breton University.

R. BRIAN HOWE AND
KATHERINE COVELL

Education in the Best Interests of the Child

A Children's Rights Perspective on Closing the Achievement Gap

UNIVERSITY OF TORONTO PRESS
Toronto Buffalo London

© University of Toronto Press 2013
Toronto Buffalo London
www.utppublishing.com
Printed in Canada

ISBN 978-1-4426-4658-2 (cloth)
ISBN 978-1-4426-1451-2 (paper)

Printed on acid-free, 100% post-consumer recycled paper with vegetable-based inks.

Library and Archives Canada Cataloguing in Publication

Howe, Robert Brian
Education in the best interests of the child: a children's rights perspective on closing the achievement gap / R. Brian Howe and Katherine Covell.

Includes bibliographical references and index.
ISBN 978-1-4426-4658-2 (bound).   ISBN 978-1-4426-1451-2 (pbk.)

1. Educational equalization   2. Academic achievement.   3. Educational change.   4. Children's rights.   5. Education.   I. Covell, Katherinell.
II. Title.

LC213.H69   2013 379.2'6   C2012-906888-8

University of Toronto Press acknowledges the financial assistance to its publishing program of the Canada Council for the Arts and the Ontario Arts Council.

 Canada Council   Conseil des Arts
for the Arts   du Canada

ONTARIO ARTS COUNCIL
CONSEIL DES ARTS DE L'ONTARIO
50 YEARS OF ONTARIO GOVERNMENT SUPPORT OF THE ARTS
50 ANS DE SOUTIEN DU GOUVERNEMENT DE L'ONTARIO AUX ARTS

University of Toronto Press acknowledges the financial support for its publishing activities of the Government of Canada through the Canada Book Fund.

This book is dedicated to John Clarke and Ian Massey of Hampshire County Education Authority, England. Their commitment and tireless efforts to improve education through children's rights and their attention to the best interests of every child has been truly inspirational.

Contents

Acknowledgments

The writing of this book and the research upon which it is based has been funded by the following, to whom we are very grateful.

Office of Research and Graduate Studies, Cape Breton University
Social Sciences and Humanities Research Council of Canada
The Chapman Foundation

We also acknowledge the anonymous reviewers whose comments were helpful and so very encouraging, and University of Toronto Press editors Doug Hildebrand and Brittany Lavery, who have been a pleasure to work with.

Abbreviations

ACLU	American Civil Liberties Union
ADHD	attention deficit hyperactivity disorder
BBBF	Better Beginnings, Better Futures (Canada)
CRC	Convention on the Rights of the Child
ECM	Every Child Matters (United Kingdom)
HCZ	Harlem Children's Zone
HRiE	Human Rights in Education (New Zealand)
HRW	Human Rights Watch
NCLB	No Child Left Behind (United States)
NCES	National Center for Education Statistics (United States)
NICHD	National Institute of Child Health and Human Development (United States)
OECD	Organization for Economic Co-operation and Development
PIRL	Progress in International Reading Literacy
PISA	Program for International Student Assessment
RRR	Rights, Respect, and Responsibility (England)
SAT	Standard Assessment Test (United Kingdom)
UNESCO	United Nations Educational, Scientific and Cultural Organization
UNICEF	United Nations International Children's Emergency Fund

EDUCATION IN THE BEST INTERESTS OF THE CHILD

A Children's Rights Perspective on Closing the Achievement Gap

Chapter One

In Search of the Best Interests of the Child

We recently saw a school-aged boy wearing a t-shirt with a picture of a school desk and the caption "ancient torture device." We smiled. But as we did so, we thought about the reality of this for so many children in today's schools. Approaches to educating our children are in a lot of respects ancient. There have been few fundamental changes in curricula, pedagogy, or educational practices since compulsory schooling began in the mid- to late 1800s. The use of individual desks, such as that pictured on the t-shirt, continues in many schools. Participatory teaching styles, with support for children's voice and with the use of practices such as role play and small group cooperative learning, continue to be rejected in favour of traditional rote learning. And torture? This is probably an overstatement for most children. Nevertheless, the fact remains that many children are disengaged from school. This is particularly the case for children from socially disadvantaged backgrounds, and these children are the ones most likely to underachieve, repeat grades, and eventually drop out. Such negative outcomes are contrary to the best interests of the child.

Education is important. It is associated with numerous positive outcomes such as more stable employment, better income, more job satisfaction, and better health. However, when children are disengaged from school, when they fail to achieve to their potential, and when they drop out, their best interests are seriously compromised. Education should not be this way. Schools should engage children; provide them with high-quality teachers and programs; provide them with a safe, welcoming, and stimulating learning environment; and ensure equal opportunity for educational success. Disadvantaged children should have the same opportunity to achieve their potential as do other children. All of this is in the best interests of the child. Why, we wondered, as the boy walked away, is education not designed with the best interests of children in mind?

The purpose of this book is to make the case for education in the best interests of the child. One might think that education already is in the best interests of the child or is at least moving in the direction of the best interests of the child. But this is not the case. If it were the case, underachievement, disengagement, and inequality of opportunity would not be the extensive problems that they are in today's schools. Modern education systems do not even have as their core purpose advancing the best interests of the child. This is hard to understand. Providing for the best interests of the child has become a lead principle in many areas of law and public policy affecting children – for example, in matters of child custody, child protection, adoption, and child health care. The principle has even become the gold standard in international law dealing with children. In the United Nations Convention on the Rights of the Child, for example, the best interests of the child is identified as a principle to be used in guiding *all* decisions affecting children. But strangely, when it comes to the core principles and purposes of schooling, it is missing in the education laws and policies of virtually all countries. It is missing as an explicit principle to guide educational practice. Moreover, it is missing in educational practice itself, as reflected in the problems of underachievement, disengagement, and inequality of opportunity for disadvantaged children.

It is difficult for us to understand why the principle and practice of best interests in education are missing. It is not for lack of knowledge. Since the early writings of John Dewey (1916, 1933), research findings on successful educational practices have been compelling and consistent across time and place. We know which practices optimize every child's chances of achieving to his or her potential. We know which practices and policies are more likely to engage children in school and to equalize opportunities for disadvantaged children. We know the vital importance of education. Education is a key means of cognitive, social, and emotional development, the achievement of personal potential and fulfilment, the learning of literacy and numeracy skills, vocational preparation, citizenship preparation, and the development of attributes for lifelong learning. Over the longer term, in modern societies and knowledge-based economies, education increasingly is needed for a productive and healthy adulthood. There is little question, therefore, that schooling and good educational practices are in the best interests of the child. The puzzle is why research knowledge about best interests is so little applied.

Disengagement and Disadvantage

When schools are not consistent with the best interests of the child – for example, when they are boring and punitive – children tune out. They become disengaged and do not do well. Children who are disengaged are more likely to become involved in disruptive and inappropriate be-haviours, including aggressive behaviours such as bullying; their aca-demic performance is more likely to suffer; and early school leaving is more like to result (Appleton et al., 2006; Roeser et al., 2008). It is seldom the case that children who are disengaged at school will achieve to their potential. In contrast, children who are engaged in school have positive perceptions and feelings about their school, teachers, and peers. Rather than spending their day involved in inappropriate behaviours, they are actively involved in school-related activities and learning (Furlong et al., 2003; Jimerson, Campos, & Greif, 2003). These children do well and they feel a valued part of the school community. High levels of school engagement are associated with positive behavioural, social, and aca-demic outcomes and with successful school completion (e.g., Furrer et al., 2006).

Children are more engaged in schools that have a positive school cli-mate (Carter et al., 2007; Covell, 2010; Stewart, 2003), that have teachers who are supportive and respectful (Klem & Connell, 2004; Sanders & Jordan, 2000), and that provide meaningful opportunities for students to be active participants in their own learning and in school activities (Covell, 2010; Finn & Rock, 1997; Jennings, 2003). But schools with these features are not that common. As Cohen and his colleagues noted in writing about the importance of positive school climate, the gap be-tween what is and what should be is vast, and it has a major impact on students' achievement potential (Cohen et al., 2009).

Children who become disengaged from school disproportionately come from socially disadvantaged backgrounds. Their family's socio-economic status makes a difference. Of course not all children living in social disadvantage will be disengaged from school or underachieving. Nor will all advantaged children be engaged and achieving to their po-tential. But social disadvantage is a significant risk factor for disengage-ment, underachievement, and educational failure (Johnson, Crosnoe, & Elder, 2001; Kalil & Ziol-Guest, 2008; Li & Lerner, 2011; Murray, 2009;

Schoon, Parsons, & Sacker, 2004). Children of higher socioeconomic status are more likely than their less advantaged peers to have parents who are involved with their schooling, who have appropriate expectations for their academic achievement, and who model and reinforce a high value on education. These children may be engaged and do well despite less than optimum educational practices. But this is not usually the case for socioeconomically disadvantaged children.

The problems of disengagement and underachievement are particularly profound for children who are at risk of failure because of their social backgrounds. This is the case for several reasons. First, schools in disadvantaged neighbourhoods are the least likely to have the characteristics that are predictive of engagement. They are often under-resourced, more likely to have unqualified or inexperienced teachers or substitute teachers, and more likely to have teachers who use ineffective instructional styles and punitive management strategies (Amrein-Beardsley, 2007; Darling-Hammond, 2006; Good & McCaslin, 2008). Second, the children who attend these schools come poorly equipped cognitively and socially to adapt to school. Poverty at home predicts poor behavioural and cognitive readiness for kindergarten (Barbarin et al., 2006; Fantuzzo et al., 2005); behavioural problems and poor achievement in elementary school (Baker et al., 2006; Hoglund & Leadbeater, 2004); poor academic performance in middle school (Malecki & Demaray, 2006); suspensions and expulsions in middle and high school (Theriot et al., 2010); and early school leaving (Ou & Reynolds, 2008). Third, material poverty tends to be accompanied by poverty of aspiration and impaired or ineffective parenting practices (Schoon et al., 2004). Children living in social disadvantage tend to have parents who themselves have low educational attainment, low aspirations for their children, and less involvement in their children's schooling. Lack of parental involvement is a well-known risk factor for lower school achievement.

Schools that function in ways counter to children's best interests serve only to exacerbate the difficulties that disadvantaged children face throughout school. It is not surprising, then, that it is the children of families living in social disadvantage who are the most likely to be disengaged from school and the most unlikely to achieve to their potential (e.g., Baker et al., 2006). Yibing Li and Richard Lerner (2011) assessed the behavioural and emotional engagement levels of almost 2,000 adolescents from Grade 5 through Grade 8. They defined behavioural engagement as participation in academic and social activities and positive behaviours. Emotional engagement was defined as positive feelings towards the school, teachers, and peers. Their data demonstrate significantly different patterns of engagement over time among children living in poverty compared with their more advantaged peers. Children from low-income families tended to either have low academic and emotional engagement across time or to show rapid declines in both types of engagement over time. In turn, these patterns of reduced engagement were linked with poor academic outcomes, substance use, and antisocial behaviours including criminal behaviours and violence. The consequences are lifelong. School failure is associated with difficulties such as poor adult adjustment, antisocial and criminal behaviours, health and work problems, and marginalization from adult society (Roeser et al., 2008; Schoon et al., 2004).

At the beginning of this millennium, the need to redress barriers to educational success was identified by UNESCO as a critical social issue across the world (UNESCO Global Monitoring Team, 2003). In the developing world, it is a critical social issue because of gaps in basic access to education, especially for girls. As reflected in the Millenium Development Goals for education, the educational needs of the developing world are much more fundamental than in the developed world. With a target year of 2015, the aim of the Development Goals is to ensure that all boys and girls everywhere will be able to complete a full course of primary schooling. Thus, the focus for education in the developing world must be to remove barriers to attendance and to ensure adequate infrastructure. Fees need to be removed, transportation to school provided, schools and classrooms built and resourced, and teachers trained.

In the developed world, the situation is much different. A critical issue here is the need to redress barriers facing socially disadvantaged children. Although children now have access to primary and secondary education, disproportionate and significant numbers of disadvantaged children have high levels of school disengagement, underachievement, and early school leaving, as summarized above. Not surprisingly, it has been suggested that widespread educational reform is essential to reducing disengagement and closing the achievement gap. We acknowledge that some differences in achievement will remain regardless of school reform. Innate capacities vary as a function of early prenatal and environmental conditions and genetic predispositions. What is of central importance, we believe, is that every child has equal opportunity to achieve to his or her potential. The U.N. Convention on the Rights of the Child requires paying attention to the rights of every child and ensuring that all children have the right to be educated such that they develop their "personality, talents and mental and physical abilities to their fullest potential" (Article 29). Schools and education systems can make a difference. If the principle of best interests were seriously put into effect in education, there would not be such disengagement, there would not be so many dropouts, and there would not be such an educational achievement gap between disadvantaged and socially advantaged children. Evidence-based education aimed at advancing the best interests of the child has the potential to make a significant difference through building educational resilience. In turn, the building of educational resilience has been shown to be an important means of reducing the achievement gap.

Reducing the Achievement Gap

Poor achievement and school failure are neither inevitable nor necessary outcomes of socioeconomic disadvantage. Rather than amplifying the existing challenges faced by poor children, schools can function to build their assets and to promote educational resilience. Educational resilience describes the likelihood of success in school among children who are at risk of failure because of family circumstances such as poverty (Martin & Marsh, 2006; Peck et al., 2008). Resilience is built in such children when schools and education systems provide them positive experience, develop self-confidence, and promote positive aspirations for the future. The possibilities are illustrated in isolated cases. We see the successful building of educational resilience in the heroic efforts of individual teachers and through the positive effects of particular programs.

Consider, for example, the case of Erin Gruwell. During the 1990s, Erin was a teacher at Woodrow Wilson High School in Long Beach, California. Dramatically illustrated by actress Hilary Swank in the 2007 movie *Freedom Writers,* Erin's story exemplifies the common attitude towards disadvantaged and at-risk students – the unteachables who are unworthy of resources or respect. Her story also illustrates the heroic efforts that must be expended by a teacher who cares, and the radical difference in children's lives that can occur when their best interests are given primacy (Gruwell, 1999). Gruwell was assigned a class of at-risk students who were completely disengaged and so disrespected by the school that they were not even allowed access to books on the assumption that they would damage or lose them. Sacrificing her personal life, her marriage, and her resources, and providing the students with books and engaging experiences, Gruwell transformed the students' lives with many of them graduating and continuing their education at college. Erin Gruwell was a remarkable teacher who made a difference.

Arts programs also can make a difference by building educational resilience in disadvantaged children. One example is in New South Wales, Australia, where the non-profit organization The Song Room has been deeply involved in providing free programs in the performing arts for children in primary schools in high-needs communities. A 3-year study of the impact of the programs has shown significant improvement among the children in academic achievement and school attendance (Vaughan, Harris, & Caldwell, 2011). In comparison with disadvantaged students in schools who were not offered the programs, the students who participated in the programs showed more engagement in school, better social skills, and a higher level of resilience. Similar outcomes among disadvantaged children have been found with music programs. An example here is the partnership among the Minneapolis Public Schools and the VH1 Save the Music Foundation and Comcast. The VH1 Foundation provides band instruments to schools thus allowing disadvantaged children to learn to play an instrument they would not otherwise have access to. The monthly "success stories" (VH1 Save the Music updates its website monthly) provide compelling evidence of the capacity of the music program to counter the effects of social disadvantage and improve a child's engagement and achievement.

Comprehensive programs such as the Harlem Children's Zone (HCZ) also have been demonstrated to reduce the achievement gap. Beginning in 1970 as a truancy prevention program, HCZ evolved into a comprehensive approach to reducing inequality of opportunity among poor African-American children. HCZ now includes parent education, school readiness programs, charter schools for all age levels, at-school health care services, and after school and weekend programs offering tutoring as well as access to arts and hobbies. From cradle to college, the best interests of the child are paramount. The results are compelling. Evaluation data show the capacity of the HCZ approach to reduce school absenteeism, increase graduation, and largely close the achievement gap in numeracy and literacy (Dobbie & Fryer, 2009).

Such cases are exceptions. It is not enough to advance the best interests of the child on the basis of isolated teachers or programs. Effective though they may be, such isolated cases obviously do not result in *all* children being provided with education such that they develop their personality, talents, and abilities to their fullest potential. Why should we expect teachers to make heroic sacrifices? Why should we expect foundations to be responsible for supplying basic resources to schools? Teachers who care should be commonplace, not so rare that we make movies about them. Effective programs should be the norm, not so exceptional that they evoke widespread media attention.

Some believe that it is parents who should take the initiative for improving their children's engagement and achievement. For example, why not simply allow parents the choice to enrol their children in better schools? The evidence suggests this is ineffective. In the United States, for example, with a move towards deregulation in education, there have been a growing number of alternatives to neighbourhood public schools for parents, including for parents who are living in poverty. Among the options, since the early 1990s, parents have been able to have their children attend charter schools or private schools funded by public vouchers (Bielick & Chapman, 2003). The evaluation data indicate two issues of relevance. First, when disadvantaged adolescents attend better schools in more advantaged neighbourhoods, there are positive effects on their social behaviour but little academic improvement (Cullen, Jacob, & Levitt, 2003). In fact, even when families move from high-poverty to low-poverty neighbourhoods in order to improve their children's academic performance, the evidence is that educational improvements are short term only (Leventhal, Fauth, & Brooks-Gunn, 2005). The achievement gap remains. Second, and perhaps more importantly, is the finding that family and neighbourhood disadvantage are associated with parents not exercising their choice (Lauen, 2007). In his extensive study of Chicago, an area characterized both by wide school choice and pervasive disadvantage, Lauen (2007) reports that poverty decreases the likelihood of students attending private or elite public schools even when such options are available.

In essence, it is not enough to count on individual teachers or special programs to build resilience and counter social disadvantage. It is not enough to count on a system of giving parents school choice. Every school and every education system should be consistent with what we know to be in the best interests of every child. This is important. At this time, too many schools and education systems do not serve the best interests of children. The building of assets and educational resilience is in short supply. However, this need not be the case. Moreover, the U.N. Convention on the Rights of the Child requires that it not be the case.

As this book will show, when political and educational authorities make a conscious and determined effort to counter social disadvantage, significant progress can be made in reducing the achievement gap. Disadvantaged children, like their advantaged peers, can be more engaged and achieve more in school when schooling is in their best interests. Progress requires reforms that are based on evidence from research. We suggest reforms at three general levels. First, because disadvantage begins so early in children's lives, and can set the child on a developmental pathway to school failure, reforms are required in early education. Most important is the creation and development of quality and comprehensive systems of early childhood education and care. Such systems need to include preschool enrichment programs that give special assistance to disadvantaged children. These programs need to be made part of formal education systems where they would have greater support and resources. Second, consistent with research on school improvement, reforms are required in classroom and schoolwide practices. Among other things, this means the recruitment, training, and retention of high-quality teachers and the hiring of school leaders who believe in the potential of *all* of their students and who are committed to converting research on best practices into reality. Third, consistent with the Convention on the Rights of the Child, reforms are required in providing for positive school cultures and children's rights education. This means not only education on the rights of the child but also educational practices respectful of children and consistent with their basic rights. This serves the best interests of the child by building a positive school climate for learning. This is especially valuable for disadvantaged children.

Overview of This Book

The book unfolds as follows. In the remainder of this chapter, we will discuss the scope of the book. Education in the best interests of the child is a huge topic. Our principal focus will be on the contradiction between the principle of the best interests of the child and the reality of unequal educational opportunity for disadvantaged children, and the major means by which the achievement gap can be reduced. In chapter 2, we explain the modern meaning of the principle of the best interests of the child. We first discuss the emergence of the principle in child custody law and decision-making, its spread to other child-related areas, and its incorporation into the U.N. Convention on the Rights of the

Child. Then, based on the wording of the Convention and the comments of the U.N. Committee on the Rights of the Child, the highest international authority in interpreting the Convention, we explain the modern meaning of the principle. Finally, we apply the meaning to the field of education and discuss how educational practices are consistent or inconsistent with the principle.

In chapter 3, we describe the major challenges for education in the best interests of the child. We begin with the problems of social inequality, poverty, and the achievement gap. In reference to a wide body of research, we then discuss the negative educational impact of social disadvantage and the various ways by which impoverished family backgrounds put children at risk of unfavourable educational outcomes. Finally, we look at schools as risk amplifiers. Rather than taking action to counteract the effects of disadvantage and building resilience, schools typically amplify the problem through reinforcing inequality and through punitive practices such as grade retention and exclusion. In failing to provide for the child's right to education on the basis of equal opportunity, they fail to act in the best interests of the child.

In the chapters that follow, we examine three areas of reform that would make a significant contribution to tackling the problem of the achievement gap. The reforms that we examine may be conceived as protective factors that work to counter the risk factors to which poor children are exposed, and to equalize opportunities. As pointed out by Carolyn Webster-Stratton and her colleagues (Webster-Stratton, Jamila Reid, & Stoolmiller, 2008), in the absence of such protective factors, the negative effects of risk factors can interact and intensify. Educational resilience is determined by the balance of risk and protective factors in the environment as the child develops. For protective factors to counter the negative effects of risk factors, they must outweigh risk factors at each developmental or educational stage. Continued provision of protective factors throughout the child's schooling is essential to counter the child's continued exposure to the risk factors associated with poverty. It is not enough to ensure protective factors during early childhood education, for example. Although doing so would be expected to provide a solid rather than fragile foundation for later success, if in subsequent years the risk factors outweigh the protective factors, the benefits may be lost. It is, then, our contention that significant and sustainable progress in closing the achievement gap requires reforms in three areas.

In chapter 4, we look at reform in the area of early childhood education and care. We first note the importance of the early years for the development of the neurological underpinnings of school readiness, and the need for early intervention to address deficits. Based on a review of research on the impact of early childhood education in the form of quality child care and preschool enrichment programs, we make the case for comprehensive early childhood education and care as a key means of countering disadvantage. We note that this is an important but incomplete step. Protective factors in place early do put the child onto a positive developmental trajectory. But the absence of subsequent protective factors in schools may render the early efforts little more than band-aids rather than inoculations against adversity.

In chapter 5, we examine reform in school and classroom practices and in education policies. In reference to numerous research studies and comparative international research, we point to the importance of high-quality teachers, committed school leaders, evidence-based programs, and policies such as promoting social integration, providing appropriate resources, and setting concrete targets. Again, we note that this is an important but incomplete step. Each of these acts as a protective factor that can build educational resilience in the child who is at risk of failure. However, sustaining high-quality practices and programs is very difficult in the absence of an overarching school culture that promotes, supports, and integrates best practices. In the absence of a shared and positive values framework, children's exposure to the protective factors of high-quality teachers and so forth may be sporadic and unreliable.

In chapter 6, we examine reform in the area of transforming school cultures. In reference to the U.N. Convention on the Rights of the Child and to research on positive school climate, we point to the benefits of educating children about the rights of the child, using the Convention as a shared-values framework for the functioning of schools, and ensuring the practice of children's rights in schools. Examining the research evidence of a case study in England, we show that a rights-based school culture indeed does promote and sustain school practices that build educational resilience in children at risk of failure because of social disadvantage. When school cultures are positive and respectful of children, the benefits are disproportionate for children of social disadvantage.

In our concluding chapter 7, we explore the question of whether it is possible to fully close the achievement gap through educational reform alone. Although exceptional cases demonstrate that schools can close

the achievement gap, we believe that substantial and sustained progress in so doing also requires improved social policies and supports
for disadvantaged families. We examine the question of why there has
been a lack of public commitment and political will to close the achievement gap. The conclusion we come to is that ambivalence among members of the education community and the general public is the key
underlying factor. Equal opportunity is supported in the abstract but
not as a concrete goal to be realized. Our final thoughts concern prospects for change. In considering long-term changes in political cultures
across the developed world, we are optimistic that with the emergence
of post-materialist values, pressure will increase for the reforms necessary to close the achievement gap.

Some words are needed on the scope of this book. First, as mentioned
earlier, education in the best interests of the child is a very broad topic.
One could examine issues concerning the best interests of the individual child or particular groups of children or children as a whole. We
confine our attention here largely to the best interests of children as a
whole and to the particular challenges facing socially disadvantaged
children. Second, disadvantage also is a huge topic. We could discuss
disadvantage on the basis of social – or socioeconomic – disadvantage, or we could broaden the discussion to include gender, disability,
sexual minority status, and membership in ethnic or religious minority communities. Each of these clearly is important. However, a full
and proper discussion would take several books. We limit our focus in
this book to the problem of social disadvantage and how poverty and
poverty-related factors affect educational outcomes. We do note, however, the association between poverty and other social factors. With
poverty, for example, there is heightened risk of childhood behavioural
disorders, learning difficulties, and learning disorders, which together
have an additive effect on educational outcomes. Moreover, poverty
often overlaps with ethnicity. African-American and Latino children
in the United States, Indigenous (or Aboriginal) children in Canada,
Australia, and New Zealand, Bangladeshi and Pakistani children in
the United Kingdom, and Roma children in many parts of Europe are
much more likely to live in poverty. Disadvantage for these children is
related not only to poverty but also to discrimination and cultural bias.
However, a full analysis of factors such as ethnicity and disability is beyond the scope of this book.

Third, there are many forms of education that could be discussed. We
could examine not only public education but also private education,

religious education, home schooling, and alternative schooling. Although we make reference to alternative schools, we confine our attention largely to public schools and public education systems. We do so for the sake of space and because this is where the vast majority of children are educated. Finally, in terms of countries, we could discuss schools, education systems, laws, policies, and research studies from across the world. But this would be unwieldy and, as noted previously, the critical issues are somewhat different between the developed and developing world. Our main focus, then, will be on developed countries and largely those in North America, Europe, and Australasia.

Finally, we limit the elaboration of examples within the geographical areas to those we believe important to highlight and for which there are reliable data. Given the broad-ranging scope of the macro-level analysis we undertake, extended discussions of all systems, approaches, and practices would be impracticable. Our aim throughout is to demonstrate the importance of applying the best interests of the child to education.

Chapter Two

The Principle of the Best Interests of the Child

The principle of the best interests of the child is relatively new. Originating in the late 1800s, the principle was first applied to law and judicial decision-making in the area of determining child custody arrangements. Its meaning was simple: The welfare or well-being of the child had to be a consideration or a primary consideration in deciding custody. Custody could no longer be awarded on the basis of a presumption in favour of either the mother or father solely on the basis of economic, religious, or cultural factors. The welfare – or best interests of the individual child – had to be a key decision-making criterion. Since then, however, the meaning of the principle has evolved to apply to a wide number of fields beyond child custody. Moreover, it has evolved to refer to the well-being not only of an individual child but also of children as a whole. Today, under international law and specifically the U.N. Convention on the Rights of the Child (hereafter the Convention or the CRC), it refers to *all* actions concerning children both as individuals and as a collectivity. All actions include all *educational* actions.

In this chapter, we review the emergence and evolution of the principle, its general meaning under the CRC, and its application to the field of education. In our analysis of education, we provide a map of education laws, policies, and practices that are consistent or inconsistent with the modern meaning of the best interests principle, as it is found in the CRC.

The Emergence and Evolution of the Best Interests Principle

Historically, in Western countries, there was no legal principle of the best interests of the child. In law and public policy, until very recently, it was assumed that children were the property and responsibility of their parents (Freeman, 1983; Hart, 1991; McCoy, 1988; Stone, 1977). In the eyes of the law and in the eyes of society, children were not recognized as independent persons with interests and rights apart from their parents. Parental power and parental rights were paramount. In ancient Roman times, for example, under the harsh legal principle of *patria potestas* (power of the father), the father had the absolute power of life and death over his children. Authorized by Roman law, infanticide, parental cruelty, and parental maltreatment were commonplace. In medieval and early modern Europe, the treatment of children was better, but only to a limited degree. Children now were more valued for their contribution to family work and for the support of their parents in old age. Parents increasingly were expected to maintain and protect their children. With this expectation, laws were established to give parents a legal duty to protect their children and provide them with the basic necessities of life. But all of this said, although children were to be treated in a more humane manner, they remained the property and the private domain of their parents. It was assumed that except in extreme circumstances, there should be no societal or governmental interference in child-parent relationships and in the private affairs of the family.

In the mid- to late 1800s and early 1900s, the property concept gradually gave ground to a new understanding. According to this new understanding, children were a vulnerable and immature class of persons who required the periodic protection of a paternalistic state against abusive or negligent parents and adults. This understanding informed the development of a number of reform movements across Western countries, including a new child-saving movement that aimed to rescue or save children from maltreatment and exploitation. The goal of the reformers was to create new laws and policies to better protect the interests and needs of children (Behlmer, 1982; Katz, 1996; Sutherland, 2000). The reformers ultimately were successful. Western governments established new child labour laws, new laws to protect children from abuse and neglect in the home, and new juvenile justice systems and courts to respond to what was called delinquency. As part of this change, the legal doctrine of *parens patriae* (state as father) – which earlier had been developed by the courts in England to protect adults who could not protect themselves – was expanded to include children who were in need of protection (Rendleman, 1971; Thomlison & Foote, 1987). According to the doctrine as it was applied to children, although parents have the primary responsibility to care for their children, the courts and the state must sometimes step in and act as a substitute parent, overriding or restricting parental authority in order that the interests of children be protected. The assumption was that the interests of children are not always the same as those of their parents. The state must step in when parents or other adult authorities are failing to fulfil their responsibilities to children.

In the late 1800s, the principle of the best interests of the child was developed as an aspect of the doctrine of *parens patriae* (Breen, 2002; LaFave, 1989; Mason, 2006). First, it was applied in the area of child custody. In the United States, as explained by LeAnn Lefave (1989), its origins can be traced back to the Territory of Dakota where, in 1877, under the Code for the Territory, the principle was invoked as a factor for the court to consider in determining child custody arrangements. According to the court, it could not be assumed that either a mother or father would automatically get custody. Consideration had to be given to the welfare or best interests of the child in question. This was an important decision that set a precedent. From Dakota, the principle gradually spread to other parts of the United States and across Western countries. Today, in virtually all Western countries, the term *best interests* – or an equivalent term – is commonly used in child custody laws and decision-making, serving either as a consideration or as the paramount or primary consideration in custody decisions.

The use of the principle did not end with child custody. During the 1900s, it spread to many other areas of law and policy dealing with children. It is widely found today in a variety of fields including adoption, child protection legislation, children in state care, the guardianship of minors, child labour laws, refugee determination, and medical decision-making (Breen, 2002; Mason, 2006; Woodhouse, 2006). Finally, the principle spread from domestic law into international law. In 1959, it was incorporated into the U.N. Declaration of the Rights of the Child; in 1979, into the U.N. Convention on the Elimination of All Forms of Discrimination against Women; and, most importantly, in 1989, into the all-important U.N. Convention on the Rights of the Child (Breen, 2002; Detrick, 1999; Van Bueren, 1992). In the Convention, the principle is regarded as one of the core principles, applying not only to particular matters such as child custody and child protection, but to *all actions* affecting children.

Incorporating the principle into the Convention was a major step forward. Unanimously approved by the U.N. General Assembly in 1989 and subsequently signed and ratified by virtually all countries of the world – only the United States, South Sudan, and Somalia have yet to ratify the CRC – the Convention is a legally binding international treaty (Detrick, 1999; Verhellen, 1994). As required under Article 4, countries that have ratified the Convention are obligated to "undertake all appropriate legislative, administrative, and other measures for the implementation of the rights recognized in the present Convention." This obligation requires implementing the general principles of the Convention including, under Article 3, the principle of the best interests of the child. Under the terms of the Convention, countries are responsible for putting the CRC into effect progressively over time and to demonstrate their progress in so doing through a reporting and monitoring system. Periodic reports are to be sent for review to the U.N. Committee on the Rights of the Child, the chief U.N. monitoring agency for the Convention. The Committee, in turn, is responsible for providing feedback in its own report called Concluding Observations, which is to be used by countries for improving their children's rights record.

As the most widely and most quickly ratified convention in world history, the CRC provides a systematic and comprehensive statement on the status of the child and on the rights of children that did not exist before. A landmark document for children, it officially puts to rest older and lingering assumptions about children as parental property or as a vulnerable class of not-yets in need of state protection. The document officially elevates the status of children to valued and independent persons with basic rights. By ratifying the Convention, countries have agreed to recognize this new status for children and to bring their domestic laws, policies, and practices into consistency with the Convention and with the principle of the best interests of the child. Although the United States has not ratified it, the CRC remains an important standard and guide for American child advocacy and professional practice involving children (Gardinier, 2010; Small & Limber, 2002). States such as Vermont, cities such as Chicago, and various professional organizations such as the American Psychological Association have passed resolutions in support of the Convention. Furthermore, although the United States has not yet ratified the CRC, the U.S. president has signed it, obligating the United States to at least not adopt policies contrary to it (Melton, 2002). In the meantime, until official ratification takes place, the CRC is a widely recognized standard for the treatment of American children.

In the Convention, apart from Article 3, the term "best interests" is referred to in six articles, which deal with specific matters. Under

Article 9, the child's best interests are the only reason to separate children from their parents and to deny a child's contact with a non-custodial parent. Under Article 18, parents will have as their basic concern the best interests of the child. Under Article 20, a child shall be given special protection and assistance if it is in the child's best interests to be removed from his or her family environment. Under Article 21, the best interests of the child shall be the paramount consideration for adoption. Under Article 37, children in the juvenile justice system shall be separated from adults unless it is in their best interests not to do so. Finally, under Article 40, children have a right to a fair hearing unless this is not in their best interests by reason of age or circumstance. But the key article is Article 3, which is a statement on best interests as a general principle. It states that "in all actions concerning children, whether undertaken by public or private social welfare institutions, courts of law, administrative authorities or legislative bodies, the best interests of the child shall be a primary consideration."

But what does it mean to say that the best interests of the child shall be a primary consideration?

The Modern Meaning of the Best Interests of the Child

The modern meaning of the best interests principle is found not only in the words of the Convention but also in comments by the U.N. Committee on the Rights of the Child, the highest international authority in interpreting the Convention. In providing feedback to countries in their reports on implementing the CRC, the Committee has elaborated on the meaning of best interests and provided the most authoritative commentary. Before we discuss this current meaning, it may be helpful to see how it evolved from the traditional understanding of the principle.

According to the traditional meaning of the best interests principle, decision-makers were obligated to consider the welfare or well-being of children when making decisions about their placements or care (Breen, 2002; Van Bueren, 1992; Wolf, 1992). As applied originally in child custody cases, the key consideration was the well-being or healthy development of the child, rather than the wishes or rights or interests of parents or of other parties. For example, in one of the earliest child custody cases in which the principle was applied – *Chapsky* v. *Wood* (1881) – a judge in Kansas awarded custody to the child's grandmother rather than to the biological father. He did so through considering a variety of factors, including the relationship of the child with each applicant and the love and affection of each applicant for the child. He then determined that awarding custody to the grandmother was in the child's best interests. The decisive factor was the child's welfare, not biology or "bloodlines" as it was then called. Up to this time, the father would have had an automatic right to custody. The judge's decision was a break with the past and a progressive ruling. Although this early conception of best interests was progressive, there were two problems. First was the strong element of paternalism. The decision-maker determined what was in the child's best interests without giving serious consideration to the input of the child. Second, there was a wide degree of discretion. The decision-maker weighed a number of factors, deliberated, and then arrived at a decision. In doing so, he or she was not constrained by important principles or signposts such as consistency with the rights of the child.

The modern meaning is similar to the traditional concept in a very basic way. It has as its core concern the well-being of the child. But beyond this, there are significant differences. One difference is that the scope of the application of the modern principle is much wider. As stated in Article 3 of the CRC, the principle is to apply to *all* actions involving the child (not only to decisions in a limited number of fields such as child custody) and to children as a whole (not only to an individual child). This is evident in the plain reading of Article 3 – *all actions* and *concerning children* – and in comments and interpretations of Article 3 by the U.N. Committee (Detrick, 1999; Hammarberg, 2008; Hodgkin & Newell, 2007). It also is the case that the term *all actions* is sufficiently broad to include inaction as well as action (Van Bueren, 1992). The decision to refrain from action is part of action. In addition, the scope is broad in that the principle is to apply to a wide number of decision-making authorities in both the public and private sectors, not simply to the courts as in the past. In Article 3, the principle is to be used by "public or private social welfare institutions, courts of law, administrative authorities or legislative bodies." Thus, in addition to judges, the principle of best interests is to be employed by professionals working with children, social workers, medical practitioners, educators, administrators, and politicians. Article 3 does not refer to actions by parents and guardians. But Article 18 states that "the best interests of the child will be their [parents and legal guardians] basic concern." So the application of the principle is very broad.

Another difference in the modern meaning is that there is less room for paternalism and discretion. In determining best interests, decision-makers are not to decide simply on the basis of what *they* think is best for children. They are obligated to take into account the views of children who are capable of forming their own views (Flekkoy & Kaufman, 1997; Hammarberg, 2008). As pointed out by Kathleen Marshall (1997), as revealed in the documents and discussions leading up to the adoption of the CRC, the framers of the Convention intended the participation of children to be an integral part of best interests. The framers regarded the gaining of the child's views to be a critical component of the process of determining best interests. To deny the views of children would be to exclude the possibility of valuable information in decision-making. The framers regarded participation to be so important that they incorporated it into the CRC as a general principle under Article 12. As stated in Article 12, children have the right to express their views freely in all matters affecting them. The only constraints on their participation are that children must be capable of forming their own views and that their expression applies only to matters affecting them. Participation, then, is a core part of best interests. However, other articles of the Convention are equally important to the determination of best interests. As noted by numerous commentators, in reference to the framers and to the comments of the Committee, the determination of best interests is to be constrained not only by the child's right of participation but also by the Convention and by the rights of the child as a whole (Detrick, 1999; Freeman, 2007; Hodgkin & Newell, 2007; Van Bueren, 1992; Wolf, 1992). The best interests principle and the rights of the child cannot be separated. Determining best interests requires careful consideration of the Convention and the incorporation of the rights of the child into decision-making.

The modern concept of best interests, as expressed in the Convention, is indeterminate from the point of view of substance. As pointed out by Michael Freeman (2007), Article 3 provides a normative statement on the need to consider the child's best interests, but it does not provide a clear and full substantive definition of what best interests actually are. Article 3 does not even provide a checklist of factors to be considered. The decision by the framers of the Convention to be indeterminate was quite understandable. First, there was the difficulty in gaining a consensus. Many countries were involved in the drafting of the CRC, and it would be virtually impossible to get an agreement and move forward should an attempt be made at a substantive definition. Second, there was an appreciation of the difficulties in deciding best interests given the complexities of issues, differing interpretations of answers to the difficulties, and the continuing evolution of knowledge on the well-being of children. So it was recognized that flexibility is required. Third, there was acknowledgment of the difficulty of accommodating different cultural and religious traditions. The framers understood this issue and appreciated the need for a statement on best interests that would be general and allow a certain degree of latitude in interpreting the substance of best interests (Alston, 1994).

But from the wording of Article 3 and other parts of the Convention, and from the comments of the Committee on the Rights of the Child, a number of points can be made about the ingredients of best interests, which prevents the concept from being excessively or hopelessly subjective. Philip Alston (1994) describes these ingredients as signposts. They include a concern for healthy child development, regard for the rights of the child, regard for evidence-based research, and the incorporation of the best interests principle into law and policy. The more these ingredients are in supply, the closer children will be to having their best interests met.

Ingredients of Best Interests

One very basic ingredient or signpost is that, like the traditional concept of best interests, the modern concept is concerned about the basic welfare or well-being of children. This is often expressed in social science and medical science literature as healthy or optimum physical, social, emotional, and cognitive development (Lloyd & Hertzman, 2009). Although there may not be reliable and conclusive scientific knowledge about all aspects of healthy child development, at a very general level, healthy development refers to physical health (e.g., achieving developmental milestones and the absence of illness), good mental health (e.g., self-esteem and the absence of psychosocial disorders), positive social and emotional development (e.g., secure attachment with a parent and positive peer relations), and healthy cognitive development (e.g., acquisition of language and capacity for reasoning). Applying best interests means optimizing child health and healthy child development, and it means preventing or reducing the risk of ill health or unhealthy development.

Healthy child development is now widely measured on the basis of child well-being indicators. Such indicators are useful for calculating the extent of well-being, progress or lack of progress over time, and the effectiveness of policy (Ben-Arieh, 2008; Ben-Arieh & Goerge, 2005). In the domain of health, indicators include healthy birth weight (between 2,500 and 4,500 grams), fruit and vegetable consumption, and physical activity. In the domain of behaviour, they include positive leisure and recreational pursuits, healthy sexual behaviour, and pro-social behaviour, as measured, for example, in lack of involvement in crime and school completion. In family relations, indicators include secure attachment with a parent, and positive discipline and socialization. In peer and community relations, they include positive interaction and participation with peers, youth volunteering in the community, and a sense of community connectedness. In safety and basic economic well-being, they include protection from injury and abuse, food security, and adequate housing. Finally, in learning, they include school readiness, achievement of numeracy and literacy, and secondary school completion. In summary, at a very basic level, the best interests of children refer to the well-being of children and progress measured in terms of child well-being indicators.

Another ingredient of best interests is regard for and consistency with the guiding principles of the CRC and the rights of the child (Detrick, 1999; Freeman, 2007; Hodgkin & Newell, 2007). This means that in applying best interests, consideration has to be given to the general principles of the Convention. Together with the best interests principle, the Committee on the Rights of the Child has identified three other principles as general principles in guiding the application and implementation of the Convention: participation (Article 12), non-discrimination (Article 2), and the survival and development of the child (Article 6). All are held to be of central importance and none is subordinate to another. The best interests principle, for example, cannot trump the other principles. It must be interpreted and applied in a way consistent with the other principles to the greatest degree possible. Providing for the participation of the capable child in decision-making, ensuring non-discrimination against the child and the child's family, and ensuring the survival and development of the child are all major ingredients of the best interests of the child. In particular circumstances, there may be a conflict among principles. This may be illustrated in the classic case of a young Jehovah's Witness who requires a blood transfusion in the interests of survival and development but who refuses it in the name of freedom of religion and participation rights. This is a difficult case with no easy answer. Principles need to be balanced. But difficult though a resolution may be, a particular case where a balancing of principles is required does not subtract from the desirability of the general call for the consistency of best interests with the other principles.

Apart from the principles of the Convention, consideration also has to be given to the specific rights of the child as described in the CRC. Thomas Hammarberg (1990) has categorized the rights of the child into the three Ps: provision, protection, and participation. Provision rights refer to the child's right to be provided with basic economic and social needs, including material welfare (Article 27), health care (Article 24), and basic education (Articles 28 and 29). Protection rights refer to the child's right to be protected from harmful or exploitive practices such as abuse, neglect, and violence (Article 19), economic exploitation (Article 32), and sexual exploitation (Article 34). Participation rights include the right to be heard (Article 12), freedom of expression and information (Article 13), and freedom of thought and religion (Article 14). Apart from these general rights, there are particular rights for special populations of children. Children living with disabilities have the right to special care (Article 23), and minority and Indigenous children have the right to enjoy their own culture, practise their own religion, and use their own language (Article 30). Securing all of these rights is a vital part of the best interests of the child. Again, in particular circumstances, there may be conflict. A child in a developing country may need to go to work to help with the family income, in line with his or her right to material welfare. This may compromise the child's right to education and to leisure. But again, the balancing of rights that may be required in particular cases such as this does not take away from the worthy overall objective of incorporating the rights of children into the principle of the best interests of the child.

In giving consideration to the Convention and the rights of the child, the best interests principle requires that consideration also be given to parents, guardians, and those acting in the position of parents (e.g., teachers). The Convention is very supportive of a strong role for parents in the care and the raising of children (Covell & Howe, 2001a; Melton, 1996). Under Article 18, parents or legal guardians have the primary responsibility for the upbringing and development of the child. Furthermore, under Article 5, countries shall respect the responsibilities of parents (or guardians or other persons legally responsible for the child) to provide direction and guidance in the exercise by children of their rights, consistent with their evolving capacities. Since parents and adult authorities are to provide direction and guidance, it is logical to conclude that the best interests principle requires considering their views as well as the views of children. This, of course, does not mean that the views of parents are the decisive factor. Parental guidance is to be in line with the evolving capacities of children, and decision-makers need to take into account children's voices as well as those of their parents or guardians.

It is important to note that applying the best interests principle is not simply the case of repeating the application of the rights of the child as described in the Convention. It is not simply the restatement of the obligation of countries that have ratified the Convention to put the rights of the child into effect. Although applying the best interests principle is certainly to be informed by the rights of the child, it also is an independent principle with an independent role. As analysts such as Alston (1994), Detrick (1999), and Freeman (2007) point out, the best interests principle performs at least three roles. First, it serves to support or clarify a particular approach to issues that may arise under the Convention. This means that it helps as an aid to the interpretation of articles in the Convention or, in the words of Alston (1994, p. 16), "it is an aid to construction as well as an element which needs to be taken fully into account in implementing other rights." Second, it acts as a mediating principle that can help to resolve conflict among rights. A judge, for example, may refer to best interests and make a determination in the Jehovah's Witness case described above. Freedom of religion may have to yield to the right to life and health. Third and of particular importance, the best interests principle forms the basis for evaluating laws, policies, and practices in matters that, although related to rights, are not directly governed by rights described in the CRC. According to Alston, in describing this third role, the principle is to apply to situations when failure to observe it would adversely affect the child's exercise or enjoyment of rights. In other words, the best interests principle is to be used to identify conditions necessary for the enjoyment of children's rights.

Another ingredient of best interests is consideration of evidence. According to the Committee, because of the need for knowledge and reliable information in applying best interests and especially in identifying conditions for the enjoyment of rights, consideration needs to given to the impact of legislation, policies, and practices on children (Freeman, 2007; Hammarberg, 2008; Hodgkin & Newell, 2007). This involves the need to examine evidence on outcomes from research findings and from what have been called child impact assessments and evaluations. Child impact assessments are those that predict the impact of any proposed law, policy, or budgetary measure that affects the enjoyment of children's rights. Child impact evaluations are those that evaluate the impact of implementing various measures. Both presume the need for careful and systematic study and research. Clear evidence that is informed by research – especially from longitudinal studies and where there is a long-standing consensus in the research literature – should have major weight in decisions and policies affecting children. For example, Article 19 of the CRC says that countries shall take all appropriate measures to protect children from all forms of physical or mental violence. In reviewing policies and laws, the application of best interests would require decision-makers to consider the research evidence on the impact of various legal and educational measures on reducing or preventing violence against children. If a particular measure has clear and overwhelming support in the research, its adoption would be very much in line with the best interests principle.

Hammarberg (2008) points out that systematic child impact assessments and evaluations have been rare. But he gives a few examples that provide models of what needs to be done. In Belgium, the Flemish parliament has enacted legislation that requires that all proposed decrees before the parliament that affect the rights of the child be accompanied by reports on their impact on children. In Sweden, the parliament has adopted a National Strategy for the Implementation of the Convention on the Rights of the Child that requires that child impact analyses be conducted and documented in relevant decision-making. In Norway, there has been a move to evaluate the impact of national budgets on children. The overall benefit of child impact analyses, says Hammarberg (2008), is to compensate children for their lack of political power in decision-making and to provide a procedure by which the best interests of children can be assessed.

Finally, another ingredient is the requirement to incorporate the best interests principle into law and policy (Hammarberg, 2008; Hodgkin & Newell, 2007). The CRC requires the progressive implementation of all of the principles and rights of the Convention. But according to the Committee, because the best interests principle is so fundamental to implementation, it is of particular importance that the principle be reflected in domestic law, policies, and national plans for children. The objective, in the case of law, is to enable the principle to be invoked before the courts and, in the case of policies, to make it an explicit aim of government action such that governments can be held more accountable. Incorporation does not necessarily mean that the principle is to be supreme in child-related law and policy. As stated in Article 3, best interests shall be *a* primary consideration, not *the* primary consideration. A major reason for the word *a* – rather than the word *the* – was

American opposition to the use of stronger language in discussions leading up to the Convention, and, in addition, concern among other countries for the need for flexibility in decision-making (Alston, 1994). The outcome was the softer phrase "*a* primary consideration," which means that children's best interests do not have to be the decisive or single overriding consideration. Other primary considerations may be given priority in particular circumstances. As an example, Elizabeth Mason (2006) mentions the case of a mother's health during childbirth where there is serious risk to the mother's life or health. It is reasonable here that the best interests of the child be *a* primary consideration but not *the* primary consideration. There are only two specific areas under the CRC where best interests are to be *the* primary consideration: decisions about adoption (Article 21) and decisions about the separation of children from their parents (Article 20). But apart from these two areas, as a general principle under Article 3, best interests are to be a primary consideration in all actions concerning children.

Nevertheless, that it is *a* primary consideration does not mean it can be easily ignored or dismissed. As explained by Hodgkin and Newell (2007), there may be important economic or cultural or religious considerations in decisions affecting children and there may be genuine conflicts between the interests of adults and those of children. For example, in dealing with the issue of possible sexual health education in a school district, decision-makers may have to weigh children's best interests in terms of health and the religious views of the community against sex education (Howe & Covell, 2010a). In the deliberation, children's interests must be the subject of active and serious consideration. If best interests prove not to be the decisive consideration, then this should be transparent and reasons given. Moreover, as noted by Flekkoy and Kaufman (1997) and by Van Bueren (1992), the burden of proof should be on those who argue that other interests should prevail against the best interests of children.

Criticism of the Best Interests Principle

Although the principle of the best interests of the child enjoys widespread support among analysts, commentators, researchers, and practitioners working with children, a number of criticisms have been made of the best interests principle. The chief one is that it is too vague, too general, and too open-ended or indeterminate to be of any value.

Because it is riddled with these problems, say the critics, it should be replaced or abandoned.

The argument is this, as expressed by commentators such as Mnookin and Szwed (1983), Goldstein and colleagues (1986), Becker (1992), Fineman (1995), Herring (2005), and Elliston (2007). Because the principle is so vague and general, it provides decision-makers with very little guidance. Decision-makers are confronted with numerous complexities and complications, making it extremely difficult to identify objective criteria in order to properly apply the principle. The problems are these. There is the difficulty of assessing short-term and long-term best interests. There is the difficulty of assigning weight to different considerations when making decisions. There is the difficulty of weighing the interests of an individual child against the interests of children as a whole and of weighing the interests of different groups of children. There is also the difficulty of weighing the views of children against the views of parents and adults. Finally, when research evidence enters into the picture, there is the difficulty of getting reliable scientific knowledge for child impact analyses. Research studies may not exist or they may be contradictory or they may give different results over time. Even if there is solid research evidence, there is the problem of weighing this evidence against the views of children and of adults, when there is conflict.

According to the argument, given all of these difficulties and the limitations of knowledge, it is inevitable that discretion, subjectivity, and the values or interests of judges and state decision-makers will enter into the deliberations. The danger is that this will result in arbitrary, biased, or bad decisions. Decision-makers may claim a rational decision has been made based on best interests but in reality, given all of the difficulties, it has been based simply on their own values. However, value-based decisions can be arbitrary because, on many issues, there often is no consensus in society about what values should inform the decision. Moreover, to the extent that there is a consensus about values, this will vary from one era to another, from one region to another, and from one culture to another. It may also be the case that although decision-makers may claim a rational decision has been made on the basis of best interests, they actually have used the principle to camouflage their own interests or biases or ideological agenda. Using the best interests principle in a custody dispute, a judge may rule in favour of a mother or father. But in actuality, the ruling reflects the judge's sympathies with the plight of women or of men.

Given these serious problems, according to some critics, it would be wise to replace the best interests principle with simpler rules that apply to specific areas. This would result in less discretion among state decision-makers and greater determinacy. James Dwyer (2006) calls these proposed rules *shortcut rules*. In the area of contested child custody, for example, Fineman (1995) has argued for the rule that custody decisions be based simply on rewarding persons who have sacrificed the most for their children in the past. Becker (1992) has argued for the rule – reminiscent of the tender years doctrine – that custody simply should be presumed to be given to mothers. In the area of medical decision-making for very young children, Elliston (2007) has recommended the rule that medical decisions be based simply on the wishes of parents unless there is a significant risk of harm to the child and unless parental decisions are outside the bounds of reasonableness. Each of these critics wants the best interests principle abandoned.

In response, Van Bueren (1992) makes a good point when she says that the term *best interests* invites this kind of criticism. A more apt and less grandiose term, she suggests, would be the *better interests* of the child. Similarly, Dwyer (2006) suggests the use of the term *best feasible option* or *best available option*. Both make this suggestion in recognition of the limits of human knowledge and rationality and in line with the modern scientific approach where findings and explanations are stated not in absolute and definitive terms but in tentative or probabilistic terms, consistent with existing data. But both also admit that it would be very difficult to craft a new term because of the common usage of best interests and because of its inspirational value and tool for child advocacy. In any case, as both acknowledge, it has to be accepted that the difficulties are real and that there is no philosopher's stone to use in order to determine what is truly or absolutely in the child's best interests. However, as pointed out by Dwyer, the best interests principle is not so lacking in guidance as the critics make it out to be. It is not boundless. It has at its core the well-being of children, and it rules out the interests of persons other than the child. Furthermore, as explained by commentators such as Alston (1994), Freeman (2007), and Hammarberg (2008), although subjectivity intrudes and although the substance of best interests is indeterminate, the U.N. Convention on the Rights of the Child provides a normative framework that mitigates or constrains subjectivity and a process or methodology that works to determine the better or best interests of children.

The CRC provides a broad ethical framework and a carefully formulated statement of values to which virtually all countries of the world have formally agreed. Within this statement of values is the endorsement of the core principle of the best interests of the child. The Convention also provides a number of signposts to help guide decision-makers to determine what is and what is not in the child's best interests. Key among the signposts is consistency with the rights of the child. To the greatest degree possible, decisions have to be in line with the principles of the CRC and with the protection, provision, and participation rights of children. As noted above, there may be occasional conflict among rights and difficulties in resolving issues. But through careful deliberation and feedback from the U.N. Committee on the Rights of the Child, progress can be made in determining the better or best interests of the child. However, as emphasized by Alston (1994), the Convention and the best interests principle also allow for flexibility and adaptability in decision-making. This is to keep pace with changing circumstances and to accommodate different cultural traditions. Thus, the framers of the Convention saw fit to cast the best interests principle at a very general level and to insert the term *a* primary consideration. But as also emphasized by Alston, flexibility is by degree only. Culture needs to be accommodated but culture cannot trump human rights. If there is a clear conflict between culture and the rights of the child – for example, the cultural approval of infanticide or genital mutilation versus the child's right to life and health – best interests must be interpreted such that culture yields to rights.

Neither the Convention nor the Committee on the Rights of the Child provide concrete answers as to what is truly in the best interests of the child. But they do provide signposts and, in the case of the Committee, point to what is *not* in the child's best interests. In surveying the reports of the Committee, Freeman (2007) identifies a number of practices, laws, and policies that the Committee has criticized as contrary to the child's best interests: corporal punishment; child abuse and neglect; a low minimum age of marriage; a low age of criminal responsibility; a punitive system of juvenile justice rather than one that focuses on rehabilitation and prevention; the discriminatory treatment of minority children (e.g., Aboriginal children in Canada and Roma children in Bulgaria); the discriminatory treatment of children born out of wedlock; child poverty (especially the poverty of vulnerable children); and conditions related to poverty such as inadequate housing, a substandard environment, and homelessness. Finally, the Committee has criticized as contrary to best interests the lack of the incorporation of the best interests principle into domestic law and the lack of public knowledge of the rights of the child. Best interests are less likely to be put into effect if the principle is not entrenched in law and policies and if the rights of the child are not known and not understood by children, parents, and professionals working with children.

In summary, although the Committee points to a number of items not in the child's best interests, it does not provide a full and definitive answer as to what is in the best interests of children. However, what is provided in the Convention and by the Committee is a process or methodology that provides direction. As concluded by Hammarberg (2008), it is the *process* that is the key to understanding the role and importance of the best interests principle. It is the process by which decision-makers take their direction from a principle that has been incorporated in law and policy, from regard for the welfare and healthy development of children, from the rights of the child, and from evidence on the well-being of children as informed by research.

Application of Best Interests to Education

What then is the meaning of the principle of the best interests of the child when it is applied to the field of education? How does the principle apply to primary and secondary schools, to education systems, and to education laws and policies that govern these systems and schools? To address these questions, we need to consider each of the signposts of best interests and their implications for education.

Concern for the Welfare of Children. At a very basic level, education in the child's best interests means that children are able to receive education. This is in keeping with the signpost of fundamental concern for the welfare or well-being of children. As is well known, education in modern society and in knowledge-based economies is very much connected to positive outcomes for children as a whole. This is well established in research, including research on the social determinants of health and on the effects of education on income, job satisfaction, and health and longevity.

According to the literature on the social determinants of health, social position or socioeconomic status is strongly associated with health (Marmot, 2004; Marmot & Wilkinson, 2006; Wilkinson & Pickett, 2010). Based on population health studies in numerous countries across the developed world, the research points to the primary importance of socioeconomic factors – income, occupational status, and level of education – in shaping health outcomes. The research concludes that the social gradient – or differences between people at the top and the bottom of the socioeconomic ladder – is more important in shaping health outcomes than even biomedical differences, genetic endowment, and behavioural risk factors such as diet. Although the steepness of the social gradient varies, depending on the degree of social inequality in a country, the population health in all countries is unevenly distributed and varies by income, occupation, and education. Although there is much more social inequality in the United States than in Norway or Sweden, in all countries, socioeconomic status affects outcomes in health and longevity.

Education is an important component of socioeconomic status. But when education is measured independently from income and occupation, a large body of research shows a significant relation between levels of education and health outcomes (Cutler & Lieras-Muney, 2008; Lantz et al., 2001; Mirowsky & Ross, 2003; OECD, 2010a). Simply put, people with more education are more likely to live longer and have better health. They are more likely to report better health, and they are more likely to have lower rates of mortality, morbidity, and disability related to health. People with less education, however, are more likely to have higher rates of infectious diseases, many non-infectious diseases, shorter survival rates when ill, and shorter life expectancy. Clearly, education is highly correlated with income level. But they are not entirely the same thing. When income levels are adjusted, education continues to be a strong predictor of better health and longevity. At the same levels of income, people who are better educated are significantly less at risk of poor health outcomes than people who receive little education or less education (Mirowsky & Ross, 2003).

Although the strong connection between education and health is well established in the research, the most important pathway through which education affects health is not clear. John Mirowsky and Catherine Ross (2003) suggest three main pathways. One is employment. People with more education are more likely to find full-time employment and to work in jobs that are more rewarding financially and personally. Moreover, they are more likely to have stable employment and higher income and to have more satisfying jobs that allow for autonomy and creativity, which are linked to better health. A second pathway is the development of stable and supportive interpersonal relationships. People with more education are more likely to be in committed long-term relationships and to have social support in their families and communities, which again are linked to better health. Finally, a third pathway is the process of learned effectiveness where more educated persons learn skills, gain knowledge, and gather resources that equip them psychologically with a sense of efficacy, that is, a sense of being able to control events and shape their lives in positive ways. A sense of efficacy includes being able to acquire and sustain good health and healthy lifestyles. It is not clear in the research which pathway is most important. What is clear is the strong relationship between education and health. The implication is obvious for children. From the point of view of health outcomes, and thus the well-being of children, receiving education is in the best interests of the child.

It is not only health. There is also the positive impact of education on economic well-being. According to the Organization of Economic Co-operation and Development (OECD), in reporting on educational outcomes across the developed world, education is more likely to result in more stable employment, less unemployment, and higher lifetime earnings (OECD, 2010a). To be sure, there is variation in the relation, depending on types of education and factors in education systems. But overall, more education is associated with more favourable economic outcomes. So from the point of view of economic well-being, education is in the best interests of the child.

There is also the positive impact of education on social well-being. For example, as found in research by Lochner and Moretti (2004), confirming a wide body of previous research, more education is associated with a reduced likelihood of criminal activity, arrest, incarceration, and destructive antisocial lifestyles. Children who do better at school and who stay longer at school are less likely to become involved in crime, gangs, and antisocial behaviour. The opposite is true for children who have less education and who experience less success at school. So from the point of view of social well-being, as gauged by the extent of criminal activity, education again is in the best interests of the child.

Education also has a number of indirect positive effects for children. For example, through the education of girls and women, education has an indirect effect on the survival and health of children. As reported by Emmanuela Gakidou and colleagues (2010), in a study of 175 countries over almost 30 years, childhood deaths and illness decrease as women's level of education increases. Education also has positive indirect effects for children in terms of promoting democracy and human rights. As reported by the OECD (2010a), across the developed world, more education is associated with higher levels of political interest and civic and political engagement. As shown in other research, more education is linked to a higher level of voting and a greater degree of overall citizen participation (Dee, 2004; Glaeser, Ponzetto, & Shleifer, 2007). More education also is shown to be associated with more support for human rights and the endorsement of human rights ideals (Cohrs et al., 2007; McFarland & Mathews, 2005). If it can be agreed that democracy and the protection of human rights – which include children's human rights – are desirable features of modern society, then more education for children contributes to these desirable ends.

So there are a number of important direct and indirect effects of education that are positive for the well-being of children. Richard Wilkinson and Kate Pickett (2010, p. 103) summarize the research by saying this: "People with more education earn more, are more satisfied with their work and leisure time, are less likely to be unemployed, more likely to be healthy, less likely to be criminals, more likely to volunteer their time and vote in elections." So at a very basic level, education in the best interests of the child means children receiving education. But it also means more than this.

Concern for the Rights of the Child. Education in the child's best interests means regard for and consistency with the rights of the child. The principle means not only that children are able to receive education but also that they receive a type of education informed by children's rights as described in the CRC. This, in turn, means that education laws, policies, and practices are consistent with the general principles of the Convention to the greatest degree possible. Thus, the principles of participation, non-discrimination, and the survival and development of the child are to be put into effect as part of best interests. In meeting the best interests of the child, then, school and classroom practices and education policies must provide meaningful opportunities for child participation, ensure the absence of discrimination, and ensure not only the survival but also the development of the child to his or her fullest potential.

Importantly also, education practices, policies, and laws must be consistent with the rights of the child. A number of articles are relevant to education. Following Eugeen Verhellen (1993; 1994), we can divide the Convention articles on education into three tracks. The enjoyment of rights on all three tracks is in the best interests of the child.

On the first track is the child's right *to* education (Articles 28, 29, and 23). Article 28 affirms that the child (every child) has the right to education and that countries have the responsibility to achieve this right progressively and on the basis of equal opportunity. Primary education is to be made available free to all, and secondary education (as well as higher education) is to be made available and accessible to every child, with financial support if necessary. In addition, under Article 28, educators are to take measures to encourage regular school attendance and reduce dropout rates, and school discipline is to be administered in a manner consistent with the child's human dignity. The Committee on the Rights of the Child has interpreted this provision on school discipline, together with other articles in the CRC, to mean that all forms of corporal punishment are unacceptable types of discipline in school (Hodgkin & Newell, 2007).

Further to Article 28, Article 29 affirms that the education of the child (every child) shall be directed to: (1) "the development of the child's personality, talents, and mental and physical abilities to their fullest potential"; (2) "the development of respect for human rights and fundamental freedoms, and for the principles enshrined in the Charter of the United Nations"; (3) "the development of respect for the child's parents, his or her own cultural identity, language and values, for the national values of the country in which the child is living, the country from which he or she may originate, and for civilizations different from his or her own"; (4) the preparation of the child for responsible life in a free society, in the spirit of understanding, peace, tolerance, equality of sexes, and friendship among all peoples, ethnic, national and religious groups and persons of Indigenous origin"; and (5) "the development of respect for the natural environment." These aims point to, among other things, the need for effective environmental education, citizenship education, and human rights education. The first aim is noteworthy because of its concern for the *whole* child, not simply the learner. As discussed at length by the U.N. Committee (2001) in its general comment on the aims of education, the article refers to the development not only of the child's intellect but also of the child's entire personality, talents, and abilities. Thus, there is concern for well-rounded development, not simply cognitive development and academic performance. This wider concern is reflected in the aim of developing respect for human rights, for parents, and for the environment. Finally, under Article 23, reference is made to the right of the disabled child to special care and assistance, including effective access to education and financial assistance where needed. The child with a disability has the right to education, as other children do, but also the right to special assistance in accessing education.

Education systems and schools that are not consistent with the best interests principle are ones that do not provide the right to education on the basis of equal opportunity. They fail to take measures to assure regular attendance, to reduce dropout rates, and to eliminate the use of corporal punishment. They are also ones that fail to develop effective programs of environmental education, citizenship education, and human rights education, and more broadly, to develop the child's fullest potential. If education systems focus solely on intellectual development, academic performance, and test scores, and not on the development of the *whole* child, they too are acting in ways inconsistent with best interests. A key problem, which we examine in detail later in the book, is that contrary to the child's right to education on the basis of equal opportunity, there continues to be a significant achievement gap in education between socially advantaged and disadvantaged children. Socially disadvantaged children are less likely to achieve to their fullest potential. In contrast, they are more likely to have higher rates of absenteeism, early school leaving, and school failure.

On the second track are the child's rights *in* education (Articles 2, 12, 13 to 16, 19, 24, 27, 30, 31, 33, and 34). Children have a wide number of rights that do not stop at the school door (Howe & Covell, 2005; Osler & Starkey, 2010, Verhellen, 1994). There is the right in school not to suffer from "discrimination of any kind" (Article 2). There are rights of participation in school. A child in school has the right to express views "freely in all matters affecting the child, the views of the child being given due weight in accordance with the age and maturity of the child" (Article 12.1). In addition, in any judicial and administrative proceeding related to the school, children have the right to be heard directly or through a representative (Article 12.2). Associated with these participation rights in school are a number of expressive rights. Subject to reasonable limits, children have rights to freedom of expression and access to information; freedom of thought, conscience, and religion; freedom of association and peaceful assembly, and privacy (Articles 13 to 16). Children also have the right in school to play and leisure and to participate in recreational activities and cultural and artistic pursuits (Article 31).

There are also the rights of protection. In school, as in families and elsewhere in society, children have the right to be protected "from all forms of physical or mental violence, injury or abuse, neglect or negligent treatment, maltreatment or exploitation, including sexual abuse" (Article 19). As the Committee has emphasized, this means, among other things, effective measures to deal with problems such as bullying and school violence. In addition, children have the right to be protected from the illicit use of narcotic drugs and from all forms of sexual exploitation and sexual abuse (Articles 33 and 34). This means effective prevention programs. Furthermore, there are the rights of provision. Children have the right to health care (Article 24) and basic economic well-being (Article 27). Again, these rights do not stop at the school door. If there is a pressing need such as to respond to a child with a physical injury or to one coming to school hungry, schools as agencies of the state have an obligation to provide or arrange for basic medical assistance and school meal programs. To ignore these issues would be to act contrary to the child's best interests. Finally, there are rights for special populations of children in school. Under Article 30, minority and Indigenous children have the right to enjoy their own culture, practise their own religion, and use their own language. This means an obligation on the part of school authorities to take measures to accommodate minority and Indigenous children.

Schools and education systems that are not consistent with the best interests principle are ones that fail to protect children from discrimination and school violence and to provide children with effective means of participation in schools and classrooms. They also are ones that fail to establish effective measures or programs against bullying, drug use, and sexual abuse, and that ignore the medical and health needs of children and the problem of child poverty and child hunger. Moreover, they are ones that fail to accommodate minority and Indigenous children in terms of their culture, religion, and language. A problem is that in many schools and education systems across the developed world, there continues to be a serious gap between the principle of accommodation in education and actual practice. As noted by Laura Lundy (2006), the problem is particularly pronounced in socially divided societies such as Northern Ireland where children at school continue to experience harassment, intimidation, and discrimination. But in virtually all countries, to greater or lesser degrees, there continues to be a gap between rights and reality.

On the third track are the child's rights *through* education (Articles 29, 42, and 44). This refers to education in which children come to learn and know about their rights and to develop respect for human rights and fundamental freedoms, including the rights and freedoms of children. The importance of this third track of education long precedes the Convention (Freeman, 1997; Hodgson, 1996). It is in line with the U.N. Charter itself and with the Universal Declaration of Human Rights. The

United Nations judged human rights education to be so important that it proclaimed 1995 to 2005 to be the U.N. Decade for Human Rights Education. It comes as no surprise, then, that the framers of the CRC made children's human rights education part of the document (Howe & Covell, 2005). Under Article 29 of the CRC, countries have agreed that the education of the child shall be directed to "the development of respect for human rights and fundamental freedoms." This development of respect presupposes that children have knowledge and understanding of human rights, which includes children's human rights. Under Article 42, countries have agreed "to undertake to make the principles of the Convention widely known, by appropriate and active means, to adults and children alike." This signals a clear obligation for countries and educators to disseminate information and to educate children – as well as adults – about the rights of the child. It also signals the need to use "appropriate and active means" to reach children in an effective way, which means fully implementing children's rights education in schools, not merely providing information through websites or brochures. The Committee on the Rights of the Child, therefore, has repeatedly urged countries to take measures to incorporate children's rights education into the school curricula. Finally, under Article 44, countries have agreed to make their reports on the rights of the child widely known to the public. This means that child advocacy groups and concerned citizens will be made more aware of the rights of the child and of their country's efforts, and thus more able to spread awareness to others, including children.

It is in the best interests of children not only that they enjoy basic rights but also that they know and understand their basic rights. Philosopher Joel Feinberg (1973; Feinberg & Narveson, 1970) has pointed out the close relationship between the possession of rights and the development of a sense of value or self-esteem.

Rights, says Feinberg (1973, pp. 58–59), "are not mere gifts or favors, motivated by love or pity, for which gratitude is the sole fitting response. A right is something that can be demanded or insisted upon without embarrassment or shame." In other words, a right is one's due. It says to people that they are valued persons worthy of respect. It conveys to people a sense of value and, in so doing, empowers people to act with confidence as equal and valued citizens who exercise their rights and responsibilities. Feinberg's analysis may be applied to children (Howe & Covell, 2005). Having rights and knowing that they have rights means that in their own eyes, and well as in the eyes of others, children are esteemed persons worthy of respect. Rights equip children with a sense of value as individual persons, apart from their relationship with parents, teachers, and adults. Learning they have rights, children learn that they are not parental property or objects of paternalistic concern. Rather, they learn that they are persons with inherent value. With inherent value, they are empowered to hold their heads up high and to participate in their school community as valued members of their school community.

Schools and education systems that are inconsistent with the best interests principle are ones that fail to educate children about the rights of the child. They are also ones that fail to provide for teacher training and appropriate pedagogy (Osler & Starkey, 2010; Verhellen, 1994). Furthermore, and of particular importance, they are ones that fail to model and respect the rights of the child. Schools may teach children about their basic rights but if they fail to model the practice of those rights – for example, fail to provide opportunities for the exercise of participation rights – children will see through the hypocrisy and fail to engage in the learning. As pointed out by Lundy (2007), allowing for student voice in itself is not enough. The participation rights of children need to be made known to children, respected, and given weight. A key problem is that, contrary to the child's rights through education, the practice of educating children about their rights continues to be largely absent in schools across the developed world (Howe & Covell, 2005). Children's rights education may exist in particular classrooms or particular schools or even in particular school districts. But contrary to the best interests of the child, it does not yet exist on a systematic and comprehensive basis.

Concern for Evidence. Education in the best interests of the child also requires full consideration of the evidence on the impact and outcomes of various education laws, policies, and practices for children. According to the U.N. Committee on the Rights of the Child, in education as elsewhere, applying best interests requires taking into account the results of child impact assessments and evaluations. This, in turn, requires that impact assessments and evaluations be done and that these be informed by well-designed research studies. In order to appropriately implement the education rights of the child, address issues, and determine conditions for the enjoyment of children's rights, evidence-based knowledge is required about child outcomes and best practices.

The Committee has expressed a number of concerns about issues and problems in the implementation of children's education rights

(Hodgkin & Newell, 2007; U.N. Committee, 2001). In putting into effect the child's basic right to education (Article 28), for example, the Committee has urged that more attention be given to goals such as ensuring regular attendance in school and reducing school dropout rates. It also has urged that major efforts be made to counter educational discrimination against minority and rural children, refugee and immigrant children, and children with disabilities and HIV/AIDS. In addition, it has recommended that serious problems such as bullying and school violence be given more attention and that steps be taken to eliminate the practice of corporal punishment in schools that have not yet done this. Furthermore, in achieving the various aims of education as described in the CRC (Article 29), the Committee has pointed to the need for greater educational efforts in providing balanced and child-centred education that develops children's personality, talents, and abilities to their fullest potential. The Committee also has emphasized the need for stronger measures to establish broad and effective human rights education in the interests of cultivating among children greater respect for human rights. Finally, in the interests of preparing the child for responsible life in a free society, the Committee has pointed to the need for effective and engaging programs of citizenship education, health education, sexual health education, and environmental education.

Tackling these various issues requires knowledge about the nature and scope of the problems, best practices in dealing with the problems, and the impact that various policy options will have on children. This, in turn, requires research and evidence about how best to proceed. This is why the Committee has referred to the need for systematic studies on problems such as poor school attendance and high dropout rates (Hodgkin & Newell, 2007). It is important, said the Committee, to identify the causes of non-attendance and dropping out. A number of factors may be involved ranging from poverty, discrimination, and teen pregnancy to overly punitive discipline policies, dull curricula and dull teaching styles, and lack of support for children with disabilities. There is a need, therefore, to determine which factors are most critical. There is also a need to identify best practices in response to the problems. In the best interests of children, education authorities need to do or refer to impact studies on the alternatives and to use evidence-based research to determine which alternative practice or policy is better at tackling the problem.

Ideally, all education policies, laws, and practices should be reviewed and evaluated for their impact on the well-being of children, taking into account existing research evidence. To the greatest degree possible, evaluations should involve methodologically rigorous studies. The point is to find the best evidence possible to guide decisions in children's best interests. This is particularly important for dealing with serious problems such as school disengagement, high dropout rates, school violence, and discrimination, which compromise a child's fundamental right to education on the basis of equal opportunity. Education systems where decisions and policies are made without the benefit of evidence-based studies of child impact and best practices, especially in these critical areas, are inconsistent with the best interests of the child. A major problem, as noted by Hammarberg (2008), is that in education as elsewhere, child impact assessments and the systematic use of research evidence are rarities.

Incorporation. Finally, education in the best interests of the child means the incorporation of the principle into education legislation and policies. Countries that have ratified the Convention have the formal obligation to ensure that the principles of the Convention (including the best interests principle), and the articles of the Convention (including the articles on education) are incorporated into domestic laws and policies. In line with this obligation, the Committee has repeatedly emphasized that the best interests principle, together with the other principles, should be reflected in legislation and decision-making, including in the area of education (Hodgkin & Newell, 2007). This is to ensure that the principle can be used in the courts and used as a political means to hold governments and education decision-makers accountable for actions in the best interests of children. The principle need not be stated such that it is to be *the* primary consideration in actions concerning children, although it can be stated this way. But at a minimum, consistent with Article 3, it needs to be stated as *a* primary consideration.

The Value of Applying Best Interests

Apart from the matter of legality and the honouring of international commitments, the explicit integration of the principle into education law and policy is in the best interests of the child. Children are among the most vulnerable groups in society. They are unable to vote and they lack political and economic power. As Freeman (2007, p. 40) puts it, "in a world run by adults, there would otherwise be a danger that children's interests would be completely ignored." We may add that in the world of education, there is the danger that the interests of children as a whole, and especially the interests of socially disadvantaged children, would be ignored or dismissed or overridden by other interests. As a vulnerable group, children do not have the resources or power to defend their interests against other interests. They therefore depend on adults in positions of authority, including education authorities. But if education authorities are not bound by the principle of the best interests of the child, if they are left with wide discretionary power, there is little assurance that they will always make decisions and policies in the best interests of children. Even if they claim to be acting in children's best interests, without formal reference to the principle as stated in the CRC, there is no assurance that they will not be interpreting best interests in a paternalistic or otherwise inappropriate way. The benefit of an explicitly stated principle of best interests, based on Article 3 of the CRC, is that it focuses attention on the core goal of promoting the optimal development of children. It does so from the perspective of making education decisions that are consistent with the rights of the child and sensitive to research evidence that identifies conditions for children to enjoy their rights in school.

Furthermore, through a careful and systematic application of the principle, there is the benefit of greater rationality and the use of principled judgment in education decision-making and policy-making (Howe & Covell, 2010a). Such a reasoning process is more likely to produce outcomes in the better or best interests of children. Under the best interests principle, instead of the wide use of discretionary power or ad hoc decision-making, education decision-makers would be required to make rational decisions in the best interests of children, informed by the rights of the child, the views of the child, and evidence-based research on child outcomes. It is true that authorities may not ultimately make decisions in the best interests of the child because the principle is to be *a* primary consideration, not *the* primary consideration. Nevertheless, the principle is to be a consideration, which means that it needs to be taken into account in an active and serious way. If at the end of the deliberation, decisions are made on the basis of other primary considerations – for example, economic or religious considerations – this needs to be made transparent and reasons made known to the wider educational and political community. In all likelihood, over the longer term as the principle becomes entrenched, it is reasonable to think that education decision-makers would be hesitant to allow other considerations to outweigh best interests, fearful of criticism and embarrassment.

Education systems that are not fully consistent with the best interests of the child are ones in which the best interests principle is omitted in legislation and policy. Unfortunately, such omission is very common. It may be the case – as it is in some jurisdictions – that the principle is referred to as a guide in particular areas of education such as the placement of children with disabilities. In the Republic of Ireland, for example, under the Education for Persons with Special Educational Needs Act (2004), authorities are required to apply the best interests principle in assessing and placing children with special needs (McPartland, 2010). In Canada, thanks to the Canadian Supreme Court's decision in the *Eaton* case (1997), education decision-makers are required to refer to the best interests principle in deciding whether special needs students are to be placed in regular or special classrooms (Howe & Covell, 2010a). But important though this requirement is, it applies to a narrow field of education. The principle fails to apply to education systems as a whole.

It also may be the case that in some jurisdictions there is mention of the principle of the educational best interests of students. In Canada, for example, reference is made in Quebec's education legislation to the best interests of the student and in the legislation of Alberta and Manitoba, to educational best interests (Howe & Covell, 2010a). But this is a narrow approach, giving attention to children as learners or students rather than to the *whole* child. As emphasized in Article 29 of the CRC, the best interests of children involve much more than how children achieve as students. What is important, says the article, are not only the child's cognitive development but also the growth of the child's entire personality, talents, and abilities. Although education in the best interests of the child certainly includes academic progress, it also involves well-rounded development and progress in areas such as respect for human rights and respect for the environment.

Finally, it may be the case – as in many jurisdictions – that certain aspects of the best interests principle are referred to. For example, there may be reference in education legislation to the principle of non-discrimination, to the child's right to participation or voice, to the child's right to education and access to education, or to the principle of equal educational opportunity. But aspects of the principle are not the same as the principle itself. Unfortunately, when we review what countries in the developed world have reported to the Committee on the Rights of the Child about education – as contained in the database of the Office of the High Commissioner for Human Rights (2011) – we find no reference to the best interests of the child as a core principle to guide systems of education. Such failure – as well as the general failure among countries to incorporate the Convention on the Rights of the Child into law – has been repeatedly noted and criticized by the Committee. This brings into question the level of commitment that countries actually have for wanting to apply the best interests principle to education.

This does not mean that there have been no efforts among educators, school leaders, and education policy-makers to develop practices consistent with children's best interests. As later chapters in this book will show, we have important examples of teachers, schools, and policy-makers who have contributed to the advancement of education in the best interests of the child. They have done so through taking seriously the idea that *all* children have the right to education and through taking steps to equalize opportunities and to implement evidence-based practices to achieve equity. The problem, however, is that action has yet to be done on a systematic and comprehensive basis. What would be of immense help to this end would be the explicit incorporation of the principle of the best interests of the child into education law and policies. This would put pressure on education systems as a whole to take concerted action on behalf of children.

In summary, education in the best interests of the child means the incorporation of the best interests principle into education law and policies and a process of decision-making in which authorities take into full consideration the principles of the Convention, the provision, protection, and participation rights of the child, and child impact assessments and research evidence. Of particular importance, consistent with Articles 28 and 29 of the Convention, it means ensuring not only a child's education but also a child's *right* to education on the basis of equal opportunity for the purpose of developing the child's personality, talents, and abilities to his or her fullest potential. However, this meaning of best interests has yet to be appreciated and put into effect.

The Meaning of Education on the Basis of Equal Opportunity

Crucial to applying the best interests principle in education is implementing the child's human right to education. According to Article 28 of the CRC, the child's right to education is to be achieved progressively and on the basis of equal opportunity. The term *progressively* is straightforward. As explained by the Committee, it means making progress over time in making financial resources available for education, improving administration, improving access to education, and improving the quality of education (Hodgkin & Newell, 2007). Many developing countries are lacking in resources and capacity and therefore need more time and support to put the education rights of children into full effect. But what does the term *equal opportunity* mean? This is more difficult. The Committee discusses various forms of discrimination as barriers to equal opportunity. But it does not define or elaborate on the actual meaning of equal opportunity.

Allen Buchanan and his colleagues (2000) provide a helpful analysis of the evolving concept of equality of opportunity. According to their analysis, there have been three alternative interpretations of the concept, as the concept has emerged in the literature and public discourse. The first and earliest is called formal equality of opportunity or careers open to talents. Here, equal opportunity means the absence of legal barriers to equality such as discriminatory laws that deny minorities and women the opportunity to vote or get an education. An example would be an early U.S. law that prohibited African-Americans from attending a regular school. In this kind of situation, equality of opportunity requires that such a legal barrier be eliminated so that there are similar prospects for persons of similar talents and abilities. But the problem with this early concept is that it fails to recognize informal barriers to equality, which are not related to law. Despite a removal of legal barriers, discrimination may still occur in informal ways such as exclusionary social and economic practices based on prejudice.

The second interpretation sees equal opportunity as the absence of both legal barriers and informal barriers to equality. Primary among informal barriers would be prejudice, stereotyping, bias, and discrimination, such as against minorities and women by employers, organizations, or businesses providing services to the public. An example would be education authorities in a particular school district, out of prejudice, having a deliberate policy of excluding children with disabilities from attending school. Equality of opportunity here means eliminating not only legal barriers but also any informal barriers that result in extralegal discriminatory policy or exclusionary actions. The problem with this concept, however, is that it does not recognize barriers to equality that are based neither on legal discrimination nor informal prejudice-based discrimination. Unjust exclusion and the denial or restriction of opportunity may still occur. For example, in schools, minority children or children with disabilities may still be denied the same opportunity as others because of the effects of poverty or harassment or bullying or a lack of educational support. The elimination of legal discrimination or prejudice would do little to ensure equal opportunity.

The third interpretation, and the one supported by Buchanan and his associates (2000), conceives equal opportunity as the absence not only of legal and informal discrimination but also of the effects of bad luck in the social lottery. This is called the level playing field conception. The logic is this. If it is granted that legal and informal discrimination are unjustified because they are arbitrary and unfair obstacles to opportunities, then it must also be granted that anything beyond a person's control that puts obstacles or limitations on opportunities is also unjustified. Persons should not have lesser opportunities because of how they fare in the social lottery – whether they happened to be born and raised in a very positive and supportive family and social environment or whether they were raised under negative social conditions and in a socially disadvantaged family. Just as it is unfair to allow legally based or prejudice-based discrimination that impairs or denies a person's opportunity, it is also unfair to allow social or even genetic factors beyond a person's control to impede the person's opportunity and life chances. Justice requires that people pursue opportunities based on their choices.

According to the level playing field conception of equal opportunity, the state must act to counter not only discrimination but also the opportunity-limiting effects of bad luck in the social lottery. This means that laws, policies, and government action must aim to level the playing field and to counteract the ill effects of factors such as poverty, racism, and disability. Buchanan and his colleagues (2000) urge that in addition to social factors, action also be directed against opportunity-limiting genetic factors, which of course is much more controversial. But what is widely embraced among subscribers to the level playing field conception is the need for strong government action against social factors. In the field of education, this means that education laws and policies need to tackle not only discrimination but also all obstacles beyond the control of students. A simple example of levelling the educational playing field, as has been done in developed countries, would be the provision of free or accessible primary and secondary education, designed to counter the negative effects of poverty on access to education. Further examples would be supports and services in place for children with disabilities, policies in place against harassment and bullying, and school practices in place designed to overcome barriers and meet the needs of all disadvantaged children.

This level playing field conception is the one supported in the Convention and by the Committee on the Rights of the Child. In describing the right to education in Article 28, the framers of the Convention chose to use the term "on the basis of equal opportunity" rather than an alternative term such as "equality of results." They did so in order to gain consensus and moving forward rather than getting mired in controversy. But their conception of equal opportunity was not the traditional one of simply acting against prejudice and discrimination. It was the broader one of levelling the playing field. Thus, in Article 28 of the CRC, every child has the right to free primary education and to accessible secondary education, with financial assistance if necessary. Also in Article 28, education authorities have the obligation to ensure regular school attendance and to reduce dropout rates. So equality of opportunity means not only the absence of discrimination but also positive action to remove barriers such as poverty. In addition to the CRC, the Committee also has embraced the level playing field concept, although it does not name it as such. As previously discussed, the Committee has emphasized the need for policy-makers and educators to take strong action against problems such as bullying and school violence. In their view, it is not enough to satisfy equal opportunity by eliminating prejudice and discrimination alone. There must also be strong educational action to level the playing field and counter all social obstacles to education that are beyond the control of children.

In summary, from the point of view of the Convention and the Committee the right to education on the basis of equal opportunity means more than eliminating discrimination. It means levelling the playing field for children who suffer from the bad effects of the social lottery. Thus, because implementing the child's right to education on the basis of equal opportunity is a vital part of advancing the best interests of the child, levelling the educational playing field is in the best interests of the child.

Chapter Three

Challenges for Best Interests in Education

The challenges for the application of the principle of best interests in education are many. One that has particular significance is the inequality of educational opportunity experienced by socially disadvantaged children. As explained in the previous chapter, according to the U.N. Convention on the Rights of the Child, children not only have the right to education but they also have the right to enjoy education on the basis of equal opportunity. Achieving equal opportunity requires that political and education authorities take action not only to eliminate discrimination but also to level the playing field such that obstacles to opportunities are removed. However, as has been well established in the education literature, children from impoverished homes and disadvantaged communities are significantly less likely to do as well at school. There is a serious achievement gap. Because socially disadvantaged children are less likely to do as well at school, over the long term, they are less likely to have favourable economic and health outcomes. This is in clear contradiction of the best interests of the child.

In this chapter, we examine the challenge of inequality of educational opportunity. We do so first by looking at social inequality and the persisting problem of child and family poverty. We then describe the impact of poverty on education and the family and school risk factors through which poverty and low income become translated into inequality of educational opportunity. Although not all children living in poverty will have difficulties with schooling, the probability of learning difficulties and behavioural problems is higher among them. Rather than taking guidance from the research literature, and rather than taking strong steps to support and engage disadvantaged children, educators typically respond to their difficulties with punitive practices such as grade retention, the use of corporal punishment, and exclusion. In doing so, they fail not only to deliver on the child's right to education on the basis of equal opportunity but also to act in the best interests of the child.

Social Inequality and the Persistence of Poverty

Educational inequality among children occurs in the context of social inequality and the persistence of family and child poverty. Throughout the developed world, despite overall economic growth since the Second World War, despite a long-term increase in average incomes, and despite an overall improvement in living standards, there remains a significant gap between high- and low-income families and children. As discussed by Wilkinson and Pickett (2010), there are a number of ways of measuring income inequality. We can measure the top and bottom 20 per cent of household income. Or we can measure the top and bottom 10 or 30 per cent. But regardless of the approach, the result is the same: There is significant inequality of income and wealth among individuals, families, and children.

Wilkinson and Pickett (2010) also alert us to more sophisticated measures of inequality. We can use the Gini coefficient and measure income inequality across a whole society rather than comparing the extremes. Under this approach, which is commonly used by economists, if all income in a country went to one person – a situation of maximum inequality – the Gini coefficient would equal 1. Alternatively, if all income were shared equally – a situation of full equality – the coefficient would equal 0. So the closer the coefficient is to 1, the higher the degree of inequality. One other approach is the use of the so-called Robin Hood Index in which inequality is calculated in terms of what proportion of a country's income would have to be taken from the wealthy and given to the poor to achieve complete equality. The index ranges from 0 (complete equality) to 100 (complete inequality). But as Wilkinson and Pickett (2010) conclude, regardless of which measure is applied, the same general pattern can be seen to emerge: The distribution of income among individuals, families, and children is highly unequal.

Although there is social inequality in all developed countries, there also are major variations by country. For example, when income inequality is measured in terms of the top and bottom 20 per cent of household income after taxes, there are vast differences in the extent of inequality among countries (United Nations Development Program,

2006; Wilkinson & Pickett, 2010). At one extreme, in Japan, Finland, Norway, and Sweden, the wealthiest 20 per cent are less than four times as rich as the poorest 20 per cent. But at the other extreme, in the United States, Portugal, and Singapore, the wealthiest 20 per cent are eight to 10 times as rich as the poorest 20 per cent. So the difference is twice as big in the United States as it is in Japan or Finland. Within the above extremes, using the same measure, income inequality is less in northern European countries such as Denmark, Germany, and the Netherlands, and more in New Zealand, Australia, and the United Kingdom. Nonetheless, although there are variations among countries in the extent of inequality, the basic point remains that in all developed countries, there is significant social inequality.

With social inequality comes child and family poverty. Again, although child poverty exists in all developed countries, there is considerable variation across countries. This variation is related to the degree to which governments intervene to mitigate or reduce poverty. Child poverty can be measured in absolute terms as the lack of a certain fixed amount of goods and services. Or it can be measured in relative terms as the percentage of children being in households under a certain minimum level of income. The relative measure has become the most commonly used measure. Although this measure tells us little about absolute material deprivation, it does give us a picture of the contrast between the lives of poor children and their affluent peers. It also is useful for comparative purposes. UNICEF (2007) has done an impressive comparative study of child poverty in 24 OECD countries, which comprise the wealthiest countries of the world. In the study, UNICEF defined child poverty as the proportion of children growing up in relative poverty measured in terms of households with income less than 50 per cent of the national median. Using this definition, UNICEF found huge national differences in levels of child poverty. At the lowest end were the Nordic countries of Denmark, Finland, Norway, and Sweden, respectively. At the highest end were the United States, the United Kingdom, Italy, and Ireland. Where the proportion of poor children in Denmark was only 2 per cent, and in Finland only 3 per cent, it was a whopping 23 per cent in the United States, well above the OECD average of 11 per cent.

There are also significant variations in child poverty within countries. For example, there are major differences by region, ethnicity, and family structure. As an illustration, in the United States, rates of child poverty are the highest in the southern and southwestern states and the lowest in the northern and northeastern states (Children's Defense Fund, 2010). In addition, by a significant margin, child poverty rates are highest among African-American children, followed by American Indian and Latino children. Where one in five children in the United States lives in poverty, the figure is one in three for African-American children. In Canada, rates of child poverty are the highest in the northern territories and western provinces and the lowest in the eastern and Atlantic provinces (Campaign 2000, 2010). One reason for this variation in Canada is the higher portion of Aboriginal children and families living in the northern and western parts of the country. The rate of Aboriginal child poverty in Canada is over double the rate of overall child poverty, with over 40 per cent of Aboriginal children living below the poverty line. But this is not just a problem for Canada. High rates of poverty among Indigenous children and families – as well as a host of other social problems – are also present in Australia and New Zealand (United Nations, 2009). In Australia, poverty rates for Aboriginal and Torres Strait Islander children are similar to or higher than those in Canada. In New Zealand, although rates are not as high, they are disproportionally higher for Maori children than for other children. It is estimated that where the child poverty rate for Pakeha children (children of European ancestry) is about 16 per cent, it is 27 per cent for Maori children and 40 per cent for Pacifica and other minority children (Office of the Children's Commissioner of New Zealand, 2008).

Child poverty rates also vary by family structure. In absolute terms, most child poverty is in two-parent families. This is not surprising because despite the rise of single-parent families, most families are still two-parent families. Nevertheless, in relative terms, children across OECD countries have a higher probability of being in poverty when they live in single-parent families (OECD, 2008). This also varies by country. The lowest rates of child poverty in single-parent households are in the Nordic countries (under 15%). The highest rates are in Japan, Luxembourg, the United States, Canada, Germany, and Poland (over 40%). The main reasons for these cross-national differences are that in countries with low rates of child poverty, there are much higher rates of maternal employment and higher levels of government support for single-parent families in terms of child care, paid parental leave, and other benefits.

It may be tempting to think that social inequality and poverty have become less of a problem in the developed world. But such is not the case. The gap between rich and poor individuals and families has

actually increased in most OECD countries over the past 20 years
(OECD, 2008). Inequality of household incomes was higher in most
OECD countries by 2005 than it was during the mid-1980s. To be sure,
this was not the case in all countries. France, Spain, and Greece – until
very recently – moved towards greater social equality. But the general
trend has been towards more inequality, which can only be expected to
continue because of the major economic difficulties starting in 2008 and
subsequent cuts or restraint in social programs. According to the OECD
(2008), over time, there has been a moderate to very significant increase
in income inequality in most countries of the developed world. With
this growing inequality, rates of child poverty have risen, particularly
in Australia, the United Kingdom, and the United States. Very recently,
in some countries, the trend has become even more pronounced. In the
United States, for example, where the child poverty rate was 16 per cent
in 2000, it was almost 20 per cent in 2008 with over 14 million children
living in poverty (Children's Defense Fund, 2010). So child poverty remains a persisting problem across OECD countries, and in some countries such as the United States, an acute and growing problem.

As pointed out by Wilkinson and Pickett (2010), there are a number
of reasons to be concerned about inequality and child poverty. Drawing on a wide body of social science research, they provide a long list
of negative outcomes from poverty. Primary among the outcomes are
an erosion of trust and deterioration in the quality of social relations;
a greater risk of mental health problems, drug abuse, physical health
problems, and shorter life expectancy; more teenage pregnancies and
births; and a greater likelihood among children and youth of involvement in antisocial, violent, and criminal behaviour. But also among the
negative outcomes of poverty is early school leaving and reduced academic achievement. Clearly, such outcomes are at odds not only with
the principle of equal educational opportunity but also the best interests of the child.

The Impact of Poverty on Education

Poverty has a profound effect on educational opportunity. As established in a large body of research, socially disadvantaged children are
less likely to be prepared for school, less likely to perform well in school
as measured through national and international tests, more likely to repeat grades, and more likely to drop out of school (Burnett & Farkas,
2009; Cooper et al., 2010; Darling-Hammond, 2010; Field, Kuczera, &

Pont, 2007; Ou & Reynolds, 2008; Raffo et al., 2010; Raver, Gershoff, & Aber, 2007).

Poverty is a barrier to educational achievement that is very difficult for children to overcome (Bramley & Karley, 2007; Darling-Hammond, 2010). The fundamental problem is that children in poor families disproportionately lack the kind of early experiences, either at home or at child care, that prepare children for school (Crosnoe et al., 2010). Starting school is particularly difficult for children whose early years are lacking in opportunities for them to develop the necessary foundational skills in cognition and in behaviour that are needed for successful adaptation to formal schooling. Because of these socioeconomically based differences in early experiences, an achievement gap is evident at the beginning of kindergarten. Overwhelmingly, the research demonstrates that children from families that are relatively high in socioeconomic resources enter formal schooling with higher language and math skills and with fewer behavioural problems than do children from families living in adverse socioeconomic conditions (e.g., Barbarin et al., 2006; Fantuzzo et al., 2005; Jackson, Choi, & Bentler, 2009; Kaplan & Walpole, 2005; Marks & Coll, 2007). It is worth noting here that poverty is the key predictor of the differential level of school readiness, not its common correlates of family or neighbourhood structure (Barbarin et al., 2006; Leventhal et al., 2005). The result is an early, persistent, and increasing achievement gap that appears to be most pronounced in language, reading, and math skills (Aikens & Barbarin, 2008; Marks & Coll, 2007). It is a gap that typically grows as educational and developmental demands increase throughout schooling.

The development of competencies in language, reading, and math begins in early infancy and grows through childhood. The effects of socioeconomic status on the development of these basic competencies are substantial and evident early (Noble, Farah, & McCandliss, 2006a). As early as age 2 or 3 years, children from low-income families have less-developed vocabulary and oral language skills compared with those from middle- or high-income families (Phillips & Lonigan, 2009). They acquire language skills more slowly, have delayed letter recognition, and have poor phonological awareness (Aikens & Barbarin, 2008; Kaplan & Walpole, 2005). These delays are very important to future competencies. Phonological awareness refers to an understanding of the sound structure of language, and it is essential for later reading ability. When children learn to read, they need to understand that the words are made up of sounds, or phonemes. Children with slowed

phonological awareness, then, are likely to be delayed readers and at risk of reading difficulties (Aikens & Barbarin, 2008). Like language and pre-literacy skills, differences in basic math knowledge are very clear in comparisons of children from middle- and low-income families in their early years (Klibanoff et al., 2006). Although the fundamental capacity to discriminate quantities is innate, how that capacity develops is based on experience (Krajewski & Schneider, 2009). As Kristin Krajewski and Wolfgang Schneider (2009) explain, two developments occur through the early years. One is that children acquire the language that allows them to differentiate quantities verbally using words such as "more" and "less." The second, and an independent development that normally occurs around age 2, is that children learn to count. Connecting the two – realizing that number words used in counting are linked to quantities – is an important milestone that is the beginning of children's math abilities. It is an achievement that occurs through experience in the family (Klibanoff et al., 2006), and it is one that is strongly linked with subsequent achievement in mathematics (e.g., Gersten, Jordan, & Flojo, 2005; Krajewski & Schneider, 2009).

The income-based disparities in the attainment of basic language and math skills mean that children from low-income families are already behind their more advantaged peers when they enter formal schooling (Aikens & Barbarin, 2008). At the outset, the scores of children from low-income families on both math and reading tests are significantly lower than those of children from middle- and upper-income families (Burnett & Farkas, 2009; Duncan et al., 2007; Raver et al., 2007). The key problem is that these low early scores in math and reading predict poor performance in later reading and math (Cadima, McWilliam, & Leal, 2010; Grissmer et al., 2010; Romano et al., 2010). With regard to math performance, for example, counting skills at the beginning of schooling are identified as a strong predictor of math learning 6 months later (Passolunghi, Vercelloni, & Schadee, 2007). Children's number concepts in kindergarten are found to predict their calculation ability in Grade 4 (Koponen et al., 2007). With regard to reading, the early deficits in phonological awareness and reading are highly predictive of subsequent literacy skills. Researchers have not only shown that many poor children continue to be unable to read at all by the end of Grade 1 (Kaplan & Walpole, 2005), but also that children who begin school with language and reading delays stay behind their peers even when there are intensive remedial or intervention efforts (Phillips & Lonigan, 2009). Not surprisingly, these early disparities in math and reading increase

throughout elementary school, making it progressively more difficult for the child to acquire numeracy and literacy skills in the later grades (Aikens & Barbarin, 2008; Crosnoe et al., 2010). As a result, the acquisition of skills is continuously slowed (Burnett & Farkas, 2009; Marks & Coll, 2007). There is little catch-up.

It seems that achievement trajectories of children from low-income families are determined by their earliest school experiences. When we compare tests scores, we repeatedly find that throughout the elementary school years, children living in poverty earn lower grades and are more likely to repeat grades than their more advantaged peers (Raver et al., 2007; Yeung, Linver, & Brooks-Gunn, 2002). This achievement gap has been noted so often that researchers have proposed that the start of formal schooling represents a critical period during which appropriate learning experiences are essential to prevent lasting damage to school engagement, motivation, and cognitive capacity (e.g., Burnett & Farkas, 2009). Children who are prepared well for schooling experience early successes in school. These successes promote constructive academic attitudes and further successes (Pettit et al., 2009). Children who are not well prepared for schooling are more likely to have negative experiences early; these appear to set the child on a developmental pathway to failure and dropping out of school (Cooper et al., 2010).

The achievement gap that grows through elementary school persists into adolescence (Malecki & Demaray, 2006). Once again, in later grades, as in elementary school, poverty is a key predictor of lower math and reading skills (Eamon, 2002). The size of the gap has been particularly clear in comparisons of national test scores. For example, in a comparison of scores in English conducted in the United Kingdom, not one 14-year-old who was living in poverty achieved the expected level of performance, whereas 83 per cent of those from a comparison sample of children living in middle-income families did (Glennerster, 2002). With this large gap in achievement, it is not in the least surprising that poverty is a strong risk factor for the failure to complete high school (Crowder & South, 2003; Harding, 2003; Ou & Reynolds, 2008; Oyserman, Brickman, & Rhodes, 2007). As Daniel Caro and Rainer Lehmann (2009) observed in their study of students in Germany, the school experiences of children from low-income families simply worsen as they age. The achievement gap that is present when children start school continues to widen and it impels early school leaving. However, such evidence does not just come from the United Kingdom or Germany;

the income-related achievement gap and its effects are seen across the developed world.

The presence of an achievement gap in performance and school completion among adolescents is well established in research. In *all* OECD countries, adolescents of low socioeconomic status are much more likely to be underperformers in school (Darling-Hammond, 2010; Field et al., 2007; OECD, 2010b). This is known through the analysis of the social backgrounds of school dropouts and through the results of how students from different social backgrounds do on international standardized tests. The findings of the Program for International Student Assessment (PISA) are particularly revealing. PISA is a large, carefully designed study involving more than 50 OECD and other countries, testing how well 15-year-olds do in reading, science, and mathematics. The results of PISA – which has conducted tests every 3 years since 2000 – show, among other things, that most of the students who perform poorly in PISA are from socially disadvantaged backgrounds (OECD PISA, 2011). For example, in the 2003 mathematics results, children from the most disadvantaged backgrounds were over three times more likely to be in the lowest scoring group. In the 2009 reading results, students from advantaged backgrounds outperformed their counterparts by 38 score points or about one year's worth of education. Although there are variations in the size of the achievement gap by country, in all the OECD countries, there is a poverty-related achievement gap. Canadian education expert Ben Levin summarizes the data best: "The reality, in PISA and in every other assessment of student outcomes, is that socioeconomic status remains the most powerful single influence on students' educational and other life outcomes" (Levin, 2007, p. 75).

The difficulties of school for disadvantaged adolescents are reflected not only in poor academic achievement and early school leaving because of academic failure. The high school years of poor teens are more likely than those of their more affluent peers to be disrupted or ended by behavioural problems, early pregnancy, substance abuse, or criminality (Duncan, Duncan, & Strycker, 2002; Farrington & Loeber, 2000; Harding, 2003; Wadsworth et al., 2008). Behavioural problems among children living in poverty are, of course, evident long before high school.

Behavioural problems are all too common among children of disadvantage. Aggressive-disruptive child behaviours, in particular, have long been identified as a significant problem in low-income families (Hoglund & Leadbeater, 2004; Jackson et al., 2009; McKay et al., 1999).

A U.S. study by Jean Baker and her colleagues (2006) is particularly illustrative of the extent of behavioural problems among children living in poverty. Their study involved assessing children from Grades 1 through 5 in a school district whose population was largely living at or under the poverty line; 70 per cent of the children qualified for free or subsidized lunches, and most lived in public housing units. An astonishing 56 per cent of the more than 1,000 children who were assessed had behavioural profiles that indicated a need for intervention. A full 17 per cent had pervasive and severe externalizing behavioural problems as well as poor social competence. Similar links between poverty and behavioural problems have been reported by many other researchers, and these include emotional problems evident as early as preschool and Grade 1 (e.g., Hoglund & Leadbeater, 2004; Jackson et al., 2009). The costs to children's academic achievement are high, and again, the problems start very early.

Behavioural problems in the early years at home are strongly linked with behavioural difficulties as children enter formal schooling (Dishion & Patterson, 2006). As Duane Thomas and his colleagues (2008) clearly demonstrate, aggressive behaviours at home predict aggressive behaviours in Grade 1. Aggressive behaviours are maladaptive. They affect the child's ability to get along with peers and teachers. They interfere significantly with the child's learning. Moreover, they persist. Researchers have reported that a majority of children who enter formal schooling with behavioural problems continue to behave poorly, and have associated academic problems throughout school (Pettit et al., 2009; Kim-Cohen et al., 2005; Kokko et al., 2006). Not only do many behavioural problems persist, but also some problems – for example, aggression – increase markedly during elementary school (Thomas et al., 2006). The consequences are serious. In elementary school, children who show behavioural problems are likely to underachieve or fail, and they suffer further setbacks by being required to repeat grades (Beebe-Frankenberger et al., 2004). With age, and with the transition to secondary-level schooling, things only get worse.

During the adolescent years, while engagement in school and academic achievement remain poor, behavioural problems tend to develop into more serious conduct disorders (Broidy et al., 2003). Conduct disorders interfere with all aspects of schooling, and they tend most often to result in the teen being suspended or expelled from school (Panayiotopoulos & Kerfoot, 2007; Theriot et al., 2010). High school completion is unlikely (Janosz et al., 2008). In fact, the link between behaviour and school completion is so strong that early school leaving is predictable by behavioural problems as early as primary school. Researchers in Canada, for example, tracked children who were persistently aggressive in primary school and found that they had a school dropout rate that was six times higher than the average (Kokko et al., 2006).

Early school leaving perpetuates the cycle of poverty. Because children from low-income families tend to leave school early, they are less able to pursue post-secondary education, successfully develop careers, or even enter the labour market. They become poor adults who raise children in poverty, and the intergenerational cycle appears hard to overcome. Those who leave school prior to graduation have poorer physical and mental health and employment status, and lower levels of income in mid-life than those who graduate on time (Caputo, 2005). Caputo's research (2005) shows this to be the case even if those who drop out of school early subsequently obtain a high school graduation equivalency certificate. The inequity of opportunity caused by early family experience and early schooling, it seems, affects a lifetime. We turn now to a discussion of why family factors are so predictive of poor academic outcomes among the disadvantaged.

Parental Risk Factors

There is consensus in the research literature that parents' educational practices – the home learning environment – are the key family mechanism through which poverty exerts its negative effects on children's achievement. Generally, the parental practices of relevance to their child's education are determined by a combination of personal and material resources (Phillips & Lonigan, 2009). Personal resources include the parents' level of education, how stressful their lives are, and their expectations for their children. Material resources include the family's level of income and the type of neighbourhood in which they live. These resources affect not only parents' educational practices but also the academic outcomes of their children (Tazouti, Malarde, & Michea, 2010). Poor academic achievement among children is associated with the following parental risk factors: low levels of education, high levels of parental stress, low expectations of the child, low income, and living in distressed neighbourhoods. Each of these risk factors has an independent effect on the likelihood that the child will achieve to potential at school. However, as we know, the reality is that these risk factors rarely exist in isolation. Most often they coexist (e.g., Fantuzzo et al., 2005; Hoglund & Leadbeater, 2004). For example, parents with low education are the most likely to be living in stressful circumstances and in disadvantaged neighbourhoods with insufficient access to resources. What this means is that many children who are living in poverty are exposed to cumulative risk (see, e.g., Gassman-Pines & Yoshikawa, 2006). This cumulative risk, or concentration of risk factors, is most predictive of adverse outcomes (Gutman, Sameroff, & Cole, 2003).

The probability that children will do well at school decreases as the number of risk factors to which they are exposed increases (Ackerman, Brown, & Izard, 2004; Cadima et al., 2010). Cadima and colleagues (2010), in their study of young children in Portugal, found that the effect of cumulative risk was clear as early as preschool. The more risk factors preschoolers had experienced, the lower their level of literacy skills through preschool and Grade 1. The effects of cumulative risk on academic outcomes persist over time (e.g., Gutman et al., 2003). Children who are exposed to the multiple risk factors associated with poverty tend to have lower grades throughout schooling. The key and interconnected family risk factors of particular importance to achievement are parental involvement, parents' education level, and parenting style.

Parental Involvement. Among the most powerful proximal influences on children's achievement is parental involvement in their schooling. This is well known and widely accepted. Many educational jurisdictions have attempted to establish partnerships among schools, families, and communities in an effort to increase parental involvement (e.g., Driessen, Smit, & Sleegers, 2005). In the United States, efforts to increase parental involvement are explicit in the policy of No Child Left Behind (NCLB, 2002). No Child Left Behind mandates schools to implement procedures that actively involve parents in their children's education across elementary and secondary school (Hill & Tyson, 2009). It does so for two fundamental reasons. One is extensive evidence that compared with middle-income parents, poor parents are much less likely to be involved in their children's schooling (e.g., Cooper et al., 2010; Jeynes, 2007; Sheldon, 2002; Tazouti et al., 2010). This link between family income and parental involvement has been well established in research not only in the United States, but also in Canada, the United Kingdom, the Netherlands, and Cyprus (DePlanty, Coulter-Kern, & Duchane, 2007; Driessen et al., 2005). The second reason is that a significant body of research identifies parental involvement in education to be a means by which the gap in achievement between disadvantaged children and their peers can be reduced (e.g., Dearing et al., 2006; Driessen et al., 2005).

The differences in parental involvement in their children's learning by socioeconomic status are well documented. First, in the important preschool years, we find that middle-income mothers are more likely than low-income mothers to engage their children in complex number activities and more frequent number-related activities. There is, then, a differential preparation for math learning (Klibanoff et al., 2006). Socioeconomic differences are also clear in preschoolers reading-related experiences – the number of hours that parents spend reading with their children and the number of books in the home (Noble et al., 2006a). Daily shared book reading in the home is associated with growth in the child's vocabulary and oral language skills (Phillips & Lonigan, 2009). The more enriched home literacy environment of the middle-income family, then, predicts greater reading achievement of their children when they enter school (Aikens & Barbarin, 2008; Noble et al., 2006a). Appropriate parental involvement continues to be very important once children start school.

Parental involvement has been identified as a key predictor of the factors that underlie academic achievement in school: children's positive attitudes towards school, motivation, sense of efficacy, and prosocial behaviour (Cooper et al., 2010; Gonzales-DeHass, Willems, & Holbein, 2005). Parental involvement also directly predicts achievement – especially in children's reading and math skills (Hill, 2001; Marks & Coll, 2007; Powell-Smith et al., 2000; Sheldon & Epstein, 2005; Sirvana, 2007), and years of school completed (Ou & Reynolds, 2008). But it is not simply that the more the parent is involved, the better a child does. As clearly identified in a recent meta-analysis, parental involvement is neither unidimensional nor necessarily effective (Hill & Tyson, 2009). First, the effects of parental involvement vary with whether it is positive or negative. Having a parent who is encouraging and helpful and shows an interest in the child's schoolwork has a very different effect on the child from having a parent who uses threats and coercion to pressure the child to get schoolwork done. Second, what is effective varies with the child's developmental stage. To prepare children for school, toddlers and preschoolers need to be engaged in playful number-related activities and reading. Volunteering in the classroom and helping with homework are effective involvement strategies for the elementary school–aged child, but probably would be seen as offensive and intrusive by the adolescent. Not only should parental involvement be positive and supportive, then, but also it needs to change over time such that it remains developmentally appropriate. This is critical whether the involvement is at home or at the child's school.

Through early and middle childhood, school-based involvement describes such activities as communicating with the child's teachers, visiting the classroom, volunteering at school, and participating in school governance. These types of parental involvement activities are associated with the child's achievement in elementary school. The visits that parents make to the school improve the relationship between the child's teacher and parent, increase the knowledge the parent has of the curriculum, and in so doing, facilitate meaningful help with homework (Hill & Tyson, 2009). This, of course, assumes that the visits the parent is making are positive and are not a result of teacher concerns about behavioural problems. School-based involvement changes in nature and quantity once children reach adolescence and progress to middle or secondary schools. At these higher levels, parents tend to decrease the amount of involvement and restrict it to attendance at school activities. As such, there is little direct relation between school-based involvement and achievement (Hill & Tyson, 2009; Jeynes, 2007; Seginer, 2006). Nonetheless, it is important for children of any age to know that their parents are interested in their schooling and that they hold expectations for good performance.

Parents living in poverty or with low incomes are less likely to engage in positive school-based strategies of involvement when their children are either in elementary or high school (Cooper et al., 2010). They attend school functions less often, are less likely to communicate with teachers, and are unlikely to volunteer at the school. Where parents of older children do have frequent contact with teachers, it tends to be concerning their child's poor performance or behavioural problems. As would be expected, this type of involvement is negatively related to positive attitudes and outcomes (Fan & Williams, 2010). There are a number of reasons for the differences in parental involvement in the school that are associated with socioeconomic status. It may simply be more difficult for poor parents to get to their child's school. For example, they may have multiple jobs, which impose time constraints, or they may have fewer means of transportation. More importantly, perhaps, the evidence suggests that poor parents generally have less optimism about their child's chances and less confidence for teacher meetings. This lack of confidence is a problem that is reinforced by the bias and disrespect from teachers that poor parents often experience

(Cooper et al., 2010; Crosnoe, Mistry, & Elder, 2002; Lareau, 2003; Newman & Chin, 2003). Finally, poor parents are likely to be contacted by teachers only when there is a need to discuss difficulties with their child's behaviour. This cannot be expected to promote increased confidence, optimism, or involvement.

Disadvantaged parents also are less likely to be involved in children's extracurricular activities. There are clear income-based differences in children's participation in before and after school athletic and other programs, lessons, religious activities, and educational summer activities (Coulton & Irwin, 2009; Dearing et al., 2006). Such programs often request parent participation. Families living in socioeconomically disadvantaged circumstances are unlikely to volunteer for or enroll their children in organized educational or recreational activities during the school year or during summer vacations (Cooper et al., 2010; Kaplan & Walpole, 2005). There are too many obstacles. The barriers to involvement include lack of financial resources and the neighbourhood features most often associated with disadvantage, particularly parental concerns with safety (Coulton & Irwin, 2009). The lack of basic resources – such as libraries and community centres – in disadvantaged areas poses a further barrier (Allington et al., 2010). The overall effect is to reduce children's opportunities for academic achievement (Bramley & Karley, 2007). Educational outcomes suffer as a result (Woolley et al., 2008). In fact, the achievement gap widens as the parents of more advantaged children enable the child's participation in a number of enriching extracurricular activities (Dumais, 2006). With little parental involvement in school or in extracurricular activities, the poor child is further disadvantaged.

The achievement gap is also widened by the lack of positive involvement poor parents show in the school-aged child's education at home. Home-based involvement at the elementary level describes such behaviours as helping with homework; ensuring time, space, and needed resources for homework completion; providing educationally stimulating toys and books, magazines, and games; and providing cognitively stimulating activities such as trips to libraries, museums, art galleries, and zoos (Hill & Tyson, 2009; Noble et al., 2006a). These are unlikely in poor families. Poor parents are much less able than are middle-income parents to provide their children with cognitively stimulating materials or activities (Cooper et al., 2010; Eamon, 2002). Books are less common in low-income homes (Allington et al., 2010), and home computers, which have been found to be a powerful tool for academic success, if not an essential one, remain prohibitively expensive for many low-income families (Lee, Brescia, & Kissinger, 2009). Using a national database, Lee and her colleagues (2009) found that students who used a home computer for an hour each day had higher reading and math scores than those without a home computer.

In addition to the provision of resources and opportunities for learning, as mentioned earlier, involvement is effective only when it is positive. Helping with homework, for example, can be a pleasant and supportive experience for a child, or a very upsetting one. The research is quite clear in showing that a supportive home environment with encouragement of learning is associated with high achievement, whereas the use of coercion, criticism, punishment, intrusion, or pressure tends to reduce the likelihood of achievement (Rogers et al., 2009). These latter negative forms of involvement are more common in families raising children in stressful economic conditions (Cooper et al., 2010; Eamon, 2002; Driessen et al., 2005).

The need for supportive and non-intrusive home-based strategies becomes even more pronounced in adolescence. What is most important during the teen years is that while children's increasing need for autonomy is respected, their parents' behaviours send a clear message that education is important and that they expect their child to succeed (Fan & Williams, 2010). This is no easy task. The parents' strategies need to change. The direct efforts at helping that were appreciated during earlier childhood are likely to be rejected and perceived as interference. During adolescence, direct parental help with homework can actually have a negative effect on achievement. What seems to be more effective is for the parent of the adolescent to avoid actively helping with homework assignments. Rather, the parent should show support for the adolescent's independent efforts to complete them (Patall, Cooper, & Robinson, 2008). The difficulty of achieving the right balance between involvement and support for independence was highlighted in a large-scale study of adolescents in the United States (Crosnoe & Huston, 2007). When parents' discussions about course taking with their teen-aged children decreased during adolescence, the adolescents accumulated fewer course credits. But when parents remained involved in their adolescents' decision-making about courses, the achievement of the adolescents was less because the involvement threatened their sense of independence, and, in consequence, their intrinsic motivation and effort. It is a fine line between support and perceived intrusion. In their meta-analysis of the strategies that promote academic achievement among adolescents, Hill and Tyson (2009) describe supportive parental behaviours as a form of academic socialization. The supportive behaviours they identify are these: parents communicating their expectations for education, emphasizing the value and utility of education, making efforts to link school subjects to current events, and discussing learning strategies and future goals with their adolescents. These positive and effective parental involvement behaviours are not only associated with income, but also with the parents' level of education. Parents with higher income and higher levels of education are more likely to create environments that value, encourage, and facilitate achievement – to effectively socialize their child's academic self.

Parents' Education Level. The education level of the parents consistently has been associated with children's school achievement (Keltikangas-Järvinen et al., 2010). Dubow, Boxer, and Huesmann (2009) provide compelling evidence of the predictive power of parents' education level. Examining the predictors of educational and occupational success in mid-life, they identified unique effects of parents' education level when the child was 8 years old. Parents' education affected children's aspirations for their own education and subsequently children's actual achievement. The higher the level of parents' education, the higher the achievement and aspirations of their children (Dubow et al., 2009). This link has been found across schooling and even into college-level students (Schlechter & Milevsky, 2010). A possible explanation for the power of parents' education level is seen in its correlates. As found by researchers in Turkey studying students' science scores, parents' education level is an important predictor of achievement (Akyol, Sungur, & Tekkaya, 2010). But also important to achievement are the correlative behaviours of more highly educated parents: the number of reading materials in the home, the act of buying a daily newspaper for home reading, and computers with Internet access in the home (Akyol et al., 2010).

We acknowledge that there is a genetic component underlying the similarities in educational aspirations and achievement between generations (Keltikangas-Järvinen et al., 2010). Nonetheless, there are strong reasons to believe the child's environment may be more important. First, as Dubow and his colleagues (2009) point out, behaviour is shaped, in part, through what is observed in the home. Parents who model a value on education and achievement through their own efforts and interests – for example, completing advanced degrees, taking classes, reading newspapers, and so forth – are demonstrating the value of education to their children. Their children are learning that education is "to be valued, pursued, and anticipated" (p. 228). Such observational learning is powerful. Second, it has been found that once children enter school, the influence of intelligence (a genetic factor) decreases, while the influence of socioeconomic status (an environmental factor) increases in importance (Krajewski & Schneider, 2009). Third, and particularly interesting in our context, researchers have found that genetic factors are more strongly linked with language development among children from higher socioeconomic families whereas environmental factors have stronger predictive power among those from low-income families (Noble et al., 2006a; 2006b). Such findings are intriguing. Ultimately, as Keltikangas-Järvinen and colleagues suggest (2010), it is most likely that a child's academic achievement is a joint function of genetic predisposition and the type of environment that parents create for their child. Genes moderate outcomes; they do not determine them.

Parenting Style. In their European study of families with 8- and 9-year-olds, Youssef Tazouti and his colleagues (2010) found a strong relation among the income level of the family, parenting style, and children's school outcomes. The more supportive parents were of their children, the higher the children's academic achievement. These relations among income, parenting style, and children's achievement are found across cultures. What has been observed repeatedly is that the educational achievement of children varies with the degree to which their parenting is warm and supportive with age-appropriate demands and expectations for academic success (Jeynes, 2007; Pong, Johnston, & Chen, 2010). Language development, in particular, is associated with maternal warmth (Aikens & Barbarin, 2008).

Many parenting practices, including academic socialization and expectations for success, are influenced by both income level and parents' level of education (Davis-Kean, 2005; Pettit et al., 2009; Tazouti et al., 2010). Low levels of income predict harsh parenting, lack of positive parental involvement in education, and poor achievement among children (Pettit et al., 2009; Spera, 2005). The problems result from the profound effects of the stress produced by socioeconomic disadvantage on parenting capacity. Parents living in the stressful circumstances that tend to accompany low education and low income have diminished capacity for the supportive and positive parenting that predicts achievement at school (Cooper et al., 2010; Jackson et al., 2009). Stress makes it difficult for the parent to be patient, to be cognitively stimulating, to establish and maintain routines, to monitor the children's activities, and to be supportive (Cooper et al., 2010; Spera, 2005). Furthermore, parents in stressful economic circumstances tend to socialize with reactive punishment more than with proactive support and socialization. The cumulative effects of stress on parenting have a profound effect on children's schooling. The more stressed their parents are, the less positive parenting children receive. In turn, there is a significantly increased likelihood that the children will be disengaged, achieve below potential, and fail school (Simons-Morton & Chen, 2009). As Hill and Tyson (2009) conclude, in the absence of effective parenting and academic socialization, by adolescence, "opportunities are often foreclosed, leading to lost potential, unrealized talent, diminished educational and vocational attainment, and widening demographic gaps in achievement" (p. 760).

In summary, the key risk factors associated with low income are low level of parental involvement, a low level of parents' education, and an unsupportive parenting style. Schools can make a difference to children in such difficult family circumstances. Schools can provide protective factors and build resilience. But too often they do not. Too often, they make things worse.

Schools as Risk Amplifiers

As described above, children from disadvantaged families tend to enter schooling with lower literacy and numeracy skills than their middle-class peers, and with increased incidence of behavioural problems. In sharp contrast to their obligations under the U.N. Convention on the Rights of the Child, few educational jurisdictions or schools respond with strategies that would help reduce this early inequality. Ignorance of effective strategies is not an excuse. As cogently summarized by Duane Thomas and his colleagues (2008), there is a wealth of evidence clearly demonstrating that the punitive management styles that are so often used in schools are ineffective in improving the behaviour or performance of children having difficulties. Children in classrooms that are managed through strategies such as predictable routines and teacher warmth and support, in contrast, show increased social competence, reduced rates of behavioural problems, and more on-task behaviours. Effective teachers in well-managed classrooms, particularly in the early grades, can do much to reduce (although not fully close) the inequality gap, and facilitate children achieving to their academic potential (Konstantopoulos, 2009; Lee & Loeb, 2000). Unfortunately, the use of positive strategies is rare. The evidence on effective practices is ignored.

A fundamental obstacle to the use of evidence-based practices is seen in the focus of teacher education. Too often, the goal of teacher training is subject competency rather than pedagogical competency or competency in classroom management (Ucar & Sanalan, 2011; Niesyn, 2009; Rosenberg et al., 2004). Evidence-based strategies to respond effectively to behavioural difficulties do exist, but they generally are not taught to pre-service teachers (Jones & Chronis-Tuscano, 2008). As a result, teachers report that their training leaves them ill-prepared for the daily realities of teaching, and they report infrequent use of evidence-based practices (Gilbert & Graham, 2010; Kiuhara, Graham, & Hawken, 2009). As teacher and researcher Mary Niesyn states, many teachers find that their students' "needs surpass the teacher's repertoire of effective strategies" (2009, p. 227). This is particularly the case in the important first years of schooling from kindergarten through Grade 3 where in response to challenging behaviours, teachers become increasingly negative (Raver et al., 2008). But in the absence of training or support, the use of evidence-based strategies is impeded by a lack of perceived competence (Niesyn, 2009; Witzel, Riccomini, & Schneider, 2008). The importance of appropriate training in the use of evidence-based practices in pre-service is underscored by findings that in-service training may not be sufficient to change teacher practices (e.g., Jones & Chronis-Tuscano, 2008). This latter issue will be considered further in chapter 5.

Disadvantaged children are especially unlikely to experience effective teachers (Halvorsen, Lee, & Andrade, 2009; Konstantopoulos, 2009). Rather than countering the risk factors associated with family disadvantage, the education system often amplifies them through the punitive practices of grade retention, corporal punishment, exclusion, and teachers' differential expectations for and behaviours towards children from low-income families. The gap at the starting gate is made wider as a result. We now examine each of the risk amplifiers in turn.

Grade Retention. Grade retention describes the practice of requiring children who have not demonstrated achievement of curricular objectives for a grade to repeat that grade. With few exceptions – Norway is one exception where it is not allowed – the practice is reported to be widespread and popular among teachers (e.g., Bonvin, Bless, & Schuepbach, 2008; Griffith et al., 2010; Silberglitt et al., 2006). Occurring most frequently in the early years, the intent of grade retention appears to be to provide children with extra time to catch up to their better prepared peers. However, as Patrick Bonvin and his colleagues (2008) note, there is little reason to expect that extra time, in the absence of effective instructional interventions, will improve the child's learning or academic outcomes. But there are many reasons given for the use of grade retention.

Low academic achievement, immature social skills, and little parental involvement have been identified as the primary reasons for grade retention (Alexander, Entwisle, & Dauber, 2003). Although low achievement among children who are required to repeat a grade is common, it is also the case that not all low-achieving children are retained. Most often, it is male children (who have higher rates of behavioural problems than do girls), ethnic minority children, and overwhelmingly children who come from low socioeconomic status homes that are retained (Bowman-Perrott, Herrera, & Murry, 2010; Griffith et al., 2010; NCES, 2006). It is, of course, the case that ethno-cultural minority and low-income status frequently coexist. As Bowman-Perrott and colleagues (2010) show, in the United States for example, compared with other groups, Hispanic families are more likely to live below the poverty line, their children are unlikely to be prepared for school, and their teachers are highly likely to recommend grade retention.

It is not surprising that children most likely to repeat a grade early in elementary school are those from disadvantaged homes who are inadequately prepared for school and who enter school with behavioural problems (Beebe-Frankenberger et al., 2004; Murray, Woodruff, & Vaughn, 2010). What perhaps is surprising is that the evidence demonstrates that it is demographic characteristics and subjective judgments, rather than objective assessments of achievement, that guide teacher decisions (Bonvin et al., 2008; Silberglitt et al., 2006).

Objective criteria for decision-making about grade retention appear to be totally absent. In fact, systematic bias appears to be more prevalent in guiding decisions than are objective criteria. The extent of subjectivity and bias is exemplified in a nationwide study of the determinants of grade retention in Switzerland (Bonvin et al., 2008). Across the nation it was the attitude of the individual teachers that significantly determined whether low-achieving children would be required to repeat a grade. Moreover, there was further bias by geographical region with retentions being an astonishing seven times higher in the French-speaking part of Switzerland than in the German-speaking area.

Like so many common practices in education, grade retention is not effective or supportable. Researchers consistently have demonstrated that not only is grade retention an ineffective means of improving out-comes, but also that it is counterproductive. As summarized by Joan Beswick and her colleagues (2008) in their discussion of systemic ed-ucational obstacles to social justice, research findings are unambigu-ous in demonstrating that grade retention does not produce academic gains. At best, there may be some very temporary academic improve-ments (Griffith et al., 2010). But even when retention is only at the kin-dergarten level – something advocated by many (Silberglitt et al., 2006) – it does more harm than good. Both short-term and longitudinal stud-ies show that any temporary benefits are soon lost and deleterious outcomes take their place. Children who are required to repeat kinder-garten subsequently perform less well on tests of literacy and numer-acy than would have been the case had they been promoted to the next grade with their same-aged peers (Hong & Raudenbush, 2005). Thus, the pattern continues. Grade level appears to be irrelevant to outcome. A comprehensive analysis of the U.S. National Education Longitudi-nal Study data showed that children who had been retained between kindergarten and Grade 8 did significantly worse on reading than a matched comparison group of children who were not retained (Griffith et al., 2010). As the authors note, their data are consistent with the find-ings from many previous studies as described in Jimerson's (2001) meta-analysis of the grade retention research conducted through the twentieth century.

In addition to reducing potential academic achievement, grade re-tention is associated with poor social adjustment, negative attitudes to school, increased problem behaviours, and decreased school atten-dance (e.g., Griffith et al., 2010; Murray et al., 2010). Indeed, evidence from Portugal – where a policy of grade retention has been in place for children who fail a test at the Grade 6 level – suggests that grade reten-tion can even increase bullying (Berger, 2007). Ten per cent of Grade 6 children, mostly males from low-income families, had been held back 2 years or more. These children were found to be twice as likely to bully as others. Of course, we cannot conclude that it is the grade retention that causes the bullying. Nonetheless, the overall pattern of linkages be-tween grade retention and behavioural problems suggests it is at least one factor. Common sense would suggest that a child who is larger and older than his or her peers, but a designated failure, might compensate for feelings of inferiority and attempt to gain self-esteem through exert-ing power over his or her younger and smaller classmates.

The problems associated with grade retention persist over time. School disengagement and early school leaving often result (Bowers, 2010; Jimerson, 2001; Jimerson & Kauffman, 2003). There is a very strong association between grade retention – even very early grade retention – and dropping out of high school (Jimerson, Anderson, & Whipple, 2002; Murray et al., 2010). As Jimerson (2001, p. 432) concluded, grade retention "is ineffective as an intervention for academic achievement and socio-emotional adjustment."

In contradiction to the evidence, counter-productive, and inconsistent with the rights of the child, the practice of grade retention continues unabated. The evidence shows clearly that grade retention is contrary to the child's education rights in three areas. First, it is inconsistent with the child's right to be provided with equal opportunity without discrimination. Second, it is inconsistent with the right of the child to education that promotes optimum development. Third, grade retention is inconsistent with the right of the child to education that promotes school attendance and reduces the likelihood of dropping out early.

Use of Corporal Punishment. Grade retention may be seen as but one ineffective and punitive response to disadvantaged children in need of help. More egregious and overtly punitive is the use of corporal punishment. It also is in clear violation of the child's right to protection from violence under Article 19 of the U.N. Convention on the Rights of the Child. Although little discussed and inadequately researched, corporal punishment in school is a practice that continues and disproportionately affects disadvantaged children. It is no wonder that the U.N. Committee on the Rights of the Child has called for a ban on the use of corporal punishment as a school disciplinary strategy. Nevertheless, this call remains unheeded in many countries.

Corporal punishment is prohibited by law in most of the developed world. Led by Poland as far back as 1783, it has been banned by law in most of Europe and elsewhere including Japan, South Africa, Australia, and New Zealand (Covell & Becker, 2011; Repeal 43 Committee, 2012). In Canada, as a result of legislative change and a Supreme Court decision in 2004, the practice is banned in all 10 provinces and the three northern territories (the only acceptable use of physical force by a teacher in Canada is in the form of reasonable force for restraint). In the United States, although the practice is banned in most of the states, corporal punishment is still permitted by law in 19 states, most of those in the south.

However, despite the legal prohibitions, corporal punishment remains a common disciplinary strategy for schoolchildren in many countries.

The following rather startling statistics are provided in a study of children in the Caribbean region where the use of corporal punishment in schools is a widely accepted practice (Baker-Henningham et al., 2009). In Barbados, 90 per cent of primary school–aged children report being beaten with an object at school. In Jamaica, 75 per cent of 11- to 12-year-old children said they have been beaten with an object by their teacher, and 80 per cent of the 74 primary school teachers who were asked said that they use corporal punishment to discipline their students. This practice also remains all too common in the United States.

According to a 2009 research report released by Human Rights Watch (HRW) and the American Civil Liberties Union (ACLU), 20 states in the United States allow the use of corporal punishment as a school disciplinary measure (Human Rights Watch and the American Civil Liberties Union, 2009). Corporal punishment typically takes the form of "paddling" during which an administrator or teacher hits a child repeatedly on the buttocks with a long wooden board. In interviews with children, HRW and the ACLU learned that other forms of corporal punishment are used also: these include slapping, pinching, being dragged across the room, and being thrown to the floor. As described in their report, the state of Georgia, which is among the 10 states with the highest use of corporal punishment, is illustrative. With the exception of three school areas (Metro Atlanta, Savannah, and Rome), Georgia's schools use corporal punishment with an astonishingly high number of children – over 28,000 according to recent statistics. According to Georgia's statutes, there are restrictions on the use of corporal punishment in schools. It is not to be excessive, unduly severe, or used as a first line of punishment, and it is not to be used at all if a physician certifies that the child's mental or emotional stability would be affected. These restrictions are so vague as to be meaningless, as evidenced in practice. Not only do the HRW and ACLU (2009) report widespread use of corporal punishment in schools in Georgia, but they also note its disproportionate use among children with disabilities and behavioural disorders (both more common among children from low-income families). Moreover, they note its use is primarily for minor infractions such as having a shirt not tucked in, being late, running in hallways, or talking in class.

The release of the HRW and ACLU (2009) report led to renewed calls by both parents and politicians for a ban on the use of corporal punishment in schools. Examples from parents and grandparents filled the Internet and many are included in the report. Describing her 5-year-old granddaughter who attended an elementary school in Georgia, Theresa E. said: "You could see the bruising. Her whole arm was swollen by the time she got to the emergency room. Her right arm. The doctor said it looked like she'd been hit by a baseball bat or had been in a motorcycle accident" (p. 23).

In a subsequent joint report by the ACLU and HRW (Murphy, Vagins, & Parker, 2010), it is noted that in some states children receive "greater protections against corporal punishment in detention facilities than they do in their public schools" (p. 3).

As emphasized in these reports, hitting children does not improve their behaviour. The opposite is more likely. Corporal punishment in school increases the likelihood of aggressive and disruptive behaviour (Dupper & Dingus, 2008). Corporal punishment does not improve academic performance. Indeed, recent research demonstrates that corporal punishment in school may have a long-term detrimental effect on children's verbal skills and problem-solving ability (Talwar, Carlson, & Lee, 2011). Teachers' use of corporal punishment functions only to decrease academic achievement, good behaviour, school engagement, motivation to succeed, and school attendance (Baker-Henningham et al., 2009). The title of the HRW and ACLU (2009) report summarizes the effects of teacher use of corporal punishment well: *Impairing Education*.

There is a wealth of evidence that corporal punishment is ineffective and harmful for any child (see Gershoff, 2002, for an excellent review). It appears to be particularly harmful for children when used in schools. Its targets are minority, disabled, and economically disadvantaged children (Baker-Henningham et al., 2009; Murphy et al., 2010). These are the children who are already having difficulties at school, and these are the children who are also the most vulnerable to exposure to violence in their homes and neighbourhoods. Corporal punishment at home is itself a source of reduced academic achievement (Murray & Straus, 2003). Multiple sources of exposure to violence have an additive effect on poor achievement in school (Baker-Henningham et al., 2009; Holt, Finkelhor, & Kaufman-Kantor, 2007). As was demonstrated in the study of children in Jamaica, when children are exposed to the three types of violence that frequently coexist (peer violence, community violence, and teacher use of corporal punishment), the negative effects are compounded. Each exposure to violence is associated independently in a dose-dependent manner with school achievement in numeracy and literacy (Baker-Henningham et al., 2009). Each reduces the child's chances of success.

Exclusions. Among the more common and most serious responses to student misbehaviour is exclusion from school. Exclusion takes two forms. Temporary or fixed-term exclusion describes suspensions in which a child is not allowed to attend school for some specified number of days or weeks. Permanent exclusion describes expulsion where children are permanently disallowed from attending a particular school (although alternate arrangements for education are usually made). There has been a general trend upward among developed countries in the use of disciplinary exclusions. Statistics from the United States, Australia, and the United Kingdom, in particular, show a very large increase in the use of exclusions. In the United States, exclusions are now one of the most common forms of discipline (Petras et al., 2011). In Australia, since the 1990s, suspensions of up to 4 schooldays have doubled, and suspensions of up to 20 schooldays have tripled (Panayiotopoulos & Kerfoot, 2007). As in the United Kingdom, the increase in exclusion is particularly marked among primary school children. Rare prior to the 1990s (ironically prior to ratification of the CRC), statistics from 2000 show that an astonishing 13 per cent of children who were permanently excluded from schools in England were from primary schools (Panayiotopoulos & Kerfoot, 2007). These children – the "trouble-makers" who must be discarded – are under age 12.

What is very clear in the statistics, regardless of education jurisdiction or age of student, is the disproportionate use of disciplinary exclusions among children living in poverty (Gazeley, 2010; Panayiotopoulos & Kerfoot, 2007; Petras et al., 2011; Theriot, Craun, & Dupper, 2010). In England, for example, exclusions are the highest among children who are in receipt of free school meals – the most common marker of family poverty used by schools and researchers (DCFS, 2009) – and in schools situated in areas of social and economic deprivation (Clegg et al., 2009). Similarly, data from the United States show a strong link between poverty and exclusion (Theriot et al., 2010). In essence, it is those children most in need of stability, supports, and continuity at school – those whose fundamental rights are already compromised – who are the most at risk of exclusion. As with the use of corporal punishment, the infractions leading to exclusions can be trivial. Although generally used as a response to antisocial behaviour, there is little attention paid to any co-morbid conditions that are contributing factors to that behaviour. For example, when delayed language development limits meaningful communication and social interaction, it can affect behaviour (Lindsay, Dockrell, & Strand, 2007). Yet a child with language delay may be excluded for inappropriate behaviour without due attention being given to the role of the language difficulties in the child's behaviour. Similarly, many developmental disorders such as attention deficit disorder can make the child appear uncooperative and aggressive and can place the child at risk of exclusion. Developmental disorders are rarely taken into account by educators when determining discipline. We are reminded of an incident reported to us by a distraught single mother in our own school district in Nova Scotia, Canada. Her 6-year-old son who suffered from Tourette's syndrome was excluded for swearing in class. It seems that the teacher was unaware of the characteristic and uncontrollable verbal tics that are associated with Tourette's.

Like other punitive measures, exclusions function to amplify the difficulties that they intend to lessen. Reports of benefits are absent. Researchers who have examined the effects of exclusions report that the primary consequences are increased academic difficulties (Arcia, 2006; Boon, 2008), disengagement from school (Butler et al., 2005), truancy (Gazeley, 2010), and early school leaving (Arcia, 2006). In addition to these detrimental educational outcomes, exclusions also function to increase antisocial behaviour and the child's risk of involvement in criminal offending (Gazeley, 2010; McCrystal et al., 2005; McCrystal, Percy, & Higgins, 2007). That exclusions actually do *cause* increased academic and behavioural problems is demonstrated in some interesting and comprehensive research conducted in Australia. In a methodologically rigorous study of over 1,000 12- to 15-year-old Indigenous and non-Indigenous students in Australian schools, Helen Boon (2008) assessed the influence of socio-demographic factors, family characteristics, and behavioural issues on low academic achievement. Her data demonstrate that although school suspensions were a strong predictor of low achievement, low achievement did not predict being suspended. Such data suggest there may well be a causal relation between being suspended from school and subsequent poor achievement.

Research showing the effects of exclusions on behaviours and reduced future success has been conducted by Sheryl Hemphill and her colleagues (2006; 2007; 2009) in Australia and the United States. Impelled by an interest in factors predictive of youth violence, Hemphill and her colleagues (2006; 2007; 2009) undertook large-scale comparisons of antisocial behaviours among 10- to 15-year-olds in Victoria, Australia, and Washington State in the United States. Using a large representative sample (the International Youth Development Study), the researchers compared child behaviour and school policies in the two demographically similar areas. As would be expected given the similarity of demographic characteristics of the two areas, the rates of antisocial behaviour generally were similar. The policies for responding to antisocial behaviour, in contrast, were quite different. In Victoria, Australia, suspensions were used only as a last resort; there was a strong emphasis on keeping children connected with school. Washington State was quite different. As in so many North American education jurisdictions, Washington State had adopted a strong zero-tolerance policy. This policy initially was given expression in its Gun-Free Schools Act. The Act, aiming to prevent school violence, initially mandated a minimum one-year suspension from school for any child who took a gun to school. Subsequent amendments to the Act extended its scope to include a range of other misdemeanors (Casella, 2003). The result was widespread use of suspensions in Washington State, a rate that was significantly higher than that of Victoria. As she followed the children, Hemphill and colleagues found increasing problems among those in the United States as a result of their suspensions.

First, school suspensions increased the likelihood of antisocial behaviour among the children in Washington State 12 months later, and to a greater degree than would be expected given the risk factors in existence (Hemphill et al., 2006). Second, there were significantly higher rates of subsequent suspensions and arrests evidenced in Washington State compared with Victoria (Hemphill et al., 2007). Third, experience with school suspensions and arrests increased the likelihood of later violent behaviour by 150 per cent (Hemphill et al., 2009). Clearly, breaking the child's connection with schooling through suspensions and expulsions severely limits the child's educational and subsequent career and employment opportunities.

The data from the studies summarized above demonstrate well the negative and spiralling effect of exclusions. Importantly, these data are consistent with other research findings showing that suspensions from school do increase the likelihood of antisocial behaviours and criminal offending. As McCrystal and his colleagues (2007) noted in their study of suspension in Belfast, Northern Ireland, exclusion from school may well be the first step in exclusion from society.

Teachers' Beliefs and Expectations. It may be that a major reason for the disproportionate use of grade retention and disciplinary exclusions among disadvantaged children stems from teacher beliefs about children in economically deprived families. Children most at risk of suffering negative stereotypes are especially vulnerable to low teachers' expectations (Jussim & Harber, 2005). Teachers tend to perceive disadvantaged children as inevitably and irredeemably less capable than their middle-class peers, and so have lower expectations for them (Beswick, Sloat, & Willms, 2008). It is important to emphasize here that these perceptions of poor competency are not based on demonstrated incompetence. Rather, teacher ratings of students' competency and achievement are affected by the child's socioeconomic status, the child's ethnicity, the education level of the child's mother, and assumptions made about the parents' value on education (Beswick, Willms, & Sloat, 2005; Hallahan & Kauffman, 2003; Hauser-Cram, Sirin, & Stipek, 2003; Rubie-Davies et al., 2010; Shaywitz, 2003). As described elsewhere (Covell & Howe, 2001a), teachers sometimes make determinations about a child's academic competency on the first day of school based on the child's dress and oral language skills. Teachers tend to prefer students from privileged and supportive families; teachers perceive advantaged children to be motivated and college-bound – worth their effort (Schoon et al., 2004).

A powerful demonstration of the influence of stereotyped beliefs on academic expectations was provided in an interesting study by Amy Auwarter and Mara Aruguete (2008). One hundred and six teachers were asked to read a paragraph describing a student having academic and behavioural difficulties. Whereas the difficulties described were identical in each paragraph, the background information about the student varied: some were presented as from families with high socioeconomic status and some from low socioeconomic status. When asked to rate the likely school outcomes for the student, teachers who were presented the information that the student was from a disadvantaged family were significantly more likely than teachers whose scenario described an advantaged child to predict a poor future. The importance of such teacher beliefs and expectancies is seen in their influence on children's self-perceptions, on teacher behaviours, and on student outcomes.

There is little question that children are influenced by their teachers' assessment of their abilities (Halvorsen et al., 2009; Schoon et al., 2004). Like parents' expectations, teachers' expectations have a direct and powerful effect on the child's own educational expectations and competency beliefs, which, in turn, directly affect academic outcomes (Benner & Mistry, 2007; Schoon et al., 2004). Unfortunately, there is some evidence that teachers' expectations have a particularly enduring effect on disadvantaged children (Jussim & Harber, 2005; Mistry et al., 2009). As Christine Rubie-Davies and her colleagues (2010) explain, the realization of success first requires the belief that success is achievable. Students' expectations strongly predict their motivation and achievement, especially in the all-important adolescent years (Tavani & Losh, 2003). In fact, the influence of teachers' expectations on students' self-expectations increases with student age (Kuklinski & Weinstein, 2001). This may well result from its effects on the classroom's emotional climate and children's awareness of the differential treatment. Low expectations are transmitted to the children through a number of differential teachers' behaviours that send a clear message to disadvantaged children that they are, and will remain, unsuccessful.

In general, when teachers hold negative attitudes and have low educational expectations for children living in poverty, they appear to have little motivation to expend the effort needed to assist them (Auwarter & Aruguete, 2008). They may have poor relationships with the child's parents (Jeynes, 2007), and they may discourage parental involvement in school (Cooper, 2010). In the classroom, they provide fewer learning opportunities and challenges, less positive attention, and less reinforcement for good performance (Benner & Mistry, 2007; Eccles, 2004; Schoon et al., 2004). Moreover, where there is the practice of streaming, tracking, or grouping, children from low socioeconomic status families tend to be placed in low-ability groups in the absence of competency assessments (Benner & Mistry, 2007). Ability groupings perpetuate and increase the effects of disadvantage whether the groupings are by school, within school, or within classrooms (Caro & Lehmann, 2009).

In a classic and very early study, Ray Rist (1970) observed a kindergarten classroom for one year. By the eighth day – before the children had had a chance to adapt – the children were divided into three ability groupings: high, average, and low. The groupings, Rist reports, were not based on IQ or comparable tests, but on socioeconomic status–related characteristics. These included the child's skin colour, style of dress, hairstyle, and even smell. The group perceived to be most promising was placed at the front of the class, and the group perceived to be the least promising was seated at the rear of the classroom. The teacher subsequently exhibited differential use of praise, reward, positive attention, support, and controlling behaviours. Children in the lowest group received the least positive and most controlling behaviours. Those in the highest group, the children sitting at the front of the class, had the most positive and supportive interactions with the teacher. Rist reports that not only was there little change among groups over the year, but also that the achievement gap between the groups increased as they progressed to elementary school. Whereas these outcomes are perhaps not surprising, it is astonishing that such teacher practices continue.

Even in Norway – among the most egalitarian countries in the world – the evidence shows that the need for teacher support among disadvantaged children is inversely related to its provision almost four decades after Rist's research. In a large-scale assessment of over 7,000 Norwegian 11- to 16 year-olds, it was found that the most disadvantaged students received the least support and positive attention from their teachers (Veland, Midthassel, & Idsoe, 2009). Compared with their peers living in middle-income families, students from lower socioeconomic status families felt socially excluded by their teachers. The negative effects of poverty on biased treatment were intensified among children who had additional disadvantages: being in the child care system, having parents with drug or alcohol problems, or being of ethnic minority status. Teachers, everywhere, it seems, are more positive with their middle-income or advantaged students. And positive expectations from teachers are a key ingredient for the achievement of potential and academic success (Schoon et al., 2004).

Low teachers' expectations are strongly predictive of poorer grades, lower test scores, and early school leaving (Benner & Mistry, 2007). In addition, teachers' expectations affect long-term educational goals such as attending college (Mistry et al., 2009). The term "self-fulfilling prophecy," originally coined more than half a century ago by Robert Merton (1948), describes the process. When teachers expect students to do poorly, they behave towards them in ways that lead to their expectations being fulfilled as described above. The overall effect of low teachers' expectations of children living in poverty has been cogently summarized as follows: "low expectations effectively perpetuate the status quo, [and] stymie equity" (Beswick et al., 2008, p. 124). Differences in interaction patterns and classroom climates that consistently favour advantaged children amplify pre-existing differences in educational opportunity among children from differing socioeconomic status levels (Kuklinski & Weinstein, 2001). They do nothing to reduce the achievement gap that is so apparent at school entry, and that continues to grow with inappropriate school policies and teacher practices.

In summary, at this time, the ingredients of the best interests of the child are missing in many schools. Punitive practices, the pervasiveness of teacher biases, and the ignoring of research evidence, indicate little regard for the rights of the child. Rather than using evidence-based practices to promote the optimal development of every child, to encourage regular attendance, and to decrease the risk of dropping out of school, policies and practices that have been shown to increase academic failure, school absenteeism, antisocial behaviour, and early school leaving continue to be used. Discretionary power given to educators in the use of inappropriate practices has been shown to result in their differential application to children living in social disadvantage. Rather than buffering the effects of poverty and its correlates at home, schools function to amplify the associated risks and increase the likelihood of poor outcomes. With such practices, schools sustain barriers to equal opportunity and increase the achievement gap.

Chapter Four

Implementing Early Childhood Education

By failing to tackle the achievement gap, education authorities help to perpetuate inequality of opportunity. Socially disadvantaged children become further disadvantaged through lack of educational success. But this outcome is not inevitable. Education systems can make a difference. To make a difference, however, there is a need among policymakers and education authorities to understand the critical importance of the early years and the early effects of disadvantage on the educational prospects of children. As discussed in chapter 3, there is a large body of research showing that all children do not reach elementary school or even kindergarten with the same learning capacities. Children who come to school in circumstances of poverty are more likely to have difficulties in learning. These difficulties begin at a very early age and they include neurological difficulties, which greatly increase the risk of school failure. But there also is a large body of research indicating that the risk can be decreased through early intervention, particularly in the form of early childhood education and preschool enrichment programs. To make a difference, authorities need not only to understand and appreciate this research but also to act on the research by putting into place effective and comprehensive programs of early childhood education and care.

In this chapter, we begin by examining the importance of the early years. We give particular attention to the negative effects of poverty on learning and healthy brain development. We then look at the importance of early intervention, the establishment of programs and services of early childhood education, and research findings on the effects of early education on the educational progress of disadvantaged children. On the basis of this research and in the best interests of the child, we make the case for the full incorporation of early childhood education into the regular education system. We conclude by noting that although this reform is a progressive step, it is an incomplete step. Major changes also need to be undertaken in schools.

The Importance of the Early Years

Success has its roots in infancy. As demonstrated in the evidence presented in chapter 3, there is a well-established link between socioeconomic status and school readiness. Simply put, the higher the level of family income, the more it is likely that children will enter kindergarten with the requisite cognitive, academic, and social competencies that spell success (Barbarin et al., 2006; Duncan & Magnuson, 2005; Hair et al., 2006; Magnuson et al., 2004; Mistry et al., 2010). The lower the family's income, the more likely it is that the child is on a developmental pathway to school failure. This link is shown regardless of ethnocultural status (Mistry et al., 2010), and it is found across the industrialized world (Hertzman &Williams, 2009). Canadian physicians Clyde Hertzman and Robin Williams report that in industrialized countries children "are remarkably similar at birth" (2009, p. 70). But after birth, in every society, differences in family socioeconomic status produce inequities in children's development (Hertzman et al., 2010). Poverty has its most profound effect on development when present during infancy (Mistry et al., 2010). The gap in opportunity for school readiness and subsequent educational achievement is evidenced early in life. To achieve consistency with the child's right to education on the basis of equal opportunity, early interventions are needed to reduce the gap in school readiness.

School Readiness. So often when we think of a child being ready for school, we focus on success at toilet training, a new lunch box, and concern about bullies. But being ready for school involves so much more. School readiness requires that the child has mastered the skills needed to meet the social and cognitive demands of the school environment. As such, school readiness has language, cognitive, social, and behavioural components. The child needs to have achieved a level of language development that allows for listening, speech that adheres to social conventions and manners, and the prerequisite skills for the development of reading and writing. These latter skills include an understanding that text represents spoken words, the knowledge that stories follow a sequence, and an interest in books (Hair et al., 2006). The cognitive component includes knowledge of the physical properties of objects, for example, weight and colour; a basic understanding of the relations between objects, for example, how two objects are different; and factual knowledge expected by the child's society, for example, numbers, names, and shapes. Social skills are needed to enable positive relationships with peers and teachers, to express feelings appropriately, and to respond sensitively to others (Hair et al., 2006). A positive sense of self and a sense of self-efficacy might also be considered requisite social skills. Finally, school readiness requires behaviours that reflect an inclination to learn: the motivation to learn, the ability to sit still and pay attention to teacher instructions, the ability to follow classroom rules and procedures, and task persistence. The development of these competencies, which co-occur within individual children, is largely influenced by the characteristics of the child's home environment (Forget-Dubois et al., 2009).

The early years of children who live in poverty tend to be lacking in cognitively enriching experiences and sensitive caregiving, and high in stress (Lengua, Honorado, & Bush, 2007; Li-Grining, 2007). Typically, poor children have little access to educational resources, lessons, explanations, recreational and social activities, or quality child care facilities (Crosnoe et al., 2010; Forget-Dubois et al., 2009). Little exposure to verbal stimulation, books, shared reading, caregiver speech, storytelling, and positive social interaction predict poor language and cognitive development (Forget-Dubois et al., 2009; Mistry et al., 2010). Poverty-related stress is far-reaching in its effect on the development of children through its association with daily hassles, family conflict, moves, and transitions (Wadsworth et al., 2008). The stress in the daily lives of poor families is often reflected in less sensitive caregiving. Parenting may be neglectful or ineffective, and it may be harsh or abusive (Covell & Howe, 2009; McCrory, De Brito, & Viding, 2010). For example, children living in poverty are at particular risk of fetal alcohol exposure and corporal punishment. These stress-related parenting practices affect the emotional stability and the social competence of the child. Most importantly, such experiences are toxic to the developing brain in ways that have a profound effect on school readiness (Covell & Howe, 2009).

Researchers have long studied the association between poverty and educational achievement. The early evidence that the association was a function of environmental rather than genetic factors came from studies of adopted children, studies of the effects of the timing and persistence of poverty in the child's early years, and intervention studies

(Noble, Norman, & Farah, 2005). Not only have consistent associations been found among socioeconomic status, cognitive performance, and educational achievement, but also they have been found to be even stronger than the association with outcomes such as health and behaviour (e.g., Duncan et al., 1998). That strength is now understandable. Recent compelling evidence from neuroscience shows that the adverse environmental experiences associated with poverty affect the developing brain.

Brain Development and School Readiness. Children with compromised brain development do not reach elementary school with the same learning capacity as others (De Bellis, 2005; Lee & Burkham, 2002; Low et al., 2005; McCain, Mustard, & Shankar, 2007).

The disparities in literacy, numeracy, and behavioural skills described in the previous chapter are associated with brain function and structure (Blair & Razza, 2007; Kishiyama et al., 2009). Insufficient cognitive stimulation and early life stress are shown to actually alter brain structure and functioning (Noble et al., 2005). In fact, it has been reported that the effects are almost equivalent to damage caused from a stroke (Kishiyama et al., 2009).

Although brain development is most rapid and dramatic through the prenatal period, it continues apace in the first few years of life. Throughout the process, networks are sculpted as neural pathways fine-tune perception, attention, cognition, and socio-emotional functioning. With the exception of genetic problems, it is the child's experiences that determine whether the developing neural networks will promote or impede the brain's ability for selective attention, appropriate information processing, and the regulation of emotions and behaviour (Joseph, 1999; Shonkoff & Philips, 2000). The good news is that since the development of the brain is experience-dependent, it generally is modifiable. Areas of the brain with a prolonged period of post-natal development, in particular, show significant plasticity. Fortunately, there is a lot of evidence that the pre-frontal cortex is one such area (Kishiyama et al., 2009). It is fortunate because major achievements in cognition through infancy and childhood depend on the development of the pre-frontal cortex (Noble et al., 2005).

The pre-frontal cortex is at the front of the brain both physically and behaviourally. It is responsible for what commonly is referred to as executive function skills – our ability to control our emotions, thoughts, and impulses; understand rules; make choices; solve cognitive and social problems; and consider future events. For school readiness, the

executive function skills are needed to help children pay attention, follow classroom rules, complete learning tasks, control their impulses,
and get along with other children and their teachers (McClelland et
al., 2007; Welsh et al., 2010). The emergence of self-regulation skills is a
crucial component of development for school readiness. The capacity
to focus attention, control emotion, and manage stress become increasingly important through the school years for the child's social and academic competence (Buckner, Mezzacappa, & Beardslee, 2009). Much of
the research in this area has examined the executive function deficits
found in children with attention deficit hyperactivity disorder (ADHD)
(e.g., Aguiar, Eubig, & Schantz, 2010; Arnsten, 2009). However, there is
a growing body of evidence that there also are differences in executive
functions skills among typically developing children (e.g., Gathercole
et al., 2008; Scope, Empson, & McHale, 2010). The behavioural manifes-
tations of these differences are not as great as those of children with a
clinical diagnosis of ADHD. Nonetheless they are significant. They are
differences that can account for the observed deficits in social, behavioural, and cognitive skills at school entry (Alloway et al., 2009), as well
as maladaptive behaviours in older children (Buckner et al., 2009). They
are also differences that primarily are associated with the adverse rear-
ing conditions of low-income families. Positive family environments
and parenting practices, which are less common in families struggling
with poverty, are important predictors of the development of executive
function skills in young children (Schroeder & Kelley, 2010). Adverse
experiences and maltreatment have been associated with both structural and functional changes in the pre-frontal cortex and executive
function skills (Beers & De Bellis, 2002; McCrory et al., 2010). It is worth
noting here that corporal punishment, particularly when it is harsh and
chronic, also is associated with structural changes to the brain that affect the executive function skills of emotion regulation, social behaviour difficulties, language comprehension, and memory (Tomoda et al.,
2009; Sheu et al., 2010).

The development of these skills, which is substantial in the preschool years, especially prior to age 3, is often delayed or deficient in
children from low-income families, as noted above (Noble et al., 2005,
2007; Welsh et al., 2010). Researchers using either neuropsychological
(e.g., Farah et al., 2006) or neurophysiological tests (e.g., Kishiyama et
al., 2009) find that social inequalities are strongly associated with reduced executive function skills in children from low-income families. It
is this poor development of executive function skills in children living

in poverty that accounts for their deficits in the numeracy, literacy, and behavioural skills that determine school readiness, as summarized in the previous chapter (Blair & Razza, 2007; Noble et al., 2005). Of particular importance are deficits in the development of working memory and attention control. These processes play a key role in literacy, math, and problem-solving skills (Blair & Razza, 2007; Li-Grining, 2007; McClelland et al., 2007).

Working memory is that which allows the temporary storage of information while it is being used (Alloway et al., 2009). For example, working memory helps children remember and follow the directions given by a teacher while working on an assigned task. Working memory is closely associated with reading comprehension (Alloway et al., 2009; Gathercole et al., 2005; Welsh et al., 2010) and with math abilities (Alloway et al., 2009; Andersson, 2006; Geary et al., 2007; Welsh et al., 2010). Children with low working memory struggle with any tasks that place demands on it. They have a great deal of difficulty with task accuracy and completion because they forget instructions. They also forget instructions about behaviour and classroom rules. The work of Tracy Alloway and her colleagues (2009) is illustrative. The findings from their examination of the profiles of children with working memory impairments clearly demonstrate that poor or low working memory is a major risk factor for underachievement or failure. The children with poor working memory in their study performed below levels that would be expected for their ages. Their achievement in reading and mathematics was very poor and their progress was slow. In addition, teachers rated them as having problem behaviours. As other researchers have noted also (e.g., Aronen et al., 2005; Gathercole et al., 2008), teachers described the children with low working memory as highly inattentive with little self-monitoring and poor attention spans, easily distracted, and lacking in problem-solving skills. The teachers in the Alloway study also complained that these children constantly forgot what they were supposed to be doing, forgot things they had previously learned, and forgot how to do things. Many "careless" mistakes and abandoned tasks were the result.

Attention control describes the child's capacity to focus on the task at hand and to complete it without succumbing to distractions (McClelland et al., 2007; Welsh et al., 2010). Arnsten (2009) describes attention control as requiring three sub-skills: (1) the ability to regulate attention based on relevance of stimuli, (2) the ability to suppress processing irrelevant stimuli and to enhance the processing of relevant stimuli, and

(3) the ability to sustain attention on relevant stimuli without allowing attention to shift. In practice this would mean, for example, the child paying attention to the teacher's instructions on how to do a math problem, accessing and using working memory to assist with the problem and remember the instructions, and staying focused on the math problem without being distracted by the behaviour of other children or thoughts of, say, recess. As with assessments of working memory, socioeconomic differences have been demonstrated to be significant in attention control and related achievement. Children from low socioeconomic homes show less attention control than their more affluent peers (Howse et al., 2003). In addition, children who are maltreated or neglected in infancy or early childhood (more likely in low-income families) show deficits in attention control (Cicchetti, 2002).

The effects of low attention control are comparable to those of low working memory. Difficulty focusing attention and high susceptibility to distraction make it very difficult for the child to access and use the items needed from working memory. In a reading task, for example, the child's attention may shift among teacher instructions, phonemes, previously learned words, and pictures in the text, or another's child's conversation. As Welsh and his colleagues (2010) note, deficits in attention control and working memory are key predictors of school success – children's capacity to follow classroom rules and teacher instructions, to control their emotions and social interactions, and to focus on and complete required cognitive tasks. The processes of working memory and attention control clearly are linked, and poor skills in each tend to co-occur in disadvantaged children (Welsh et al., 2010). However, while each makes independent contributions to the child's difficulties, the effects are additive (Gathercole et al., 2008; Scope et al., 2010; Welsh et al., 2010).

Interestingly, whereas the effects generally are additive, some research suggests they may not always be global. Deficits in attention control may not always be manifest simply in less attention, but also in maladaptive attention. Research on the effects of maltreatment illustrates this. Seth Pollak and his colleagues (Pollak & Tolley-Schell, 2003; Pollak et al., 2005) report that physically abused children – who disproportionately are children living in poverty – show atypical attentional responses to stimuli that suggest threat. They show great difficulty shifting their attention away from angry faces, presumably at the expense of needed attentional processes. The implications for poor classroom functioning are obvious. Angry peers or an angry teacher may capture and hold the attention of an abused child. Close attention to anger cues is adaptive for the child in an abusive environment. But this is not so in school. Being distracted by the salience of the anger signals and finding it hard to refocus attention, it is highly unlikely that the child will complete or do well in classroom tasks. In such cases it is not that the child is simply inattentive, but that her attention is maladaptive in context. We can only imagine how difficult it must be for a child who is maltreated at home to be in a class where corporal punishment is the disciplinary strategy of choice.

In summary, the research findings are clear and consistent in demonstrating that the development of the pre-frontal cortex varies with environmental factors. Deprivation and stress, such as that which characterizes the early years of children living in poverty, are associated with adverse development. Poor school readiness is the result. But this is not inevitable. Enriched environments with appropriate levels of cognitive stimulation and emotional support can alter the pathway and promote healthy neural development (Kishiyama et al., 2009). Interventions can make a difference.

Services and Programs of Early Childhood Education

Without early intervention, the learning difficulties of the early years are likely to continue into later childhood and adolescence. The achievement gap is likely to persist or widen. However, as found in research studies on early intervention, there is evidence that the difficulties can be addressed and the achievement gap reduced, although perhaps not entirely closed (Karoly, Kilburn, & Cannon, 2005; Neuman, 2009). The success of intervention is more likely during the early years when children are more receptive to intervention and when the brain has greater plasticity. The forms of early intervention are many, depending on the nature of the difficulty and the focus of the program or service, whether it is on the child or on the family as a whole. The programs range from parenting education and home visitation to various forms of family therapy and early childhood education and care. We focus our attention here on services and programs of early childhood education.

There are many types of early childhood education and care, which is a new international term for what traditionally, has been called child care or day care. The new terminology reflects current concern for the need for early learning among preschool children as well as for custodial care. Within the broad umbrella of early childhood education and care are two basic categories: (1) general programs and services of child care for all children, which may be publicly funded and operated, or publicly subsidized, or privately funded and operated, and (2) targeted and specialized preschool enrichment programs or compensatory programs, which typically are publicly funded or subsidized. General or regular child care is not designed specifically as an early intervention program for children at risk, although it may have this effect. Rather, it is designed primarily to assist busy working parents with their parenting and employment needs. But when the program or service is of high quality and includes disadvantaged children, it can serve as an effective means of early intervention. Preschool enrichment programs, however, are purposefully designed to help children who are disadvantaged and at risk. Among other things, they are programs developed to improve the cognitive and social skills of disadvantaged children such that they become more confident, more prepared for school, and more equipped for success at school. The programs typically involve teachers and professionals working with at-risk children to develop skills and improve school readiness and sometimes also with parents to promote health and parenting skills. Examples of programs include Head Start in the United States, Aboriginal Head Start in Canada, Sure Start in England, and Early Start in the Republic of Ireland.

Regular child care is by far the larger of the two categories. Today, the majority of children over the age of 3 years in developed countries are provided with early care not in their own homes with their own families but in some form of child care outside their home (UNICEF, 2008). It may be in a centre or a private residence, it may be full-time or part-time, it may be formal or informal, it may be regulated or unregulated, and it may be for a fee or subsidized. But whatever form it takes, as described by UNICEF (2008) in a comprehensive report on child care, approximately 80 per cent of 3- to 6-year olds and 25 per cent of children under the age of 3 experience some type of out-of-home care. The proportions vary from country to country. The enrolment of 3- to 6-year-olds in OECD countries such as France and Italy approaches 100 per cent while it is under 50 per cent in Switzerland. For children under age 3, enrolment is about 60 per cent in Denmark and Iceland, but under 5 per cent in Mexico. The proportions vary but the overall trend is upward. The forces driving the upward trend include the growing participation of women in the workforce, economic pressures on governments, the belief that preschool education is an investment for future educational success and for the future success of knowledge-based economies, and, for some countries, the belief that child care services are a means of reversing falling birth rates by providing support to families.

In all of the countries, there is widespread agreement that early childhood education needs to be not only accessible to children and families in need but also of high quality. This is in the best interests of children and especially in the best interests of disadvantaged children. There is also widespread agreement among researchers and experts as to what high quality means. American researchers W. Steven Barnett and Ellen Frede (2010) summarize the meaning of high quality care as follows. First, the staff needs to have appropriate qualifications and training. This has been shown to improve the interaction between staff and children and, therefore, to improve the learning of children. Staff should have a bachelor's degree or equivalent and specialized training in early childhood education. Second, staff-to-child ratios and the numbers of children at a centre or site need to be appropriate. There should be no more than 20 children in a group and no more than 10 children per staff member or teacher. With very young children, the numbers and the ratios should be even smaller. This is to allow children greater opportunities for interaction with staff and more individualized attention.

Third, there need to be appropriate early learning standards. This involves clear expectations for learning and development and appropriate programs to address children's physical well-being and motor development, social and emotional development, language development, and cognition and general knowledge. Fourth, attention needs to be paid to the health, safety, and support of the whole child. This involves such things as providing nutritious meals, having good safety standards, and encouraging parental involvement. Regular communication between parent and centre is particularly helpful in facilitating the provision of supports to the child as needed. For example, if the child had a difficult night or is not feeling well, she or he may need extra attention, comfort, or nap times. Fifth, there needs to be a system in place for evaluating, monitoring, and improving the service or program. Quality depends on feedback and on methods such as periodic site visits by assessors. Beyond these characteristics, say Barnett and Frede (2010), children should be engaged in a wide variety of age-appropriate projects and fun activities, and they should have warm and close relationships with staff and other children. Staff should continuously monitor the progress of the children, making adjustments when necessary, and preparing children for school through age-appropriate play, language development, and cognitive stimulation.

Preschool enrichment programs are the smaller of the two categories. They were pioneered and developed first in the United States as means to compensate impoverished and at-risk children for their disadvantage and to improve their educational and social outcomes. The intent was to level the playing field by giving disadvantaged children in preschools a "head start" or "better beginning" or "brighter beginning." Through cognitive and social skills training, the children would have a better start, be more prepared for school, and have greater educational achievement down the road. The first large-scale and government-initiated program was Head Start, launched by the U.S. Department of Health and Human Services in 1965 as part of President Lyndon Johnson's War on Poverty (Low et al., 2005; Rose, 2010). One of the longest running programs in the United States to address poverty, Head Start was designed as a community-based and income-based program where parents had to have an income well under the poverty line in order to qualify. The aim of the program was to provide children aged 3 to 5 years with educational services and cognitive and social skills training such that Head Start children could catch up with other children and be better prepared for school. But Head Start involved more than education. There were health services for children in the form of screenings and check-ups. There were also social services in which professionals worked with the parents, gave them support and education, and facilitated their involvement in their children's education. Under the terms of the program, it was mandatory that there be parental involvement.

Beyond Head Start, there has been the development of numerous other enrichment programs in the United States (Karoly et al., 2005; Neuman, 2009; Rose, 2010). Among the leading examples, in Michigan, there was the creation of the famous High/Scope Perry Preschool program in 1962 (which lasted until 1967). It targeted 3- and 4-year-old children living in poverty, providing half-day services, and aiming to promote the children's intellectual, social, and emotional learning. The staff-to-child ratio was one teacher for every six children. In Chicago, there was the establishment of Child-Parent Centers, beginning in 1967 (and still in operation). They provided half-day services for high-poverty children aged 3 and 4 years and required parental involvement in the programming. The staff-to-child ratio was one teacher and one aide for every 16 children. In North Carolina, there was the establishment of the Abecedarian Project preschools, which started in 1972 (and operated until 1985). The Project offered full-day, full-year, centre-based care for high-poverty and mainly African-American children from infancy up to 6 years of age. Also in North Carolina, there was the creation of the Bright Beginnings program, which began in 1996 (and is still running). It is a literacy-focused and full-day preschool program for 4-year-olds with a strong emphasis on parental involvement and community support. Finally, at the national level in the United States, there was the establishment of federally funded Early Head Start in 1994 (also still in operation), which evolved out of Head Start. It provides educational services for very young children from low-income families, up to age 3. It also provided support services for the families of the children involved, including parenting education, home visitation, and health care referrals.

Influenced by American developments, programs and services also have been put into place in other developed countries. For example, in Canada, Australia, and New Zealand, enrichment programs have been developed for Indigenous children living in poverty and their families (Prochner, 2004). In Canada, Aboriginal Head Start was established in 1995 for children and families off-reserve and expanded in 1998 to include children living on reserves. This was a federally funded national program, designed to provide educational and health services for Aboriginal families and children aged 3 to 5. The program was similar to American Head Start in that an important goal was to promote school readiness and success. But it was different in that there was a major emphasis on services and supports being culturally appropriate. Likewise, in Australia, there was the establishment of a national preschool program in 1987 called Multifunctional Aboriginal Children's Services. In New Zealand, there was a similar development in 1982 with the creation of the *kohanga reo* (language nest) program for Maori children and families. Like the Australian and Canadian programs, this was a comprehensive preschool program to promote school readiness but within the framework of family supports and attention to culture and identity.

Programs also have been put into place for children and families living in poverty apart from their ethnic status. In Canada, in 1991, after lengthy consultation, the government of Ontario developed the Better Beginnings, Better Futures program (Corter & Peters, 2011). It was an ambitious and large-scale program put into place in eight socially disadvantaged communities across the province. It was designed to prevent children living in low-income families from experiencing poor developmental and educational outcomes by promoting their positive social, behavioural, and educational development and enhancing their family and community environments. Similarly, in England, based on the American Head Start model and influenced by the Ontario program, there was the establishment of Sure Start in 1998, with the aim of providing educational services for children under age 5 living in poverty together with health services and other supports for the children's families (Rutter, 2006). Rolled out in six waves between 1998 and 2003, this enrichment program was targeted at the 20 per cent most socially deprived areas in England.

Like regular child care, quality has been emphasized as a key component of well-functioning enrichment programs. According to Susan Neuman (2009), the characteristics of high-quality programs are similar to those of regular child care except that the education and care have to be "more than just an extra boost toward learning" (p. 103). Because the children in the programs are so highly disadvantaged, vulnerable, and in need of major compensation to make up for their impoverished beginnings and learning difficulties, the programs need to be more intense and perform at a higher level. Neuman identifies four key characteristics. First, programs need to be longer. If high-poverty children are to catch up with their peers in language and other skills and be ready for school, time is a crucial commodity. One important means to extend time is to have full-day and full-year services for the children and their families. But even more critical, consistent with knowledge about the importance of the early years, brain development, and early intervention, programs should begin at an earlier age, as in Early Head Start or the Abecedarian Project, where the age is from infancy to 3 years. Children most at risk are in need of programs before they are 3 years old.

Second, programs need to be more focused on improving the development of working memory and attention control. Quality programs give attention to developmentally appropriate learning that is focused on educational outcomes. Activities should be targeted to the goals of helping children to develop language skills, expand vocabulary, and learn dispositions necessary for successful entry into school. Third, to enable such a focus, programs need to involve smaller groups of children and to be staffed with highly qualified and highly trained caregivers or teachers. Dedicated and skilled teachers are required who are able to spend time with each child and give each child the individual attention that she or he needs in order to overcome the difficulties of the early years. Children who have closer relationships with the teachers have fewer problem behaviours, better social skills, more motivation, and a higher level of achievement. Fourth, programs need to incorporate a system of child-centred and results-oriented accountability. Programs need to be monitored and evaluated on the basis not of factors such as teacher lesson plans but of the children's progress and performance. The primary focus has to be on outcomes for children.

Evaluations of the Impact of Early Childhood Education

Findings from a large body of research show that when early education services and programs are well designed, well implemented, and of high quality, they have an overall positive effect in improving children's cognitive and social skills, literacy development, school readiness, school achievement, and rates of high school completion and college entrance (Barnett, 2008; Britto, Fuligni, & Brooks-Gunn, 2006; Camilli et al., 2010; Neuman, 2009; Nores & Barnett, 2010; OECD, 2006; Ramey & Ramey, 2006; Rose, 2010). These findings come from a variety of sources including longitudinal studies, evaluations with experimental designs involving randomized control trials, evaluations with quasi-experimental designs, descriptive studies, case studies, and meta-analysis of a large number of studies. Some of the research results are mixed or inconclusive. But when the results of the studies are examined together, they show a positive impact of early education in countering the effects of social disadvantage. We now examine evaluations of regular child care and enrichment programs in turn.

Regular Child Care. As summarized by Barnett (2008), typical child care – care without high standards and high quality – has been found in research evaluations to have small or no effects on children. Home-based care, for example, has been found to have no effect on cognitive development while centre-based care has small effects on cognitive and language development. Some studies have even found centre-based care to have a small negative impact on children in terms of aggression and behavioural problems. However, when the child care is of high quality, the situation is different. A number of American studies, for example, have found gains for children in their cognitive and language abilities, especially for disadvantaged children (McCartney et al., 2007; NICHD Early Child Care Research Network & Duncan, 2003; Vandell, 2004). In a recent American study by the National Institute of Child Health and Human Development (NICHD), quality child care was found to be positively correlated with the child's cognitive development at age 4½ and

15 years (Vandell et al., 2010). The effects were modest but they were enduring and significant, although in this particular study no substantial differences were found in effects between advantaged and disadvantaged children. All children benefited.

Similar benefits have been found in evaluations in Europe and Australasia. In a recent summary by John Bennett (2008) of long-term studies in Australia, France, New Zealand, Sweden, and the United Kingdom, quality child care was found to have positive effects for all children and especially for poor children. The Swedish study, for example, found that the earlier the child enrolled in child care, the stronger the effect on educational achievement by age 13. The New Zealand study reported that high-quality care predicted higher levels of achievement in reading and mathematics in children by age 12. The British study concluded that quality care has a significant impact on children's cognitive development and sociability, particularly for disadvantaged children and particularly if disadvantaged children attend centres where there is a mixture of children from different social backgrounds.

Enrichment Programs. Although there is evidence that enrichment programs can have positive outcomes for children, not all programs have received full and rigorous evaluations, and some have findings that are mixed or inconclusive. Canada's Aboriginal Head Start program, for example, has shown some positive results for children in their educational progress but only on the basis of local project assessments (Public Health Agency of Canada, 2010). To date, there are no national evaluation data. In England, the Sure Start program has shown promise but it has yet to produce conclusive long-term results. A national evaluation began in 2001 in which children in disadvantaged areas with local Sure Start programs were compared with equivalent populations in non-disadvantaged areas (Rutter, 2006). By 2005, few significant differences were found in the educational progress or health of the children or in family functioning. In assessing this result, Michael Rutter (2006) concludes that the program was implemented in too diverse a manner to allow generalizations about its effects on disadvantaged children. The key problem, he says, is that there has not been one program of Sure Start in England, but a diversity of programs because of the open-ended nature of the program design by local communities. Local areas have been allowed to develop programs as they have seen fit. Because there has not been a single program to assess, the mixed and inconclusive results are to be expected.

Inconclusive results also have been found in evaluations of America's longest-running enrichment program – Head Start (Fuller, 2007; Low et al., 2005; Neuman, 2009). Contrary to early hopes, the first evaluation of Head Start – the Westinghouse study conducted in 1969 – found that the program had little effect on the cognitive development of children who participated in the program. The study reported that there were small effects in Grade 1, but these effects then faded out. However, this evaluation was strongly criticized because of flaws in its design. The groups of children in the study were not comparable: The children in Head Start were far poorer than the non–Head Start children. More recent and better-designed studies have found more favourable results. The most recent evidence comes from the congressionally mandated National Impact Study, with findings released in 2010. It shows modest but positive short-term results on some outcome measures, although not on all measures (Barnett, 2008; Barnett & Frede, 2010). The effects were largest for narrow literacy skills (e.g., naming letters) and smallest for broad cognitive measures (e.g., tests of vocabulary). But according to the study, by kindergarten and Grade 1, there was no persistent positive impact on children. However, in accounting for the lack of persistent effects, Barnett and Frede (2010) point to major problems in the quality of Head Start. The program has suffered not only because of funding problems but also because of a low level of teacher qualifications and pay. It is reasonable to conclude, they say, that if teacher pay and qualifications were improved, such as in Oklahoma where assessment has been much more positive, overall evaluations of Head Start would be more positive.

In Canada, evaluations of Ontario's Better Beginnings, Better Futures (BBBF) program have shown a similar pattern of positive outcomes along with some mixed results (Corter & Peters, 2011). Longitudinal research was conducted on the effects of the program for two groups of children from low-income families at different sites – younger-child sites (children from birth to age 4) and older-child sites (children from age 4 to age 8). Evaluations were done at both sites and at comparison sites during an initial period (1993–1997) and then as part of a follow-up (2003). The initial evaluations showed positive results both for the younger and for the older children (as well as for their families and local neighbourhoods). There were significant improvements in their academic performance, social functioning, and behaviour. However, the follow-up evaluations indicated positive outcomes at the older-child sites but not at the younger-child sites. For the older children, the evaluations showed that the positive outcomes strengthened over time as the children passed though Grades 3, 6, and 9. By Grade 12, the data showed continuing progress for the children, indicating the lasting positive effects of BBBF. But for the younger children, there were no similar lasting effects. These data point to the importance not only of targeting enrichment programs to early age groups but also to providing sufficient resources. As Corter and Peters (2011) point out, the investment per child during the preschool period of the Better Beginnings, Better Futures program was simply "not enough to reach a critical level of intensity" (p. 5).

Evaluations of other major enrichment programs in the United States have been much more conclusive. They have shown positive results both in the short term and long term (Barnett, 2008; Barnett & Frede, 2010; Bennett, 2008; Neuman, 2009). Early Head Start, for example, received a comprehensive and favourable evaluation from the U.S. Department of Health and Human Services (2010) for outcomes during the periods 1996–2001 and 2001–2005, based on a random sample of over 3,000 families in 17 sites. The study showed modest but positive and enduring effects on the learning of the children as well as on the provision of more supportive parenting. By the end of the program, at age 3, the children performed better on measures of cognition, language, and socioemotional functioning than did their peers who did not participate in the program. In addition, the parents in the program were found to be more attentive and more supportive of their children's emotional, cognitive, and language development. From age 3 to age 5, the Early Head Start children were more likely than their peers to participate in Head Start or other preschool programs. Finally, by age 5, as the children were beginning kindergarten, preliminary results showed that many of the positive effects endured, indicating that Early Head Start contributed to school readiness and improved family functioning. Although no effects were shown on some measures such as aggressive behaviour, overall, the impact was positive.

But the most impressive evaluations were from methodologically rigorous and long-term studies of three programs: the Abecedarian Project, the High/Scope Perry Preschool program, and the Chicago Child-Parent Centers (Barnett & Frede, 2010). First was the highly regarded Abecedarian Project of North Carolina. Designed on the basis of randomized controlled trials, the evaluation involved a long-term study of 112 children beginning at infancy (Carolina Abecedarian Project, 2010; Barnett & Frede, 2010; Ramey & Ramey, 2006). All were at high risk of developmental problems and delays in learning. Of the children, half were placed in a full-day, five days per week, and five-year program of high-quality early education. Each child had an individualized prescription of educational activities, which focused on social, emotional, and cognitive areas of development with particular attention to language. The other half was a control group. Progress was monitored at ages 3, 4, and 5 years, and then periodically until age 21. Compared with similar children in the control group, the Abecedarian children showed significantly higher levels of school achievement in reading and math, a higher rate of high school completion and college enrolment, higher earnings, better health, less involvement in crime, and less dependence on social assistance.

The High/Scope Perry Preschool program of Michigan also received a very positive evaluation (Barnett, 2008; Barnett & Frede, 2010). Again, the research design of the evaluation was based on randomized controlled trials. The study assigned 128 children either to a half-day preschool of high quality (with home visits by the teachers) or to a control group. The children attended the preschool for 2 years. Classes and staff-to-child ratios were much better than in typical preschool programs, averaging one staff person to six children. All staff had professional qualifications and experience. Evaluation results after 2 years showed significant gains of the children in language and cognitive development. The study then followed 123 of the 128 participants into their adolescence, young adulthood, and later adulthood. Evaluations showed significant results at each developmental stage. Compared with their peers in the control group, the Perry Preschool children scored higher on achievement tests during middle school, had a higher high school completion rate, had less involvement in crime, and had fewer behavioural problems as reported by teachers. Through age 40, they had higher earnings and more stable employment and less likelihood of criminal involvement and dependency on social assistance.

Finally, the Chicago Child-Parent Centers program showed very positive results (Barnett, 2008; Reynolds, 2000). The study involved a large sample of children – the original sample was 1,539 and the main study sample was 1,286 – which were followed from preschool into adolescence and adulthood. Multiple evaluations were conducted over time, and all found positive effects on the children's learning, similar to the effects found in the Perry Preschool study. There also was a significant reduction in grade retention, higher test scores through to middle school, declining enrolment in special education, and higher rates of high school completion. In addition, the study found a reduction in juvenile offending and crime.

Despite all of these positive outcomes, concerns have been raised about the high costs of such programs due in part to the higher standards of staff qualifications and low staff-to-child ratios. To address this concern, cost-benefit analyses have been done on the Chicago program as well as on the Perry Preschools and Abecedarian Project. Although it is difficult to calculate the long-term economic returns of the programs with precision, the analyses have shown each of the three programs to be cost effective (Barnett & Frede, 2010). The ratio of benefits to costs of the Perry Preschools, for example, was a stunning 16 to 1. From the point of view both of economic returns and the best interests of the child, the long-term benefits are quite significant.

Overall, the three programs have been shown to have strong positive effects on children and stronger and more lasting effects than either Head Start or regular child care (Barnett, 2008). It is important to note, however, that even in these highly regarded and proven programs, the effects lessen as the children get older. Although the impact on cognitive abilities and educational progress remains substantial over time, the effects become smaller as children move into higher grades in school.

The Chicago, Abecedarian, and Perry Preschool studies have received the best evaluations, showing a very strong evidence base for programs of early enrichment. But there have been a number of other preschool programs providing a strong evidence base as well. Neuman (2009) summarizes several studies of ongoing and successful programs in the United States. The Brookline Early Education Project in Massachusetts, for example, has been found to produce positive results on children's social and academic skills. The Early Training Project in Tennessee has been shown to result in greater educational achievement and a declining enrolment in special education. Similarly, the Milwaukee Project has been reported to produce improved educational performance and a declining enrolment in special education. Studies of the Avance program in Texas have demonstrated its capacity to decrease the high school dropout rate and to somewhat improve children's social skills and school readiness. Finally, the Bright Beginnings Program of North Carolina has been shown to have a positive impact on school performance and a decrease in grade retention. Particularly important to the success of these and other preschool programs have been quality teachers, teaching support, and classroom support. When there are well-trained and qualified teachers and staff, supports in place for teachers and staff, and classroom support for language and literacy, programs are more likely to be effective (Dickinson, McCabe, & Essex, 2006; Barnett & Frede, 2010).

In summary, a large body of evidence has been accumulated showing the positive effects of quality preschool on the learning and development of disadvantaged children. Long-term findings reveal that when early childhood education is of high quality, there are substantial gains in educational achievement and high school graduation rates and decreases in behavioural problems, grade repetition, and entry into special education.

Current State of Early Childhood Education

To a greater or lesser degree, virtually all developed countries have put into place programs and services of early childhood education and care. Support for preschool children and support for parents in the raising of young children have now become widely regarded as a responsibility of government. There are major problems, however, in the availability and quality of early childhood education (OECD, 2006; UNICEF, 2008). In some developed countries, programs and services are well established, well funded, and of high overall quality. But in many other countries, they are not well developed, uneven in access, under-funded, and spotty in quality.

On the positive side, the Nordic countries have developed some of the most advanced systems of early childhood education and care in the world. Their level of public spending on programs and services is at the top end of spending among developed countries. According to data from the family database of the OECD (2010c), in a comparison of 28 countries in spending on early childhood education services (as a percentage of GDP), the Nordic countries all ranked in the top seven. The top two countries were Denmark and Iceland, with a level of spending over twice the OECD average. Expenditure levels also were quite high in Sweden, Norway, and Finland. But apart from high spending, there is broad coverage and a high level of quality of care. Sweden, in particular, has put great effort into the building of a strong system of public, universal, and high-quality child care through a network of various kinds of preschools (Covell & Howe, 2009; Moss & Petrie, 2002). It is a system funded through payroll taxes paid by employers, general government revenues, and for parents who can afford to pay them, nominal fees that cover 15 per cent of the cost. Its coverage is wide because municipal authorities, who have the responsibility for the delivery of services, are required by law to provide child care spaces for all children – including all disadvantaged children – between the ages of 18 months and 6 years. Sweden's early education services, which are part of the formal education system under the authority of the Ministry of Education, are very much concerned with quality. Municipal authorities are required by the national government to ensure high standards in terms of staff-to-child ratios, programming, health and safety, and the qualifications of staff.

In contrast, in most developed countries, availability and quality are lacking. This is particularly the case in the United States and Canada. Their level of public expenditure on child care and early education is at the low end of spending among OECD countries and far behind all of the Nordic nations (Covell & Howe, 2009; Heymann, Penrose, & Earle, 2006; OECD, 2010c). As reported by the OECD (2010c), public spending in the United States (as a percentage of GDP) has been a quarter that of Denmark and a half that of Iceland. Expenditure in Canada has been even less than in the United States. But apart from spending, the programs in Canada and the United States suffer in terms of coverage, availability, affordability, and quality. Both countries are similar in that there is no universal and public program of early childhood education and care. Instead, most child care services are provided for in the private sector through informal care by relatives or sitters, or in unregulated day care homes. There is no national legislation and there are few national standards. Instead, because child care is the responsibility of the states and provinces, each with different resources and priorities, there is major variation and a hodgepodge of programs (Friendly, 2007; McCain, Mustard, & Shankar, 2007; Neuman, 2009). Finally, in both countries, there is a similarly modest degree of financial assistance provided to parents and centres by governments through subsidies and tax deductions. It generally is woefully inadequate.

The lack of quality services and programs weighs heavily on all families. But it is particularly a problem for low-income families and children. In the United States, for example, there has been a growing gap in recent decades between the exploding need for child care, on the one hand, and its availability, on the other (Barnett & Frede, 2010; Heymann et al., 2006; Neuman, 2009). This has been the result of a combination of many factors: the increasing entry of women into the labour force, rising economic inequality and the growth of low-paying jobs, growing numbers of single-parent families, welfare reform during the 1990s requiring many single parents to work rather than receive public assistance, and inadequate government funding and support for early childhood education. It is true that federal and provincial/state funding for services, programs, and subsidies to low-income families has increased. But it has been inadequate to meet the expanding demand, forcing many low-income parents to find informal and unstable child care by relatives, friends, and neighbours (Neuman, 2009). As is well known in the research, this form of care typically is not of high quality, decreasing the probability of school readiness and increasing the prospects for educational failure.

A problem in the United States is that although there are many examples of quality child care services and effective preschool enrichment programs, these are relatively few and far between. It is estimated that about 40 per cent of American 3-year-olds and two-thirds of 4-year-olds participate in some type of child care program or preschool (Barnett & Frede, 2010). But research shows that few of the existing programs and services are of high quality (Barnett, 2008; Britto et al., 2006; Neuman, 2009). Most programs lack quality in terms of low safety and health standards, inadequate support for learning and stimulation, high staff-to-child ratios, poorly paid and unqualified staff, and a high rate of staff turnover. According to UNICEF (2008) and Barnett and Frede (2010), in contrast to what quality early education and care could achieve for disadvantaged children, programs with low standards may actually bring them harm. "What is particularly sad about this state of affairs," say Barnett and Frede, "is that preschool education has the potential to produce exactly the opposite result" (2010, p. 22).

This lack of quality is a problem in many other developed countries. In a large-scale study of early childhood education in 25 OECD countries, UNICEF (2008) compared and assessed services on the basis of 10 indicators or benchmarks. The benchmarks included spending levels on services, staff-to-child ratios, qualifications of staff, training of staff, subsidized and regulated services, and national plans of action for disadvantaged children. Only one country – Sweden – achieved success on all benchmarks. Five countries – Iceland, Norway, Denmark, Finland, and France – achieved a high score on the basis of success on eight or nine benchmarks. But 12 of the 25 countries – Belgium, Hungary, New Zealand, Slovenia, Austria, the Netherlands, England, Germany, Italy, Japan, Portugal, and the Republic of Korea – received only a poor to mediocre grade by reaching four to six of the benchmarks. Seven countries received a failing grade by achieving only one to three benchmarks – Mexico, Spain, Switzerland, the United States, Australia,

Ireland, and Canada. That the majority of countries had mediocre to failing grades speaks volumes about the overall commitment to early childhood education and care and the best interests of the child in developed countries.

Early Education in the Best Interests of the Child

In light of the critical importance of the early years and the demonstrated benefits of early childhood education and care in reducing the achievement gap, David Low and his colleagues (2005) have made the case that early education should be given very high priority and integrated into the kindergarten to Grade 12 formal education systems. Their argument is that this would result in better educational outcomes for children and, thereby, better health outcomes for the population. Their argument is made in reference to the United States, but it can apply to many other countries as well.

The case they make is this. In the United States, there has been and remains a very high degree of public and political resistance to policies whose primary purpose is to remedy social disadvantage through redistributing income and wealth. There is a strong American aversion to the idea of *handouts* and to concepts such as equality of results. But at the same time, there is a high level of support for the principle of equality of opportunity. People should have an equal chance to pursue their chosen ends and not be held back by factors outside their control. This principle applies especially to education where children should have an equal chance to learn, achieve educational success, and achieve later success in work and life. It is unfair, according to prevailing opinion, that children, through no fault of their own, should face barriers that deny or restrict their opportunity for education. It is agreed that no child should be left behind. This, says Low, is the point at which to build an effective argument for early childhood education. Since the American public already agrees that no child should be left behind, it should be possible to convince the public that a strong system of early childhood education and care is in the interests of no child left behind and consistent with the principle of equal opportunity. It should also be possible to convince the public of the need to integrate early education into the regular kindergarten to Grade 12 state school systems, as has been done in Sweden. This is part and parcel of building a strong system of early education. Early education and care is more likely to receive the necessary support and funding when it is part of the regular school system. This kind of argument, Low suggests, is more likely to be accepted by the American public because it is a *hand up* rather than a *handout* and because it is in accord with the traditional concept of equality of opportunity.

The argument made by Low and his associates (2005) is pragmatic and convincing. Policies to remedy social disadvantage are more likely to be successful when they are framed in terms of opportunity rather than results. This applies, however, not only to the United States but also to many other developed countries. The political cultures of Canada, Australia, and France, for example, may not be as individualistic as the one in the United States, but the values of individual freedom and equality of opportunity are strong.

Beyond pragmatic arguments, there is the principled argument that strong systems of early childhood education and care are desirable because they are in the best interests of the child. This is a compelling argument either on its own or in addition to pragmatic arguments. In the U.N. Convention on the Rights of the Child, there is no explicit right of the child to early education. Article 28 states that children have the right to education. A full reading of the article shows that this means that children have the right to free and available primary education and to available and accessible secondary education. There is no mention of early childhood education. Article 18 states that countries shall take "all appropriate measures to ensure that children of working parents have the right to benefit from child-care services and facilities for which they are eligible." Again, there is no mention of early childhood education and care. Reference is only made to child care services for working parents who are eligible, according to a country's eligibility requirements. There is no reference to early childhood education as a right for all children who are in need of services.

However, according to the best interests principle, as discussed in chapter 2, children's best interests are to be determined in reference to the child's well-being and healthy development, the rights of the child, and evidence-based research. All of these considerations point to quality early education as in the best interests of the child. First, receiving good education is part of the healthy development of the child, including the disadvantaged child. Second, children have the right to education on the basis of equal opportunity, including children who come from impoverished homes. Third, there is solid and consistent evidence from research studies that quality child care and preschool enrichment programs can make an important contribution to reducing the achievement gap. It may be recalled that one important role of the best interests principle is to identify conditions for the enjoyment and exercise of the rights of the child. With strong and comprehensive systems of early childhood education in place, disadvantaged children are more able to enjoy their right to education on the basis of equal opportunity. Their ability to enjoy this right increases when early education is integrated into the regular school system where it is given elevated status and funding, consistent with the importance of the early years. As explained by the U.N. Committee on the Rights of the Child (2005), early education should be viewed as part of a continuum of formal schooling, not as a separate and less important service.

But apart from the matter of integration, consistent with the best interests of the child, services and programs of early education should be universal and accessible to all children. In putting into place services and programs, governments have the choice of establishing either targeted or universal programs. Many governments have chosen the former, concentrating resources on high-poverty children and families. This has been done, for example, in the United States with Head Start and in the United Kingdom with Sure Start. The argument for doing this is understandable. Under conditions of limited resources, targeted programs are designed to give disadvantaged children priority. If universal programs were implemented instead, it is argued, resources would be spread too thinly to ensure quality and the achievement gap would continue without substantial closing.

However, assuming the programs are of high quality, the arguments in favour of universal programs are stronger and more consistent with the principle of best interests. The arguments are summarized by UNICEF (2008) as follows. First, there is the advantage of children from different social backgrounds being brought together rather than being segregated. This is a means both of preventing social exclusion and of promoting common citizenship. Furthermore, as was noted previously in the British study of quality child care in the United Kingdom, there are greater positive effects of the care for disadvantaged children when there is a mixture of children from different backgrounds. Children learn from their peers as well as from their teachers. Second, universal services tend to garner wider public and political support and to involve greater concern about the quality of services. They are thus more likely to be sustainable and resistant to pressures for budgetary cuts or fiscal restraint. Third, that universal programs are in place does not mean that priority still cannot be given to disadvantaged children.

There is nothing to prevent the allocation of *additional* funds for services that are used mainly by children from low-income families or for incentives to encourage the best teachers to work with disadvantaged children. Fourth, targeted programs may not reach all at-risk children living in poverty who are in need. A disadvantaged child in need of an enrichment program, for example, may come from a family with an income slightly above a particular income line. But a universal program would not have this problem. It would cover all children.

The problems with targeted early education programs are well illustrated by their use in the United States (Barnett & Frede, 2010). Most publicly funded preschool programs in the United States are targeted programs. This is the case for the federal Head Start and Early Head Start programs and for most preschool programs funded at the state level. However, only a minority of children living in poverty at age 4 attend a public preschool enrichment program and only a small minority at age 3 attend such a program. If subsidized child care was included in the statistics (most of which are of poor quality, as discussed previously), then the proportion of poor children attending would be closer to half. But there remain many children in need of quality care and enrichment programs who are not getting them. Why is this so? Barnett and Frede (2010) point to the following reasons to explain why poor children are left out of targeted programs. Some families avoid programs that are limited to the poor because they do not want to be stigmatized or because they are concerned about the negative consequences of having their children associate only with peers who are also poor. Other families are left out because their income is above the eligibility requirements. Family incomes fluctuate over time. In one year, many families may be eligible for services but the next year they are not. Furthermore, eligibility rules may tighten over time, and families who are in need of services but slightly above a particular income line may not get the services they need. Thus, for a variety of reasons, targeted programs do not reach disadvantaged children. Because of the failures of the targeted approach, analysts such as Barnett and Frede urge the adoption of universal services in the United States. We agree.

Universal early childhood education and care of high quality is in the best interests of the child. Such education benefits all children and especially disadvantaged children. It is an important means both of reducing the achievement gap and of advancing the child's right to education on the basis of equal opportunity.

An Important but Incomplete Step

There is no question that establishing strong and universal systems of early childhood education and care is a critically important step in building educational resilience and in levelling the playing field for disadvantaged children. By promoting school readiness, enhancing cognitive and social skills, building confidence, and compensating for early learning difficulties, such systems are in the best interests of the child. Given the importance of the early years and the importance of early educational intervention, it is essential that early childhood education and care be well funded and given top priority in overall education systems. But it is not the full answer. It is not the final step in educational reform.

The reason is this. Although early childhood education and care has been shown to be effective in reducing the risk factors for impoverished children and in promoting school readiness, the effects on social disadvantage are not necessarily sustained. The difficulties instigated by poverty may be lessened but they do not entirely disappear. The better start that disadvantaged children can receive through effective preschool needs to be reinforced and bolstered in school if there is not to be slippage or reversal. It is important to keep in mind that evaluations of enrichment programs such as Early Head Start showed a modest positive impact on early learning and later educational success. The results were not overwhelming and not necessarily sustained through formal schooling. It also is important to keep in mind that even in the most effective of the enrichment programs, the effects lessen as children get older.

Educational resilience is built when protective factors outweigh risk factors throughout the child's schooling. If poverty continues through childhood, then protective factors must continue also in schools. Protective factors such as high-quality teaching, evidence-based programming, and effective policies in schools are needed to maintain any progress made through preschool. For disadvantaged school-aged children who have not received quality early childhood education, these protective factors may still function to build educational resilience. In the absence of protective factors at school and with the continuing influence of poverty, the children affected may very well still experience learning difficulties, lose confidence and motivation, have behavioural problems, and drop out of school. Resilience is more a function of environmental than personal characteristics.

In sum, the positive effects of even the best of early childhood education programs may be limited in duration or even countered by poor school practices. To ensure the best interests of all children, schools need to recognize the problem of poverty and their own capacity to counter its negative effects on children. Schools need to make a difference. As will be discussed in the next chapter, schools, teachers, and education systems can make a significant difference in levelling the playing field. The odds for success may be less without quality preschool. But this does not mean that schools do not play an important role.

Chapter Five

Improving School Practices

Fourteen-year-old Chris Emery had pretty much given up on school. His parents were struggling financially. His grades were low and his disengagement high. Chris planned to drop out and become a cook. But four years later, a successful high school graduate, he was on his way to college to study neuroscience. What happened? Chris changed schools. Moving to "the Met" in Providence, Rhode Island, Chris went from disengaged to inspired, from failure to success. Chris's story is not unique at this school. Comprising students from low-income families who have failed at conventional schools, the Met has an almost perfect graduation and college attendance rate (Symonds, 2006). Schools can make a difference when they make a conscious effort to do so and when they take seriously the best interests of the child. The story of Chris Emery tells us it is never too late.

Early childhood education programs, however successful, are not enough. The best interests of disadvantaged children also require that schools engage children and provide them with effective education on the basis of equal opportunity. Too often this is not the case. Schools need to improve educational outcomes through putting into place evidence-based practices and policies that counter disadvantage and build resilience. Why should schools build resilience? First, under the principle of the best interests of the child, as noted previously, schools are obligated to provide the conditions that promote the optimum development of every child. Building resilience among disadvantaged children increases the likelihood that they will achieve successful educational outcomes (Covell, Howe, & Polegato, 2011). Second, as so well explained by Jean Brooks (2006), schools should build resilience because they can. Children spend much of their days and much of their childhood in schools. Schools have the capacity to build resilience in children and in so doing, to offset the effects of family disadvantage. Resilience cannot be developed simply through will power within the disadvantaged child. It can, however, be built through the provision of protective factors at school. Educators have a choice. They can continue the practices that amplify family risk and increase the likelihood that disadvantaged children will fail (Boon, 2008). Or they can effect changes that will improve the achievement of disadvantaged children (Brooks, 2006).

In this chapter, we examine the evidence demonstrating how schools and education systems can make a difference. We first look at teacher quality and the recruitment, preparation, and retention of effective teachers. We then look at evidence-based practices in classrooms and schools including the facilitation of meaningful child participation, the practices of effective school leaders, the implementation of program reforms, and the initiation of whole-school reform such as the Met. Finally, in reference to international comparative research, we examine effective or promising education policies that improve outcomes for disadvantaged children. The policies we highlight are promoting social integration, providing special assistance to children at risk, providing appropriate resources, and setting concrete targets for reducing the achievement gap.

Quality Teachers

There has been a surge of interest in identifying factors that improve educational outcomes for children living in poverty. Among the factors that have been identified in the research literature, none is more important than quality teachers. We first note that a highly qualified teacher is not necessarily a high-quality teacher (Goldhaber & Anthony, 2007). Highly qualified teachers are considered to be those with appropriate certification and content knowledge (McLeskey & Billingsley, 2008). High-quality teachers are those who engage in evidence-based practices and hold positive attitudes towards their students. As Cook and his colleagues so cogently point out, the research can be full of evidence-based practices that may be legislated, taught, advocated, and aggressively promoted, but if teachers don't want to use them, they will not do so (Cook, Tankersley, & Landrum, 2009). The beliefs, attitudes, and motivations of a teacher appear to be as important as certification in predicting child outcomes.

Teacher Quality. As U.S. President Obama has stressed, what determines whether children succeed at school "is not the color of their skin or their ZIP code or even their parents' income … it is the quality of their teacher" (Rothstein, 2010, p. 32). There is widespread agreement among education researchers that this indeed is the case, particularly for children living in poverty (Amrein-Beardsley, 2007). As reported by Montt (2011) in a cross-national study of student achievement in 50 countries, no factor is more important than teacher quality in reducing achievement inequality. Some teachers are simply more successful at improving children's school performance than are others. If a child is fortunate enough to have high-quality teachers in successive years in the early grades, the gains in achievement are substantial. Teacher effects are cumulative (Konstantopoulos, 2009). However, the problem is that high-quality teachers are rarely found in high-poverty schools (Amrein-Beardsley, 2007; Futernick, 2010). But when they are, the difference they make to children's motivation and achievement is extraordinary.

What makes a high-quality teacher? This question has been pursued systematically for more than a decade by Teach for America, a non-profit organization that recruits college graduates to spend 2 years teaching in schools where the majority of the children are from low-income families (Farr, 2010; Ripley, 2010). Their database is impressive. Comprehensive records, interviews, and observations from a database of almost half a million disadvantaged children and over 7,000 teachers have been used to identify the characteristic behaviours of high-quality teachers (Ripley, 2010). The key six are as follows.

One: high-quality teachers set big goals for their students. The goals are ambitious, measurable, and meaningful to the student. Two: they attempt to involve parents in the child's schooling and in motivating the child to work hard. The aim is to convince the child that hard work pays off, that they can achieve their goals, and that in so doing their lives will improve. Three: high-quality teachers plan purposefully and exhaustively. They start by determining their goals for the student's achievement and behaviour and work backwards from there. They examine how success will be defined for the student and what strategies will achieve it. Four: they constantly monitor the student's progress and their own actions; adjustments in direction are made as needed to ensure that all actions contribute to student progress. Five: high-quality teachers continuously increase their effectiveness by reflecting critically on the pace of the student's learning, attempting to identify any root causes of problems, and then implementing solutions. Finally, high-quality teachers work relentlessly. Maintaining a conviction that it is possible for the student to overcome the obstacles posed by family circumstances, the teachers refuse to give up because of poverty, budgetary shortfalls, or bureaucracy. What distinguishes these teachers is, in essence, their belief that they can close the achievement gap and their motivation to do so.

Amanda Ripley (2010), who interviewed these and other teachers, noted that when she talked with those identified as high-quality teachers, they discussed their concerns for their students. If they complained about things, it was concerns such as the difficulty of parental involvement. Other teachers, she reports, spent much of the interview complaining about their job. Their concerns were with how much they were expected to do, how little time they were given to do all that was expected of them, how they had too much responsibility, and how parents simply do not know how to raise their children.

Similar findings on the characteristics of teacher quality are described by Douglas Reeves (2003) who has worked extensively with high-poverty schools. High-quality teachers never assume the student is incapable. They promote achievement by monitoring their students' work consistently and using that information to provide feedback to the children and to change their teaching strategies as needed. In the schools Reeves studied, this was done both at the individual and group level. High-quality teachers collaborate to promote achievement. They adopt common assessments to ensure fairness and consistency in grading, and they meet to discuss how the students are doing. Where it is seen as desirable, they use a cross-disciplinary focus on a topic to help every student learn. For example, if a discussion among teachers indicates there is a need to focus on teaching fractions, ratio, and measurement, the music teacher will develop activities that show how musical rhythms result from relationships among whole-notes, half-notes, and quarter-notes; the art teacher works on perspective and the use of scale in representational art; and the physical education teacher gives the students an option of running either a millimetre or a kilometre. On this latter option, as Reeves says, "when they make the wrong choice, it is a lesson most students remember well" (p. 13).

Underlying the characteristic behaviours of high-quality teachers as described by Farr (2010) and Reeves (2003) are teachers who truly care about their students. This affective dimension is reflected in the provision of social support. Whereas all children benefit from supportive teachers, they are of special importance for those children who live in social disadvantage and at risk of failure (Wu, Hughes, & Kwok, 2010). High-quality teachers are sensitive and supportive. They keep their promises, pay attention to the children, listen to them, demonstrate understanding and empathy, are available to spend time with them, and are affirming (Brooks, 2006). They celebrate achievements. School hallways are full of displays of achievement data, and school trophy cases are filled with examples of good work – essays, science projects, social studies projects, and math papers (Reeves, 2003). In sum, high-quality teachers behave with the interpersonal sensitivity and warmth and use the instructional strategies that researchers have shown to promote student achievement (e.g., Liew, Chen, & Hughes, 2010; Moolenar, Sleegers, & Daly, 2012; Teemant, Wink, & Tyra, 2011).

The difference made in the achievement of children from low-income families when they have high-quality teachers can be so great as to be literally unbelievable. Presenting such findings can leave researchers open to intense criticism. Reeves (2003) says it best: "Critics inevitably roll their eyes and allege that this surely must be a flash in the pan, the product of a frenzy of test preparation ... the exclusion of underperforming children ... a massive teaching conspiracy ... [or] the methodology of the research" (p. 17). Yet there is an abundance of research showing that one person can make a large difference in a child's life – one person who believes in the child and helps the child develop to potential (Cuthrell, Stapleton, & Ledford, 2009). Why not the child's teacher? Perhaps because although many teachers say they enter the profession to make a difference, the reality is that many do not willingly accept that responsibility. First, as described in chapter 3, many teachers hold a deterministic and counterproductive view of child development. They simply do not believe that they can do anything to alter the developmental path laid out by the child's family background. Second, they cling to earlier notions of children. They do not see children as bearers of rights, but as property, and therefore the responsibility of parents. These beliefs are exemplified in comments made by teachers in a study in New Zealand (Thrupp et al., 2003): "You could be accountable if you don't deliver all aspects of the curriculum. But for their achievement, no" and "Success isn't a thing about school, success is a thing about families and what happens at home." (p. 475). These are not quality teachers. All too often such teachers are concentrated in high-poverty schools.

Attracting Quality Teachers. Concerns about teacher quality are many and widespread. Across the developed world there have been numerous efforts to improve children's educational outcomes by improving teacher quality. Some have focused on attracting quality teachers to high-poverty schools, some on attracting higher quality candidates into education, and some on reforming teacher training.

Writing on the need to close the achievement gap, Audrey Amrein-Beardsley (2007) issued a "double-dog dare" to U.S. education leaders and policy-makers to increase the quality of teachers in disadvantaged schools. Her focus was on identifying how to attract the best possible teachers to the children who need them most. Her survey of teachers identified three incentives. One incentive described the characteristics of the school principal. What was attractive to teachers was a principal who was caring, supportive, open-minded, committed to student learning, qualified, and knowledgeable. A second incentive was a sense of community among the teaching staff. Shared values and attitudes were important, and – as with the principal – qualifications, knowledge, and commitment to students. The third, and arguably most important, was financial incentives. Teachers say they would be more willing to teach in disadvantaged schools if they were offered higher salaries, more opportunities for promotion, and/or increased benefits. Amrein-Beardsley (2007) suggests following the state of Georgia here. In Georgia, teachers who move to high-needs schools are given a $10,000 signing bonus. While less common in the United States, financial incentives are a common practice globally to encourage a more equitable distribution of teachers among schools (Stewart, 2010/2011).

Vivien Stewart (2010/2011) undertook an analysis of how the different OECD countries have dealt with the global concern of improving education. Not surprisingly, countries in the developed world have focused their efforts on improving teacher quality. Using outcome performance data, she was able to identify best practices. Her findings are very interesting. In sharp contrast to North American practices, countries that do well in education are proactive. Rather than concentrating on reducing attrition and firing poor teachers, they focus on attracting, preparing, and sustaining high-quality teachers. Finland is one such country.

Finland has raised the standards for new teachers and thereby the status of the profession. This has resulted in an increase in the number of applicants and the ability to be selective in acceptance; only one in 10 applicants is accepted into teacher training. England also has made a conscious and successful effort to increase the status of the teaching profession. It has introduced teacher awards programs on television and encouraged alternate routes into teaching. As with Finland, these efforts have increased both the number and quality of applicants. In turn, the ability to be selective in acceptance increases the possibility of training candidates who are most likely to become high-quality teachers. Steven Farr and his colleagues at Teach for America have been able to identify personal characteristics that predict an excellent teacher for children from low-income families (Ripley, 2010). These could be used as a guide for applicants to teacher training. The highest quality teachers, they found, were those who demonstrated perseverance by overcoming challenges in their own lives and by having a passion for long-term goals; they had achieved measurable goals in the past and were high in measures of life satisfaction. The absence of high grades in the candidate's schooling history is notably absent.

Preparing Quality Teachers. In many countries teacher training is woefully inadequate. Writing about teacher preparation in New Zealand, for example, Martin Thrupp and his colleagues (2003) describe its uncritical nature and point out that even such simple and consistently agreed upon concepts as the power of teachers' expectations, how social factors affect children, and the importance of classroom climate are ignored. There is little if any critical thought given in teacher training programs to the purpose of education or to the importance of social and emotional learning (Cohen et al., 2009). Writing about the United States, Arnove (2010) laments the excessive emphasis on subject matter to the detriment of pedagogy. Learning how to promote student participation, for example, should be fundamental. Teachers need to learn how to engage students in open-ended activities, offer choices, provide challenge, provide support by ensuring children have the knowledge and skills necessary for self-regulated learning, and how to use non-threatening evaluation practices in which difficulties and errors are seen as opportunities for learning (Lombaerts & Engels, 2009). Even basic training on how to facilitate small group cooperative learning among students is largely absent from teacher preparation (Gillies, 2003). Also absent, and very much wanted by teachers, is training on classroom behaviour management strategies (Thompson & Webber, 2010).

Most teacher training programs focus only on subjects that will be taught and tested on (Cohen et al., 2009). Graduates from such programs may be highly competent in math or science, for example, but ignorant of child development, influences on achievement, how to manage challenging behaviours, and even how to teach. The evidence clearly points to the need for teacher preparation to include how to teach in diverse environments, how to involve parents, how to maintain a positive classroom climate, how to manage behaviour, and how to appreciate the realities of daily life for children from low-income families (Cuthrell et al., 2009; Ratcliff & Hunt, 2009). It must, moreover, be ensured that the negative attitudes and stereotypes, which are so harmful to children living in poverty and their parents, are overcome (Baum & Swick, 2008). None of this is happening.

Martin Haberman (2010) describes well how little teacher practices have changed over the past few decades. He suggests the only change in behaviour is that teachers now require students to answer questions through Google or comparable Internet search engines. In his words: "It is a source of consternation that I am able to state without equivocation that the overly directive, mind-numbing, mundane, useless, anti-intellectual acts that constitute teaching not only remain the coin of the realm but have become the gold standard" (p. 45). These practices are antithetical to learning.

Ignoring the evidence and continuing to prepare teachers to teach in maladaptive ways runs counter to the best interests of the child and to the teacher. When teachers are prepared to teach subjects rather than to teach children, disadvantaged children are disproportionately affected. As described in chapter 3, they are subjected to biases, policies, and practices that promote their failure. Ill-prepared teachers also have difficulties. They are more likely to experience stress and burnout and lack the positive classroom experiences that influence their sense of efficacy and their ability to teach well (Klassen & Chiu, 2010; Morgan et al., 2010). The good news is that Vivien Stewart (2010/2011) reports that at least some countries have successfully modernized teacher education to make it more evidence based. But the pace of change is less than glacial.

The best example Stewart (2010/2011) describes is Singapore. Teachers there are trained to create learning environments that foster skill development among their students (rather than rote learning), and institutions that provide teacher education are held accountable for teacher competencies. Such accountability is very rare. In Canada, as Stewart observes using the example of the province of Ontario, teacher education institutions are viewed as too difficult to reform. The hope is that professional development days will effect change. But there is little reason for this hope.

Although important and useful to sustaining effective teaching, the sporadic days of specific information giving that typify much professional development are unlikely to compensate for inadequate pre-service training. Too often, professional development topics are perceived to be irrelevant by teachers, and many teachers simply avoid participation (Stewart, 2010/2011). In fact, teachers – particularly those in schools in which children are not doing well – have very limited access to the type of professional development that *is* helpful (Opfer & Pedder, 2010). Teachers need opportunities to continuously update their skills and knowledge of evidence-based practices (Looney, 2011). For example, there are many new approaches to incorporating video games into the classroom that have been demonstrated to be engaging and effective, but teachers may not be aware of or comfortable with them (Covell & MacLean, 2012). For professional development to be effective in improving teacher attitudes and instructional strategies, it needs to be sustained and intensive (Opfer & Pedder, 2010). It has also been shown to be helpful if professional development includes modelling of effective teaching, mentoring, and coaching (Bolam & Weindling, 2006; Harrison, Lawson, & Wortley, 2005; Teemant et al., 2011). Importantly, professional development needs to promote a shift from instructional strategies that are suitable only for transmitting facts to facilitative approaches that allow understanding (see, e.g., Grieve, 2010). This is rare. However, as evidenced in the interventions described earlier in this chapter, teacher professional development is often relied upon to enable effective classroom practices and curriculum delivery.

Retaining Quality Teachers. One of the best practices Stewart (2010/2011) identified is the spending of a higher proportion of education funding on classroom teachers, trading off class size, special services, and facilities. The funding is spent three ways. One is raising salaries. Stewart finds that high-quality graduates enter teaching only if entry-level salaries are comparable to other available careers. A second is the use of merit pay. As noted above, it is common in many areas to provide bonuses to teachers who agree to teach in disadvantaged or otherwise hard-to-staff schools. This use of funding reflects a conscious effort to equalize the distribution of quality teachers. Many OECD countries (Finland and Canada are exceptions) also reward teacher excellence with financial bonuses. Appropriately, teacher excellence is not determined simply on the basis of student test scores, but on meeting a wide range of school improvement goals, professional contributions, and most importantly, indicators of student well-being. The third use of funding is in the provision of time for non-teaching activities. Teachers are provided professional development time, time to meet with colleagues for mutual exploration of improvements, and time to meet with families to assess routes to improvement. Again, Singapore exemplifies best practices. Teachers in Singapore have time in the school day for professional development (100 hours per year), and for working with students outside the classroom. The trade-off – the larger class sizes – does not appear to lessen student performance.

Effective Classroom Practices

Quality teachers are ones who use effective classroom practices consistent with the best interests and rights of the child. This means that both instructional and behaviour management strategies should be child-centred.

Instructional strategies that allow child participation are the most effective. The right to participate is a fundamental right of children under the U.N. Convention on the Rights of the Child and an integral part of the best interests principle. It also is of key importance to children's learning in school. In her analysis of teacher quality, Brooks (2006) includes the importance of teachers who promote meaningful participation in the classroom. This practice is not widespread. Reflecting the current value placed on testing and standards, the emphasis in many classrooms remains on rote learning and memorization (Howe & Covell, 2005). The result is disengaged, bored, and unmotivated students whose basic rights are not being respected. We all need opportunities for self-direction and children are no exception. Even very young children need a sense that they can control events and can produce desired outcomes through their actions. That sense of control promotes effort and task persistence (see, e.g., Bandura, 1993). Regardless of their cultural or family circumstances, children need to be listened to and to be provided with increasing self-determination with age (Helwig et al., 2003). Having some control over events and being listened to at school is particularly important for children living in poverty who have little experience with participation at home (see, e.g., Aunola et al., 1999).

Teachers' instructional styles tend to fall on a continuum from highly controlling to autonomy supportive (Jang, Reeve, & Deci, 2010). Those teachers who are autonomy supportive engage and motivate students by listening to them carefully, acknowledging their perspectives and feelings, identifying and nurturing their interests and talents, providing challenges, and ensuring that they can pursue relevant and interesting activities (Jang et al., 2010; Radel et al., 2010). These pedagogical practices increase the students' intrinsic motivation – the desire to complete a task because it is inherently rewarding – effort, and success (Radel et al., 2010). In contrast, teachers at the controlling end of the continuum – those who believe that they must transmit knowledge and who attempt to coerce students to absorb that knowledge through punitive measures such as threats and criticism – function only to reduce motivation and effort.

That students should be allowed, where possible, to pursue what is of interest and relevance to them in the classroom, does not, of course, mean that there should be no leadership or structure provided (Jang et al., 2010). The classroom that is in the best interests of its students has both autonomy support and structure. Teachers need to provide leadership, structure, and guidance. It is meaningful participation that is in the best interests of the child, not full self-determination and not the confusion or chaos that result from inadequate structure. The role of the teacher is to provide a learning environment that allows students to effectively construct knowledge. An effective example of this is seen in project-based learning.

Project-based learning has attracted attention as a key route to developing the sort of generic skills students will need to be successful in our rapidly changing technological society – collaboration, communication, and problem solving. Such is the faith in project-based learning's capacity to accomplish this that the government of Hong Kong has initiated education reforms that require its use (Cheng, Lam, & Chan, 2008). It appears to be growing in popularity in many other education jurisdictions. The approach fits well with children's preferences for learning and with their developmental needs for self-direction. What is particularly good about the growing use of project-based learning is that is has great potential for helping to reduce the achievement gap.

Since the 1970s social-justice driven initiative, the Jigsaw Classroom – impelled by the ineffectiveness of desegregation policies in the United States to reduce prejudice – it has been known that small heterogeneous group cooperative learning increases the social and academic skills of disadvantaged children (Howe & Covell, 2005). The same appears to be true for project-based learning. As in the Jigsaw Classroom, project-based learning most often involves having children work in small groups in which success is dependent on group effort, shared responsibility, and group cooperation. Ultimately, knowledge is constructed through social interactions among the group (Cheng et al., 2008). What differentiates project-based learning is that it is student driven. Students select an issue about which they are curious, and then in their groups, they design their own multidisciplinary inquiry and plan and conduct their research (Bell, 2010).

In contrast to traditional methods of teaching, which tend to repress the child's natural curiosity, the promotion of self-directed learning enhances and reinforces it. As discussed by Stephanie Bell (2010) and Gregory Kucharski and his colleagues (Kucharski, Rust, & Ring, 2005), evaluation research shows numerous benefits of project-based learning. First, in terms of affect, motivation for learning, engagement, and self-esteem are significantly higher among students whose teachers use project-based learning. Second, in terms of behaviour, attendance is higher and task focus is better. Third, in terms of performance, significant evidence demonstrates that students engaged in project-based learning do much better on standardized test scores than do traditionally educated students. They also demonstrate enhanced research and problem-solving skills. Importantly, meta-analyses show that when heterogeneous-ability groupings are used, and used appropriately, there are disproportionate benefits to low-achieving students (Cheng et al., 2008; Lou et al., 1996). Low-achieving students obtain encouragement, assistance, and stimulation from their high-achieving peers. In addition, self-esteem is enhanced by the experience of success. That is often a first for disadvantaged children. These findings suggest that project-based learning is of particular benefit to children living in poverty who typically would be in the low-achieving category. Moreover, as Bell (2010) notes, it is an approach to learning that works well at entry to preschool. If used then, the achievement gap could start to be lessened early.

Anecdotal evidence from Ranvilles Infant School in Hampshire County, England, illustrates one mechanism by which project-based learning may achieve its positive outcomes. (We have been visiting this school over a 6-year period as part of a longitudinal research project; the information here is based on our observations and interview data with teachers and the principal in June 2011.) Over the past 2 years, project-based learning has been used in all classes at Ranvilles to teach the children the required learning outcomes for their ages (4–7 years). As would be predicted, there has been an increase in student engagement and achievement and a drop in absenteeism since its inception. In addition to group work in the classroom, each project includes a "home-learning component." Parents are first sent general information about home learning (traditionally called homework), and then sent information in an attractive way that is relevant to the nature of the project to describe what the project is. Finally, parents are sent specific details on what is needed for the project. This latter communication includes a child's challenge, a parent challenge, and a joint challenge for project completion. It also includes hints for the task at hand and possible resources. To preclude difficulty for disadvantaged children (the school is in a mixed socioeconomic neighbourhood), the school provides all supplies the children need to work on their project. Projects are completed over a 6-week period, and a celebration is held at the school at the end of each. Parents are notified of the celebration date and time when the initial information is sent home.

The increase in parental involvement since the inception of this approach has been extraordinary. There is at this time almost full parental cooperation and attendance at project celebrations. Teachers report significantly improved relationships with parents. The success in increasing parental involvement may well be due to the respect shown to parents in the way they are asked to be involved. Not only is it more engaging and empowering to be asked to guide home learning than to supervise homework, but also the parents' role is specified and supported to facilitate their involvement. It also is non-threatening. For example, one of the child challenges for new students (aged 4 years) was to choose their favourite nursery rhyme and design either a prop or a costume to illustrate it. The parent challenge was to talk about their child's chosen rhyme and practise singing it with the child. The joint challenge was to create the prop or costume designed. These were then used at the celebration where the children sang and showed their parents the portfolio they created with drawings, photographs, and the nursery rhymes on which they were based. Interestingly, the increased parental involvement in the child's learning has generalized. In a project "I Spy from the London Eye" in which children learned about and created representations in various media of what could be seen from the London Eye – a large structure similar to a Ferris wheel – many parents reported taking their children to London (a 2- to 3-hour journey) to assist with and improve their project outcomes. Finally, at the end of each project, parents are given a survey on which they are asked to provide their thoughts and comments about the project and to rate the extent of enjoyment they and their child experienced. Again, this reflects a degree of teacher respect for parents' opinions that is not often encountered by disadvantaged parents.

Effective and child-centred classroom management strategies can also reduce the achievement gap by lessening the likelihood that children who start school with behavioural problems will be punished or excluded. Authoritarian, punitive, and reactive classroom management strategies are neither effective nor in any way in the best interests of the child (Maag, 2002). Proactive and positive strategies, in contrast, are. Like instructional practices, classroom management strategies are more effective if children are involved in their design. Teachers who collaborate with their students at the beginning of the year to develop classroom rules and consequences for infractions are the most successful (Campbell, 2009). Students who are involved in the development of rules are more likely to adhere to them. Teachers report also that this type of collaboration with their students fosters a climate of mutual respect and positive relationships. Improved achievement is the result. Despite such evidence (Downer, Rimm-Kaufman, & Pianta, 2007; Pianta et al., 2002; Thomas et al., 2008), the more common practice continues to be punishing the disruptive child.

Effective Schoolwide Practices and Reforms

Beyond what happens in the classroom, the achievement gap may be reduced through effective schoolwide practices and reforms. Implementing school reform in support of disadvantaged children is a complex and difficult undertaking. But it can be accomplished through the introduction or incorporation of a number of practices identified in the research literature. Among these are remedial programs and full service schools. Such specific programs, however, usually produce only modest benefits. Whole school reform is much more promising although difficult to implement. But before we examine this, we first address the importance of strong and effective school leadership.

School Leadership. A large body of research has emerged over time showing school leadership to be a highly important factor in improving the educational performance of children (Cuthrell et al., 2009; Gurr, Drysdale, & Mulford, 2006; Harris, 2008; Harris & Allen, 2009; Leithwood, Harris, & Hopkins, 2008; Lyman & Villani, 2004; Ryan, 2005; Waters, Marzano, & McNulty, 2004; Ylimaki, Jacobson, & Drysdale, 2007). As reported by Kenneth Leithwood and his colleagues (2008) in summarizing research findings from a wealth of empirical studies, school leadership is "second only to classroom teaching as an influence on pupil learning" (p. 28). Successful leaders, whether they are individuals (school principals or head teachers) or teams, have been found to have a significant influence both on educational outcomes in general and on outcomes for disadvantaged children in particular.

Leithwood and his colleagues (2008) draw on extensive international literature and summarize the research findings in reference to seven strong claims about successful leadership. They report that although all of the claims have empirical support, the first two claims are particularly compelling. The first claim, as already mentioned, is that next to classroom teaching, school leadership is the most important factor in promoting student achievement. Evidence from qualitative case studies and various types of large-scale quantitative studies shows that leadership serves as a catalyst for effective school organization, student engagement, and student learning and achievement. Leithwood and colleagues note that there has not been a single documented case of a failing school being successfully turned around without the presence of talented leadership. The second claim is that "almost all successful leaders draw on the same repertoire of basic leadership practices" (p. 29). These are practices that are related to the central leadership tasks of improving the performance of teachers and staff (and, in turn, the students) and of helping teachers and staff to improve their work with performance-enhancing values, beliefs, skills, motivations, and knowledge. In accomplishing these tasks, the evidence points to the following leadership practices: building vision and setting direction, understanding and developing people (e.g., teacher skills, knowledge, dispositions), redesigning the organization (e.g., the work environment, structures for collaboration, structures for school-parent and school-community linkages), and managing the teaching and learning program (e.g., hiring teachers, providing teacher support, and monitoring school activity and student progress).

The third claim that Leithwood and colleagues (2008) make is that successful school leaders "demonstrate responsiveness to, rather than dictation by, the contexts in which they work" (p. 31). This does not simply mean being sensitive to context. Rather, it means that successful leaders apply contextually sensitive combinations of the leadership practices described above. The fourth claim is that leaders "improve teaching and learning indirectly and most powerfully through their influence on staff motivation, commitment and working conditions" (p. 32). Influencing teacher motivation and commitment are particularly important, given the effects on children of quality teachers. The fifth claim is that "school leadership has a greater influence on schools and pupils when it is widely distributed" (p. 34). This simply means that leadership has more impact when it involves a team of leaders rather than an individual. The sixth and related claim is that "some patterns of distribution are more effective than others" (p. 35). This claim is substantiated by research showing that schools with the highest levels of student performance have high levels of influence from multiple sources. In virtually all schools, principals are reported to have the greatest influence, for the better or for the worse. But the influence is for the better when the principals allow for a team approach to leadership, or for what James Ryan (2005) calls *inclusive leadership*. Finally, the seventh claim – and one of major interest – is that "a small handful of personal traits explain a high proportion of the variation in leadership effectiveness" (p. 36). These traits – present also in high-quality teachers – include open-mindedness, readiness to learn from others, flexibility in thinking, persistence in the pursuit of achievement, and optimism. Such traits, say Leithwood and colleagues (2008), help to account for the fact that under very difficult conditions, successful leaders are able to press forward and improve their schools.

So there is compelling evidence on the importance of successful school leadership, which may be assumed to benefit disadvantaged as well as advantaged children. But evidence also comes from research that examines school leadership specifically in high-poverty schools (Cuthrell et al., 2010; Harris, 2008; Lyman & Villani, 2004; Ylimaki et al., 2007). Rose Ylimaki and her colleagues (2007) report on case study findings from high-poverty primary schools in Australia, England, and the United States. They find that although the settings and the challenges in the three countries were very different, the school leaders who made the greatest difference had a quite similar array of leadership traits and practices. These turned out to be much the same as the traits and practices identified by Leithwood and his associates (2008). Of particular importance were the traits of passion and empathy. The leaders were passionate about making a difference in the lives of disadvantaged children, and they were empathetic about the barriers that poverty can produce. Nevertheless, say Ylimaki and colleagues (2007), the successful leaders did not allow poverty to be used as an excuse for poor achievement. Instead, they engaged in the practices identified by Leithwood and colleagues for school success such as building vision, developing people, and managing the teaching and learning program. They paid particular attention to making the physical environment of the school more attractive and safe, making the school more open to parents, and building supports for teachers and staff.

Linda Lyman and Christine Villani (2004), in their review of the research on high-poverty schools, also provide a list of the traits and practices of successful leaders. Much of what they report is similar to what is said by Ylimaki et al. (2007) and Leithwood et al. (2008). Successful leaders demonstrate passion and commitment to improving the educational achievement of disadvantaged children. They do this by inspiring and mobilizing teachers for the same purpose, providing supports, monitoring student progress, and making major efforts to involve parents. But more than other analysts, Lyman and Villani (2004) probe deeply into the beliefs and thinking of successful leaders about poverty and poor children. Effective leaders, they report, do not engage in *deficit thinking*, which is thinking that poor children are so dysfunctional that they lack the capacity to achieve in school. Rather, these leaders hold the strong belief that *all* children can achieve. They do not believe that poor children and their parents are poor because of their own inadequacies. They do not think that their situation is hopeless. Instead, they believe that poor children are disadvantaged by their social environments and that they can overcome their disadvantage through being treated with respect in child-centred educational environments and with evidence-based practices. In short, they believe that schools can make a difference. With these beliefs, say Lyman and Villani, successful leaders have high expectations for *all* children to succeed, and they make concerted efforts to mobilize teachers and staff and to introduce program reforms on behalf of disadvantaged children.

Program Reforms. Program reforms to improve outcomes for children living in poverty generally can be categorized into two basic types: those that aim to improve cognitive skills and those designed to decrease aggressive and disruptive behaviours. To improve cognitive skills, much attention has been paid to the use of remedial programs that are designed to improve reading. Most often these start in the third year of elementary school, a time identified as the watershed year for future success (Biancarosa & Snow, 2006; McGill-Franzen et al., 2006). The results have been mixed. The following examples illustrate the possibilities and highlight the challenges.

First, we note that recent longitudinal research from Finland suggests that computer-assisted interventions are beneficial in enhancing at-risk children's reading and spelling skills (Saine et al., 2011). Following the progress of 7-year-olds from Grade 1 to Grade 3, the researchers found that children who used GraphoGame – a computer-assisted reading intervention – compared with those who received more traditional remedial reading interventions, showed significantly greater gains in reading and spelling. GraphoGame trains children through phoneme awareness and letter knowledge to read words. Through playing the game, children learn the visual operations of putting individual letters into an orthographic unit (visual word form), their transformation into a sound (input phonology), and its articulation (output phonology). The researchers conclude that computer applications, unlike traditional remediation reading programs, provide children with the kind of individual, continuous, and motivating practice in phonological skills that promote improved reading. Their conclusion is plausible, and the use of computer-assisted remedial programs is very promising. However, it is traditional programs that are more often used, and there seem to be a number of challenges in their provision that may account for their less successful outcomes. The primary three are discussed here.

McGill-Franzen and her colleagues (2006) were concerned with the number of disadvantaged children in Florida who were being held back in Grade 3 because they lacked basic competence in reading. Attempting to identify successful remediation attempts, they examined two reading programs that were being used to improve the children's literacy. They found neither was able to raise the children's reading skills enough to prevent grade retention. The problem they discovered with both of the programs was they were designed for whole-class instruction. As they state, whole-class instruction in high-poverty schools is not effective. Neither is the use of common curricula materials. Unfortunately, whole-class instruction with common materials is common. What does motivate effort and increase competence is collaborative learning activities with a peer, and self-direction in reading (Biancarosa & Snow, 2006). This is evidenced in a program in New South Wales, Australia.

Focus on Reading 3–6 uses texts of interest to the target children, encourages self-directed involvement, and encourages collaborative learning in pairs. Importantly, it also promotes awareness of Aboriginal culture. The evidence to date suggests positive responses from teachers and students (Rowles, McInnis, & Lowe, 2010). The challenge with Focus on Reading 3–6 is the specialized training teachers need to implement it. Teachers are required to spend significant time (16 days), and money away from school obtaining certification (Rowles et al., 2010).

Another evidence-based program has been tried in Canada with Aboriginal children (Hayward, Das, & Janzen, 2007). COGENT (cognitive enhancement program) is designed to improve the child's executive function skills of working memory and attention control. Its aim is to improve the child's cognitive development such that what is learned can be generalized and transferred to novel situations. Hayward et al. (2007) report that initial testing of the program with disadvantaged children in India was very promising. Motivated by the need to improve the reading skills of Aboriginal children, Hayward and her colleagues offered the program through a school year to children in Grade 3 who had a history of reading failure to assess its effectiveness in improving their performance. Although there was some evidence of real improvements in individual children, the integrity of the program was compromised by the high absenteeism rate of the child participants. As the authors note, intervention or remediation programs assume consistency and continuity of program delivery. Without that, success is less likely. But clearly success is possible. Cognitive skills can be enhanced with self-directed and collaborative learning using relevant materials – whether computers or traditional materials – together with initiatives to increase school attendance among disadvantaged children.

Programs also have been used in schools to prevent or reduce aggressive and antisocial behaviours. These too can play a major role in reducing the achievement gap. Socioeconomic disadvantage puts children at risk for behavioural problems at the start of school, as discussed previously. Over time and through subsequent grades, these early conduct problems lead to school-level antisocial behaviours and aggression (Thomas et al., 2006). Without appropriate intervention, failure is the most common outcome since problem behaviours and achievement are incompatible. Since the early work of Mayer (Mayer & Butterworth, 1979; Mayer et al., 1983), there have been many examples of programs that successfully reduce antisocial behaviours using the fundamental principles of positive reinforcement from behavioural psychology. Christina Erickson and her colleagues (Erickson, Mattaini, & McGuire, 2004) provide an excellent summary of some of the primary programs in Europe and North America – PeaceBuilders, Effective Behaviour Support, Community Builders, Peace Power, Positive Action, and the Olweus Bullying Prevention Program. A more recent program that is showing success with children at risk is the Incredible Years Teacher and Child Training Program – Dinosaur School Curriculum (Webster-Stratton et al., 2008). This program has been shown to be particularly effective with socioeconomically disadvantaged children with significant conduct problems at school entry.

Although school based, many of these programs also involve parents and communities. What they all have in common is their focus on training teachers to alter their behaviour management strategies in ways that improve the learning environment and build the social competence of the children. As Mayer (2001) describes, reducing problem behaviours starts in the classroom. The first step is for each class to establish simple rules on how to behave that are developed collaboratively with the children, as described above. Consistent corrective consequences, modelling of appropriate social behaviours, and an emphasis on positive reinforcement across the school are other key components of successful management.

In a recent comparison of the effects of the Olweus Bullying Prevention Program in Norway and the United States, Dan Olweus and Susan Limber (2010) note that despite the evidence of the effectiveness of such programs, most schools do not implement them. They found that only 25 per cent of schools in Norway did so, and surprisingly, given the focus on violence in schools in America, only 4 per cent of U.S. schools had adopted a bullying prevention program. Most schools remain reactive and continue to use punitive strategies with individual children. Motivation may be lacking. None of these programs can be implemented successfully unless there is agreement and support from all staff; none can be sustained unless there is the capacity to adapt the program to the needs of the particular school (Erickson et al., 2004).

Most program reforms have been small scale and piecemeal. The difficulties associated with their widespread implementation have been extensively analysed by Michael Fullan (2007). The key consideration is the culture of the school, as we discuss in the next chapter. The essential point to be made is that the prospects for sustainable reform are greatly enhanced when the culture of the school and of the surrounding community and society are such that there is a genuine willingness, motivation, and commitment to improve educational outcomes for children and to act in the best interests of the child.

Broadening Mandates. There has been an increasing trend towards expanding the mandate of schools to incorporate additional programs, services, and initiatives. These are aimed at improving the overall health and educational well-being of children and include the provision of unified programming between preschool and school, the provision of after-school programs, the establishment of health centres, and the expansion of schools to offer a wide range of health and social services on site. Evaluation data on each are mixed or incomplete, but each holds promise for reducing the achievement gap between children from low-income families and their more advantaged peers.

One initiative has been the move to unified programming across early childhood education and kindergarten. In some jurisdictions, schools and school boards have partnered with the providers of early childhood education and child care to establish unified or integrated programs for the purpose of easing the transition for young children from preschool to kindergarten and the early grades. This involves aligning standards, curriculum, teaching methods, expectations, and assessments so that children can benefit from more continuity and stability. There has been little research on the impact of unified programming on the educational progress of socially disadvantaged children. But it is logical to assume that all children benefit when schools and early education providers work together to harmonize and integrate programs. In Canada, the Ministry of Children and Youth Services (2008) in the province of Ontario has undertaken a study of promising practices in implementing unified programming. Examining developments at 22 sites across the province, the promising practices identified include consistency between schools and preschools in their systems of governance and accountability, harmony of regulatory requirements, shared vision and shared knowledge of child development, collaborative and respectful relationships between teaching staff and early education providers, and appropriate funding for program planning and development. Although more research is required to assess child outcomes from such integration, it is reasonable to expect benefits for children living in poverty and for all children.

Another development has been after-school programs. Historically, such programs have been offered by community-based organizations. The programs have provided a safe place for children to be between the closing of school and the time their parents return from work. Some have offered tutoring and help with homework; others have focused more on recreational activities and positive social interaction. The benefits of such programs for children seem obvious. However, there has been no evidence to date of systematic evaluations that indicate whether these informal after-school programs contribute to the reduction of the achievement gap. More recently, there have been significant changes in after-school programs in the United States that have required formal programs and thus allowed evaluation research. Aiming to raise achievement test scores, No Child Left Behind requires school districts to provide supplemental educational services to students in schools that have failed to meet target academic standards – many of which are high-poverty schools. Federal funding of more than one billion dollars is provided for this use (Dietel, 2009). Since these services must be provided outside the school day, after-school tutoring programs appear to be the most common delivery system. Considerable evaluation research has resulted. Has the achievement gap been reduced? The answer seems to be: maybe or somewhat. Overall, the findings suggest very modest improvements in the academic performance of students who attend these programs (Zimmer, Hamilton, & Christina, 2010). The problem seems to be that very few eligible students attend, and those that do, do not attend consistently or long enough for improvement (Dietel, 2009; Frankel & Daley, 2007; Huang et al., 2008; Zimmer et al., 2010). The researchers report that attendance rates vary from 15 to 25 per cent of eligible students, that those that do attend may attend for less than one hour a day, and that attendance rates decrease with student age. The potential for effectiveness is evident, but it appears changes that motivate attendance are necessary. Perhaps this type of tutoring, which primarily involves mathematics and reading skills, also needs to be revisited.

After-school programs that allow students from low-income families access to computers might be more attractive to them and more effective in raising achievement. The lack of access to computers and to the Internet poses a real challenge for children living in poverty (Celano & Neuman, 2010). Many schools, especially high-poverty schools, have too few computers to allow each student the time needed to develop proficiency. For many children, the only additional access is at local libraries. However, public libraries are not always accessible to children in poor neighbourhoods, and even when they are, they have limited time between the end of the school day and the closing of the library, time during which they must compete with adults for use of computers.

The most comprehensive expansion of a school's mandate is seen in full service schools, also called full service community schools in the United States, and full service extended schools in the United Kingdom. Full service schools are schools that are specifically designed to reduce the achievement gap (Dryfoos, 2010; Dyson & Todd, 2010). They do so by including on-site services such as after-school programs and health services, not only for students, but also for their families and very often for other members of the community. These schools depend on effective partnerships with one or more community organizations that share the goal of improving the achievement of disadvantaged children by strengthening families and communities as well as by direct assistance to the children (Blank, 2004). Roles are defined with teachers continuing to be responsible for teaching academic subjects, and the community organization for providing supports and health and social services.

Martin Blank (2004) describes an effective model of full service community schools in a high-poverty area in the United States. The school, he explains, is open 6 days each week from 7:00 a.m. until 9:00 p.m. The partner – the local children's protection services – provides a number of programs and services. For example, parents are offered classes in computers, English language instruction, food preparation, and health issues. For the children, the partner provides homework help and a variety of cultural and recreational enrichment activities during the school's extended hours. There is also a health centre on site that offers medical and dental services, including mental health services for the children and their families. This type of cooperative functioning does not happen easily. Committed leadership, excellent planning, and sufficient resources are needed, as well as extensive trust and cooperation by all the educators and service providers involved. Overall, the evaluation of these additions to schools indicates that they are generally beneficial to children, their parents, and teachers. One area in which they are particularly effective is in increasing parental involvement (Blank, 2004). However, the improvements in children's academic achievements generally remain slow and modest, and ultimately appear to depend primarily on quality teachers (Dryfoos, 2010). If improvement is not happening at the instructional level of the school, programs added may well be limited in their capacity to effect positive change. Whole-school reform may be more promising.

Whole-School Reform. Attempts at whole-school reform largely are seen at the secondary or high school level. There are two fundamental types of reform. One is reform of existing schools through some form of restructuring. The second is seen in the design of alternative schools – schools that are designed from scratch with a particular objective. The Smaller Learning Communities approach exemplifies the former, and the Met, the latter. Each has as its aim the improved achievement of students who are at risk of dropping out or school failure.

There is some evidence that at the high school level, disadvantaged students show greater achievement in smaller schools (e.g., Steifel et al., 2000). In response, significant human and financial resources have been invested in dividing large high schools (those with over 1,000 students) into what are called Smaller Learning Communities (Levine, 2010a).

Intended to reduce the achievement gap, large high schools are restructured into smaller, more personalized learning environments – schools within a school. This reform measure has been enthusiastically adopted throughout the United States (Armstead et al., 2010). Why there is such enthusiasm is unclear. First, it is noteworthy that very few students describe the Smaller Learning Communities experience as positive (Armstead et al., 2010). Second, although some evaluations have indicated modest gains in the achievement of disadvantaged students in these schools, the achievement gap remains large (Lee & Friedrich, 2007). As Thomas Levine (2010) concludes after reviewing the evaluation research to date, there is really no evidence to support the view that the Smaller Learning Communities approach significantly improves academic performance. There are, he explains, three obstacles to its success. One is a lack of improved instructional style. Teachers do not significantly change their practices when they move to working with smaller classes; content coverage, grouping practices, and teaching strategies remain constant with many continuing to use whole-class and teacher-directed learning activities (Haughey, Snart, & Da Costa, 2003). A second is the lack of equity among the "communities." Levine observes that there has been a tendency to stratify high- and low-achieving students to the extent that there is a real danger of recreating the stratification and segregation that exists within traditional high schools. One result of this stratification has been inequity of curricula and expectations for achievement among groups. The third obstacle is the difficulty of change. It is not easy to transcend school history. The school's norms, routines, relationships, and its fundamental culture are not changed with the restructuring. Starting over may be much easier than restructuring.

In 1994, educators Dennis Littky and Elliot Washor were given a rare opportunity to design a school from scratch. The result was the Met in Rhode Island. The Met represents an excellent approach to school reform. Given a free hand to design the school as they saw fit, Littky and Washor were able to design a school that was, in many respects, in the best interests of the child. Drawing on evidence from education research, developmental neuroscience, and developmental psychology, the Met embodies best practices in education. The success of the Met is evidenced in the extraordinary rates of graduation and college attendance of students from low-income families (Symonds, 2006).

The Met has been described as the most unorthodox of schools (Symonds, 2006). It has no required courses and no regimented schedules. Rather than teaching facts and subjects, this school teaches students.

Each student is assigned to an adviser with whom he or she works for the 4 years of attendance. The adviser's role is to determine what inspires the student and to facilitate the student's pursuit of self-directed learning. Students spend 2 days each week away from the school campus exploring their interest in internships. Essentially, the approach is student-directed project-based learning on an individual basis with a high-quality teacher. We return to Chris Emery for an illustration of the process.

Before attending the Met, Chris, who was introduced at the beginning of this chapter, had decided to drop out of school and become a cook. His adviser helped him find an internship at a commercial bakery, and later at the Met's kitchen. There he became interested in the link between food and health. He decided to compare the food served in the school's kitchen with that of a local fast food restaurant. Not surprisingly he discovered that the fast food was much higher in fat and sodium. More importantly, perhaps, his love of research was born. His adviser responded to this evolution of interest by arranging a science internship for Chris at Brown University. Soon Chris was working in the neuroscience lab, taking a course, and making plans for graduate school. We do not know what Chris' path would have been without the Met. But the probability, given his past and his family history, was school dropout and lowered quality of adult health, employment status, and life satisfaction.

It is not likely that every child who attends the Met has such a success story. Moreover, historically, many alternative school designs have failed. Lawrence Kohlberg's just community school, the Cluster School, is a prime example. The school, founded in 1974, was unsuccessful in living up to its goal of promoting and enhancing democratic values (Reimer, Paolitto, & Hersh, 1983). Similar difficulties were seen also with the Learner-Centered Schools, schools developed to promote the development of the whole child within a democratic and supportive community (Lieberman, Falk, & Alexander, 1995). The Met, in contrast, has been doing well. However, its widespread adoption seems unlikely. Among the many challenges facing alternative schools is the difficulty of effecting fundamental change in the culture of schools and the pedagogical practices of teachers in the absence of teacher preparation to teach the diverse student population, and to teach in nontraditional ways. Across educational research and particularly with regard to the achievement gap, the most consistent finding is the need for, and the lack of, quality teachers.

Effective and Promising Education Policies

It is not only quality teachers and effective classroom and schoolwide practices that can make a difference. Education policies – as formulated and implemented at national, regional, and school district levels – also can help to level the playing field and reduce the achievement gap. It used to be thought that schools and education systems made little difference to educational outcomes. For example, in the highly influential 1966 report on educational opportunity in the United States – the Coleman Report – it was suggested that when children's social backgrounds were taken into account, schools and school systems had little effect on outcomes (Coleman et al., 1966). Children with low socioeconomic status backgrounds entered school behind other children and they left school behind other children. It was concluded that schools and education systems had little impact in altering the profound effects of family background. But since the Coleman Report, it has been established in international comparative research that education systems and the policies that guide these systems can make a significant contribution to equalizing educational opportunity and outcomes for children (Causa & Chapuis, 2009; Darling-Hammond, 2010; Field et al., 2007; Levin, 2003; Montt, 2011; OECD, 2010b; OECD PISA, 2011; Willms, 2006, 2010).

This research is based on cross-national studies of educational outcomes and on analyses of international test results for literacy, numeracy, and science, as provided in international programs such as the Programme for International Student Assessment (PISA) and the Progress in International Reading Literacy Study (PIRLS). In line with a large body of previous research, the research finds a significant relation between socioeconomic status and student performance. But beyond this, it finds that the strength of the relation varies not only across schools but also across countries and education systems (Darling-Hammond, 2010; OECD PISA, 2011; UNICEF, 2010). For example, in performance in science, based on the 2006 PISA results, the achievement gap was much narrower in Finland and Korea and much wider in Hungary and Luxembourg (OECD PISA, 2011). In the 2009 reading results, the gap was much less in Finland and Canada and much greater in Austria, the United States, and France. These and other results show that although most students across OECD countries who perform poorly in PISA are from socially disadvantaged backgrounds, some students from disadvantaged backgrounds excel in the tests and do so in varying degrees depending on the country. This demonstrates that overcoming socio-economic obstacles to achievement is possible and that there are varying degrees of success across countries and their education systems in levelling the playing field and promoting resilience.

This, in turn, points to the importance of education policies that direct and guide the practices of education systems and schools. The evidence shows that political and education authorities can make a difference in equalizing opportunities by formulating policies that have been shown to work in closing the achievement gap. Policies may be highly publicized such as in the United States with No Child Left Behind or in the United Kingdom with Every Child Matters. But what is most important is not the declared aim of the policies but their outcomes in terms of equalizing opportunity.

Based on a comprehensive comparative study of the relation between achievement equality/inequality and policy interventions, Simon Field and his colleagues (2007) and other OECD researchers (2010b) have identified and analysed a number of effective or promising policies for levelling the playing field. Field et al. refer to these in terms of "ten steps to equity in education." These extend beyond attracting, preparing, and retaining quality teachers. The policies we believe to be of particular importance are promoting social integration, providing special assistance to those who fall behind, promoting the inclusion of minority and immigrant children, providing resources commensurate with achieving equity, and establishing concrete targets for progress in equalizing opportunity.

Promoting Social Integration. An important finding from international research is that disadvantaged children do not perform as well in education systems where there is considerable social differentiation (Field et al., 2007; Montt, 2011; OECD PISA, 2011; Willms, 2006, 2010). Social differentiation simply refers to the situation of children from different social backgrounds attending different schools. The research shows that when poor children are concentrated in certain schools, they are more at risk of lower achievement. But when they are enrolled in more socially mixed or integrated schools, they are more likely to do better. This is because in schools where the social composition is more mixed, children from low-income families are better able to benefit from the greater likelihood of quality teachers and more resources. They are also more able to benefit from peer relations. As with early childhood education, children in schools learn not only from their teachers but also from their peers. When the peers of disadvantaged children are from higher income backgrounds and more educationally advanced, disadvantaged children are better positioned for improved learning.

Social differentiation occurs for a number of reasons. One reason is the simple tendency for different social groups to live in different areas. So as traditionally occurs, children go to school in their neighbourhood and local community. Poor children attend particular schools, and more affluent children attend other schools. But there also are policy reasons for differentiation. As one example, under policies that allow early tracking, children as young as age 10 or 12 years are put on different education tracks on the basis of their past performance. This can have the effect of social streaming – higher socioeconomic children attending academically oriented schools and children from low-income families attending vocationally oriented schools (Field et al., 2007; OECD, 2010b). As another example, under policies that allow schools – especially secondary schools – to select their students on the basis of tests or past academic attainment, children also can be socially streamed. Children living in families with higher incomes tend to be selected for more academically focused schools, leaving children from low-income families to attend other schools. Finally, as another example, under policies that allow school choice, streaming can also occur. School choice – where parents are allowed to send their children to school outside the catchment area of their local school – has become a trend in recent years due to a number of factors. One is political pressures by parents for choice. Another is the thinking of some governments that choice will result in better school performance through market competition. But the policy can produce social differentiation. The reason is that more affluent and well-educated parents can exploit the policy of choice and choose schools where the social mix is more one of higher income and educationally advanced children. They believe that in such a mix their children simply will do better.

Although social differentiation occurs in all countries, it is stronger in some countries than in others because these countries have policies that promote it or allow it. Central European countries such as Hungary, for example, have policies allowing for early tracking. In contrast, in Norway, Sweden, and Finland there are policies of comprehensive education that give emphasis to social inclusion. Under comprehensive education, the aim is to maintain schools where children of different social backgrounds remain together. Tracking does not occur until the later secondary grades when children are aged 15 or 16. Where early tracking has the effect of enlarging the achievement gap, comprehensive education has the effect of lessening it. More generally, under policies that promote or allow for social differentiation, whether it is done through early tracking or academic selection by schools or school choice, the achievement gap is wider. This is because disadvantaged children are put into schools where they are less able to benefit from the positive effects of more educationally advanced peers, where it is less likely there are high-quality teachers, adequate resources, and a stimulating learning environment, and where they lose motivation for school, internalize lower attainment expectations, and fall further behind (Hanushek & Woessmann, 2006; OECD, 2010b).

Policies of social integration are a positive means of countering the negative impact of social differentiation. This does not mean extreme measures of establishing an even social mix of poor and affluent children in all schools. Poor and wealthy families typically live in different neighbourhoods, and schools that are made up of children from local communities have many benefits. But social integration policies do mean at least three measures to limit social differentiation (Field et al., 2007; OECD, 2010b). First, it means that systems of early tracking need to be abandoned in favour of comprehensive schooling, as in the Nordic countries, Spain, and Poland. Tracking may still occur but the age and grade when it begins need to be high in order to avoid or minimize the negative effects of different streams. Finland offers a good model where tracking can only begin at age 16. Second, it means that regulation is needed on the use of academic selection by schools. The onus would be on schools to show that academic selection does not result in a significant degree of social differentiation in the school system. Third, it means that careful management is needed of school choice. Again, the onus would be on schools to show that choice does not produce social differentiation. If a combination of school choice and academic selection by schools is allowed, regulation might require that school authorities have an obligation to ensure a reasonably balanced social mix through such means as providing financial assistance to schools to attract disadvantaged children, or establishing alternative selection methods such as lottery arrangements. But however it is accomplished, the main thrust of policies of social integration is to preserve a reasonably even social composition in schools in order to equalize opportunity.

Providing Special Assistance. Another finding from international research is that disadvantaged children do better when policies are in place to provide them with special assistance when they are at risk of falling behind in school, losing motivation, and dropping out (Brunello & Checchi, 2007; Field et al., 2007; Levin, 2003; Hammond et al., 2007; OECD, 2010b). An initial part of the policy is to establish early warning systems for detecting this chain of events. One means of detection is to create and use special databases to monitor individual student performances and to identify students who are falling behind. As has been put into effect in the United States by the National High School Center, this involves gathering information on student attendance, test results, and active participation in school activities. Armed with such information, schools and school districts can take action.

Once students at risk are identified, they are provided with special assistance through programs such as tutoring, counselling, and mentoring, especially during the difficult transition from lower to upper secondary school (or junior/middle to high school). In turn, once this program has been completed, as has been done in some countries, other programs are made available in order to reintegrate the students into mainstream academic education. If the students in question remain uninterested in academic education and are still at risk of dropping out, attractive vocational training programs may be offered. All of these programs have been found to be effective or promising when they are of good quality, intensive, and sufficient in length. Such support, it has been concluded, is much better than the counterproductive policy of simply making students repeat a grade, as previously discussed.

Another positive policy intervention, although less discussed in international research, is providing assistance in the form of social and health services for students in need. As explained earlier in this chapter, full service schools have been found to produce modest but positive benefits. These benefits may be enlarged when national policies are put into place to provide services on a more comprehensive basis. This was the case, for example, in the United Kingdom with the national policy of Every Child Matters (ECM), launched in 2003. The overall aim of the ECM policy was to strengthen support for children, especially vulnerable and disadvantaged children, through integrated services where various social agencies – school and education authorities, health agencies, justice agencies, social services – collaborate and coordinate efforts on behalf of children at risk. This approach correctly assumes that it is much better to collaborate than to work separately, which can result in at-risk children falling through the cracks. Under the policy, school and other authorities were required to work together to identify the needs of each child, develop children's plans, and improve outcomes for children, including improved engagement, participation, and achievement in school. According to Alma Harris and Tracey Allen (2009) in a study of the implementation of ECM, the accomplishments of the policy were uneven across schools and across school districts. However, they also report that the policy was highly effective when there was strong school leadership, when Every Child Matters was a central priority for the school, and when school leaders had a clear vision for its implementation. With strong school leaders, teachers and staff are more likely to be mobilized to make the policy a success and to provide support for children that otherwise would not be provided.

Promoting Inclusion. Another effective policy intervention is to promote the inclusion of minority and immigrant children who may not only be living in poverty but also facing the problems of discrimination, cultural bias, and sometimes the learning of a new language. In most developed countries, immigrant students of first and second generation are more likely to grow up in poverty and not to achieve as well on standardized tests and in school as a whole. The same applies to many ethnic minority children in countries such as Australia, the United States, and Canada. Many of these children – for example, African-American, Latino and Indigenous children in the United States – are more likely to feel alienated in schools with different cultural practices and to not feel accepted, which compounds the problem of poverty.

As summarized by Field and his colleagues (2007), there are a number of policies that have been found to work in tackling the issue. One is to avoid the practice of streaming and putting these students on low-status tracks. It is much better for their educational progress and equity if they receive their education in mainstream classrooms. Another is to make concerted efforts to improve language skills where needed. This may be accomplished through special preparatory classes before the school year begins or through intensive additional language training during the school year. Another policy is to provide for special teacher training and professional development. This would involve preparing teachers to work with children from diverse backgrounds and to develop teaching methods and styles that fully embrace cultural diversity. Finally, another policy is to ensure that educational materials, curricula, and school practices are culturally appropriate and in strong opposition to discrimination and bias. This is a promising means of making minority and immigrant children feel included in their school, thus enhancing their prospects for a higher level of achievement.

Providing Resources. Another identified policy and one of key importance is providing appropriate educational resources (Darling-Hammond, 2010; Field et al., 2007). Providing and distributing resources is, of course, a huge policy challenge in all countries. Policy-makers are called upon to target educational expenditures across stages of education (pre-primary, primary, secondary, and post-secondary education), across geographical regions (rural, urban, and suburban areas), and across socioeconomic areas (poor, middle-income, and high-income areas). From the point of view of advancing equal opportunity, the question is what allocation of resources is most favourable to closing the achievement gap. According to Field and colleagues (2007) and to the OECD (2010a; 2010b), the answer lies not only in the level of funding – which is highly important – but also in an allocation that gives priority to early education and to expanded support for disadvantaged students and schools. It is essential that early childhood education is strongly funded and that students in high-poverty schools receive the support they need in terms of high-quality teachers and programs. It is essential also that funding is directed at what has been shown by research to work in closing the achievement gap. What has been shown to work are quality programs of early childhood education, measures to attract and retain high-quality teachers, measures to promote social integration, and programs of special assistance to children who fall behind.

A major problem in most countries, however, is a huge gap between the distribution of resources as required for equity and the distribution as currently exists. First of all, there is no question that across the developed world, education has received substantial and increasing levels of funding from most governments. Data from the OECD (2010a) show that most developed countries have invested heavily in education in recent decades and that spending per student has increased steadily. The average of education spending in OECD countries in 2010 was over 13 per cent of public expenditures, a higher proportion than ever before. But there has been considerable variation. Where Denmark, Iceland, and the United States spend over 7 per cent of their GDP on education, Italy and the Slovak Republic spend less than 4.5 per cent. If spending is measured on a per student basis, where the Nordic countries, Austria, Switzerland, and the United States spend over U.S. $10,000 annually per student, the Slovak Republic, Chile, and Brazil spend less than U.S. $4,000 per student. However, from the point of view of equity, there are several problems. One is that the distribution of resources favours the higher stages of the education continuum. As reported by the OECD (2010a), the OECD countries spend nearly twice as much per student at the level of post-secondary (or tertiary) education than they do at the primary level. Average annual spending per student is U.S. $6,800 at the primary level, U.S. $8,000 at the secondary level, and U.S. $17,000 at the post-secondary level. Although part of the spending at the university level is for advanced research rather than education, the differences remain significant. It needs to be kept in mind that disadvantaged children disproportionately drop out of secondary school and do not attend college or university in the same numbers. To counter the achievement gap, it is in the earlier stages of education – at the primary and lower secondary levels – when substantial resources are most needed to implement evidence-based programs and take measures to assist poor children. This is more difficult when resources are put elsewhere.

Furthermore, as also reported by the OECD (2010c), public expenditures are significantly less for early childhood education than for later stages of education. Where OECD spending on early childhood education ranges between 1.4 per cent and 0.2 per cent of GDP, spending on later education varies between 7 per cent and 4.5 per cent of GDP. Also, as discussed in chapter 4, there are huge differences among OECD countries in the amounts that are spent on early childhood education. Where early education spending is 1 per cent of GDP or higher in Denmark, France, Sweden, and Finland, it is under 0.4 per cent in the United States and Australia, and under 0.2 per cent in Canada and Greece. The greatest variation is in spending for children under age 3. Spending is highest in the Nordic countries by a large margin and lowest in North America and southern Europe. The overall low level of spending is greatly at odds with the research on the importance of the early years and of the need for early educational intervention. If equity were a priority, policy-makers across the developed world would follow the lead of the Nordic countries and invest significantly more resources on early childhood education and basic education at the primary and lower secondary levels.

Another very serious problem with the current allocation of resources for primary and secondary schools is that it is highly uneven demographically (Darling-Hammond, 2006, 2010; Field et al., 2007; Good & McCaslin, 2008). Schools in poorer areas generally receive fewer resources. A major source of the problem is that in most countries there is decentralization of education – in varying degrees – and considerable autonomy at the regional and local levels. Depending on the country and on its system of government and education, authorities at the regional, state/provincial, and/or county and municipal levels are able to use monies raised through local taxes to fund local school districts and schools. Because some areas are affluent and others poor, there are disparities and sometimes major disparities in the quality of teachers, facilities, equipment, and programs. Depending again on the country, such disparities are typically offset by some type of compensatory grant (or fund or equalization payment) from the central government (and/or state or provincial government) to poorer areas, school districts, and schools. However, although the disparities are offset, they are far from offset in terms of achieving or even approaching equity. In varying degrees, inequality of educational resources is a problem in virtually all countries.

The problem is particularly serious in the United States where there is long-standing regional as well as social inequality (Darling-Hammond, 2006, 2010; Good & McCaslin, 2008). Although compensatory funding has been in effect in the United States since the 1960s, there remains major disparity in the amount of resources that various schools and school districts receive. This is due partly to a significant amount of education spending that has little to do with research evidence on improving educational outcomes or reducing the achievement gap. Susan Neuman (2009) refers to the practice of earmarks – programs targeted to individual districts for politically motivated reasons – and to the funding of many ineffective programs. Fewer resources are thus available. It is also due, however, to the neglect of poorer regions and their lack of political power. In any case, because of funding shortages or limitations, poor schools are less able to provide their students with computers, textbooks, and programs of special assistance for those who fall behind. Most importantly, they are less able to recruit and retain well-qualified and well-trained teachers, often relying instead on uncertified teachers, inexperienced teachers, and substitute teachers. As Montt (2011) has reported in his cross-national study, inequity in the distribution of quality teachers is among the most important of factors in accounting for achievement inequality. So it comes as no surprise that in the United States, where resources have not been invested in enlarging the pool of high-quality teachers and in creating a more equitable distribution of high-quality teachers across schools, the achievement gap is greater.

Policy-makers are much more likely to make progress in equalizing opportunity when resources are provided not only for high-quality teachers but also for equalizing their distribution across schools. In Finland, for example, major investments have been made in doing this (Darling-Hammond, 2010). Resources have been allocated for highly qualified and well-paid teachers, high-calibre and extensive teacher training, and an equitable distribution of high-quality teachers across schools. Finland has complemented this strong emphasis on teacher development with resources for the building of strong programs in support of disadvantaged children. For example, systems have been established for the quick identification of children who fall behind, programs of tutoring and mentoring have been put into place to assist them in catching up, and systems of collaboration have been developed between teachers and multi-disciplinary teams of social workers and health professionals to help children with social and health problems that compromise their education. With a strong commitment of resources for teaching and special programs, Finland is well known for having among the smallest achievement gaps in the world.

France and Belgium have tried to achieve a more equitable distribution of resources through creating special educational zones of support for disadvantaged schools. In France, for example, there has been the establishment of educational priority zones where additional resources are given to schools comprised largely of students from disadvantaged backgrounds (Field et al., 2007; Story, 2007). In these zones, primary and secondary schools receive extra funding to improve student achievement if they are able to attract a sizable number of disadvantaged students. Despite the funding, however, early evaluations of the system found that student performance did not improve significantly, and that the students, parents, and teachers in the zones felt stigmatized, undermining the effectiveness of the schools. Contrary to the aim of social integration, it was found that there was an outflow of middle-class children from the schools because of the stigmatization and performance problems. In addition, there was the difficulty of attracting well-qualified and effective teachers.

In response to the problems, reforms were introduced in 2006. The reforms expanded funding and required more screening and evaluation of the schools, more accountability, more individualized approaches to teaching, less grade repetition, and more effort to increase parental involvement in the school. Of particular importance, the reforms required the recruiting of better qualified and better trained teachers, more teacher professional development, and financial incentives to attract high-quality teachers to the schools. Although evaluations of the reforms have yet to be completed, the program is promising because many of its elements are in line with the research evidence. However, stigmatization remains a potential problem and, with this, the flight of well-qualified teachers and students living in families with middle incomes from the schools. According to commentators, a major source of this problem is the labelling of the schools as disadvantaged or deprived (OECD, 2010b). One possible way to overcome it, they say, is to characterize the schools in more positive language such as schools in need of improvement. But another and probably more effective means would be to tie funding in all schools to the social composition of the student population. Thus, there would be a spectrum of schools with varying social mixtures. The result would be that particular schools would be less likely to be singled out with a label.

Setting Concrete Targets. Finally, another promising policy measure is the setting of concrete numerical targets for making progress. As Field and his associates (2007) note, such a measure can be a powerful means of focusing attention on the issue of equity and concentrating efforts on outcomes. Setting targets gives precision to assessing progress and thus adds to pressure on education authorities to get the task done. In different ways, educational targets have been brought into use in Australia, Finland, Sweden, Germany, and the United States. However, as Field and colleagues also point out, targets for achieving equity need to be used with caution. It needs to be kept in mind that there are varying degrees of social disadvantage, varying degrees of challenge for schools in addressing disadvantage, and different degrees of difficulty in measuring equity. Setting targets in one narrow and easily measureable area (such as test scores in math) might take attention away from broad but desirable objectives (such as critical thinking or problem solving) that are less easy to measure. Schools may end up putting their efforts into easily testable subjects, and teachers may end up teaching for tests and neglecting other important matters. Moreover, if the targets are overly ambitious and not reasonably attainable, target setting will not have its desired impact.

Given these problems, Field and colleagues (2007) recommend that although a policy of target setting for equity should be used, its use should be limited to where the goals can reasonably be attained and to where international comparisons show large disparities among countries in achieving equity. Target setting, suggest Field et al. (2007), should be used in two primary areas. One is reducing dropout rates. Progress is easy to measure and goals are reasonably attainable. The other area is to improve basic skills in literacy and numeracy, which also is attainable and easy to measure on the basis of PISA results. For example, PISA results show that there are major differences among countries in basic reading skills at age 15 and that there are significant achievement gaps (OECD PISA 2011). With this information, countries could easily adopt national targets to raise those skills and reduce the gaps, using PISA results to track progress and using evidence-based practices to improve outcomes. As disadvantaged children are disproportionately poor readers, the setting of targets would create pressure for concentrating efforts and making progress.

There is evidence of international comparisons having such an effect (Levin, 2010a). Since PISA began its reporting in 2000, international interest has grown in how countries have done on student achievement tests. Education communities and education policy-makers have become increasingly conscious of the test results and have made efforts to learn from the results and from successful measures used in other countries to improve performance. Levin (2010a) provides the example of Poland that improved its record through examining progress made in countries such as Finland and limiting the use of early tracking and streaming, as had been done earlier in Finland and other Nordic countries.

Strict Accountability and Testing. One policy that is not mentioned in international research is establishing a system of strict accountability for schools and teachers based on the results of tests. There is good reason for this omission. There is no question that schools and teachers should be held accountable for the educational progress of children, and there is no question that tests have their place in measuring progress and equity. When, however, a system of systematic testing and strict accountability becomes the central means of achieving progress, major problems arise, including inconsistency with the best interests of the child.

A prime example of a policy of systematic testing and strict accountability is in the United States with No Child Left Behind. The objectives of the policy are reasonable. In line with the long-standing American principle of equality of educational opportunity, the primary goals of NCLB include raising educational standards and reducing the achievement gap (Ravitch, 2010; Wells, 2009). The creation of NCLB and the federal NCLB legislation were in large part the product of past criticism and dissatisfaction with educational performance in the United States since the 1960s. The architects of NCLB wanted to achieve more progress. The problems with NCLB are less with the objectives than with the means of realizing them. Rather than using carrots, the policy is one using sticks and heavy sanctions to achieve results. The policy requires that from Grade 3 all children are tested annually for proficiency in numeracy and literacy, that states provide highly qualified teachers to all students, and that schools and teachers are held accountable for adequate yearly progress. If schools repeatedly fail to make yearly progress, they can be labelled as *in need of improvement*. At this point, they are required to create an improvement plan and carry it out. If they fail to do so, they can lose funding, students can transfer to other schools, and there can be a wholesale replacement of the teaching staff. Through such means, the declared ultimate aim of NCLB is to achieve 100 per cent proficiency among students by the year 2014.

From the point of view of achieving equity, there are several problems with the policy design. First, the definitions of *proficiency* among students and of *highly qualified* teachers are left up to individual states (Ravitch, 2010; Rebell & Wolff, 2009). States can receive federal funds and keep costs lower by having lax definitions. So quality control is not assured. Second, although there is a major emphasis on making progress in achieving results, the provision of resources commensurate with making progress has not been forthcoming (Lagana-Riordan & Aguilar, 2009; Rebell & Wolff, 2009; Wells, 2009). With growing inequality of income in the United States and with policy changes such as welfare reform, poverty has become an increasing challenge for children's educational success. But in the absence of funding to assure high-quality teachers and evidence-based programs in high-poverty schools, the demand for higher standards increases while the supply of resources fails to keep pace. As a result, to date, there has been minimal accomplishment with NCLB. Achievement levels have risen only slightly over time and the achievement gap has not been substantially reduced (Rebell & Wolff, 2009). As Diane Ravitch (2010) has remarked, NCLB provides a quick-fix and politically popular solution to problems that require substantial resources and evidence-based measures to assist disadvantaged children. As seen in Finland, the achievement gap can be low and achievement levels high without the kind of high-stakes testing called for by NCLB (OECD PISA 2011).

But the problem is deeper than this. An excessive focus on test results puts at serious risk the best interests of the child. As discussed in chapter 2, it is in the best interests of the child to be provided with education on the basis of equal opportunity. Under Article 29 of the U.N. Convention on the Rights of the Child, education is to aim at developing the child's personality, talents, and abilities; at developing respect for human rights; and at preparing the child for responsible life in a free society. Education that features extensive testing is not mentioned. This is not to say that tests are not important as a means of achieving the aims of education. The use of tests, in combination with other indicators such as school attendance, absenteeism, level of school engagement, and emotional and social well-being are helpful tools in measuring progress and equity. The problem is not with tests but with tests in a narrow range of subjects being the centrepiece of educational assessment and school performance. The preoccupation with testing makes schools into factories for teaching facts, overshadowing the importance of deeper learning and leading to problems such as stress and excessive competition among students and among schools (Howe & Covell, 2005). Furthermore, as noted by Tony Wagner (2008), even those students who do perform well on the tests may not have acquired the skills that are required for the societies and economies of the twenty-first century – critical thinking, problem solving, collaboration, and initiative.

According to the U.N. Committee on the Rights of the Child, in its general comment on the aims of education and in its country reports, education should not be solely focused on academic development, grades, and competition (Elwood & Lundy, 2010; Hodgkin & Newell, 2007; U.N. Committee, 2001). Rather, education should be concerned – along with academic development – with the well-rounded development of the *whole* child, which means among other things, social and emotional development, self-esteem, self-confidence, and the development of respect for the rights of others. The Committee has expressed concern, therefore, with countries such as Japan for extensive testing and the excessively competitive nature of its education system. This, says the Committee, threatens the development of the child to his or her fullest potential, thus putting at risk the best interests of children.

In addition, extensive testing and the publication of test results can lead to outcomes unfavourable for disadvantaged children. The publication of results and their release to the media, as occurs in England, for example, can damage equity through identifying schools as either good schools or bad schools (Field et al., 2007). Labelling a school as a bad school can have the effect of undermining the morale and confidence of children who are already disadvantaged. It may also result in middle-income parents sending their children to other schools, increasing social differentiation among schools, and thus bringing about inequity, as discussed earlier. At the very least, even if labelling were not a problem, there are serious concerns with testing that policy-makers need to examine. They have seldom done so, however. For example, as reported by Elwood and Lundy (2010) in their analysis of testing and assessment practices in the United Kingdom, policy-makers have failed to ensure that current practices are consistent with the best interests and rights of children. Elwood and Lundy remind us that policy-makers have an obligation under the CRC to do child impact evaluations of practices dealing with children. Despite major concerns that have been expressed in the United Kingdom about extensive testing, there has been no evaluation of its effects. Children in the United Kingdom continue to be the most frequently tested in the world. At the very least, the issue should be studied.

An Important but Incomplete Step

Just as the provision of comprehensive early childhood education is an important but incomplete step, so too are the beneficial classroom practices, school reforms, and policy interventions that have been described. It certainly is the case that teachers, school leaders, special programs, and evidence-based policies can make a difference in tackling disadvantage. Nevertheless, an important problem remains. The good practices and reforms described generally are piecemeal rather than systematic. They pertain to efforts here and there by individual groups of teachers, schools, and policy-makers. Disadvantaged children may or may not experience good teachers or good educational practices. Efforts need to be more systematic, comprehensive, and informed and supported by positive school cultures for learning. Heroic teachers, heroic school leaders, and evidence-based programs do make a difference. They can make *more* of a difference in the context of a school culture that leads to children being engaged in school, feeling a sense of belonging, feeling a sense of support, identifying with their school, valuing their education, feeling motivated to learn, and feeling optimistic about their future.

A positive school culture may be seen as a distal or indirect protective factor. It functions to allow the sustainability of the more proximal protective factors of high-quality teachers and overall. effective programs and policies. As in the ecological model of development initially described by Urie Bronfenbrenner (1979), the school culture affects the school climate, teacher-student relationships, and all school practices and outcomes. A positive school culture with a shared-values framework can have a profound effect on the resilience and achievement of disadvantaged children

This begs the question of what makes up a positive school culture for learning. What values and beliefs should guide the school community? The answer, which is developed in the next chapter, is a set of shared values and beliefs based on respect for the rights of the child. Children, and especially disadvantaged children, need to feel valued and respected. In a school learning environment where they feel valued and respected, they are more likely to do well. We will show that it is in the best interests of children to be educated in schools where there is a school culture that embraces the rights of the child. Because such schools function in a learning environment grounded in mutual respect, they send the important message to *all* children that they are valued members of the school community and worthy of success. Feeling worthy of success, they are more likely to succeed.

Chapter Six

Transforming School Cultures

Education in the best interests of the child requires more than the revising of practices or the restructuring of schools. It also requires the transformation of school cultures or what Michael Fullan (2001, p. 44) calls *reculturing*. The practices that take place inside a school do not exist in a vacuum: They exist in the context of a school's culture, which strongly affects the motivation and willingness of members of a school to act in certain ways. School culture refers to the shared values, beliefs, norms, assumptions, and expectations in a school that inform and guide school functioning and practices. When school cultures are negative, the best interests of the child are compromised. Values and beliefs are such that little effort is made to improve educational outcomes for children and to equalize opportunities in learning. Disadvantaged children suffer as a result. When school cultures are positive, however, the prospects for disadvantaged children are greatly enhanced. Values and beliefs are ones that spur efforts to improve learning and to implement practices and policies in the best interests of the child, including the disadvantaged child.

The challenge is to transform school cultures: Positive cultures need to replace the so many negative ones we see in schools today. We contend that critical to reculturing is incorporating into school cultures the shared values and beliefs that embrace the U.N. Convention on the Rights of the Child. Children's rights education is valuable, we believe, because it builds in children a sense of their inherent worth. With a greater sense of their value as bearers of rights, children are more likely to experience educational success.

In this chapter, we explain how children's rights education can make a difference. We begin by discussing the meaning of positive school culture and its importance in improving educational achievement. We then explain the benefit of recognizing children's rights education as the core of positive school culture and of using the Convention on the Rights of the Child as the shared-values framework for schools. Attention is given here to the reforms necessary for implementing a shared-values framework based on the rights of the child. We then examine the linkage between school culture and school climate and the effects of positive school climate on learning. Particular attention is given here to the importance of positive school climates for disadvantaged children. We then discuss initiatives in children's human rights education and evaluations of a large-scale initiative in Hampshire, England, called Rights, Respect, and Responsibility or RRR. We conclude with a discussion of obstacles to the sustaining of children's rights education.

The Concept of School Culture

Adopted from anthropology and organizational studies, the concept of school culture emerged in the education literature during the 1980s as a means of explaining the character and functioning of schools (Prosser, 1999; Van Houtte, 2005). Education researchers were in search of factors beyond structural and organizational variables to account for school effectiveness. The concept of school culture was seen to fit the bill. In the research literature that developed, the concept of school culture sometimes has been used interchangeably with the concept of school climate, a related concept that had emerged earlier in the literature. As explained by Mieke Van Houtte (2005), although the two concepts are related (both deal with the character of schools) they do not mean the same thing. *School culture* refers to the normative framework of the school community: the shared values and core beliefs that guide the school comprise school culture. *School climate* refers to the quality of the environment or atmosphere of the school as experienced by individuals – children, teachers, staff, parents, visitors – in the school; it is not about the shared values but about the shared perceptions of the environment of the school.

The concepts of school culture and school climate are thus distinct, but they are also connected. School culture is a deeper force in the life of a school, affecting the climate of the school, the practices of teachers and staff, and in turn, the potential for achievement of the students. For example, when a school culture is positive and strongly supportive of children and their learning, the climate also is likely to be positive. In such a culture, children are more likely to perceive support and to have positive feelings about the school, which in turn, leads to improved learning and achievement. The linkage between positive school climate and higher levels of achievement is well established in research (Konishi et al., 2010; Zins et al., 2004). Conversely, when a school culture is negative and indifferent or ambivalent to children and their learning, the climate is likely to be negative. Children are less likely to perceive support and more likely to have negative feelings about the school, and to achieve less.

Descriptions of positive and negative school cultures have been provided by researchers and commentators such as Fullan (2001; 2007), Peterson and Deal (2009), Deal and Peterson (2009), Hargreaves (1995), and Dufour and his colleagues (2006). Positive school cultures, they say, have the following ingredients. First, there is a strong value on learning. Everyone in the school – including teachers and principals – is seen as a learner and schools are seen as learning communities. It is believed that everyone is capable of learning and that learning can be enhanced through improving curricula and educational practices. There is a willingness to change and adopt new ideas on improvement. Second, there is a strong belief in collaborative relationships. This means that teachers should cooperate and work together and with the principal and other staff for the common purpose of improving learning. There should be shared responsibility for student learning through such means as regular teacher meetings to discuss and improve student progress. There should also be shared school leadership where principals collaborate with teachers on decision-making. Third, there is a belief in results. This involves high expectations on students, a strong emphasis on making progress, regular assessment of progress, and assessment of teacher effectiveness in improving the learning of students. It also involves high value on research evidence and its use in getting results. Fourth, there is a belief that schools should be centred on the well-being of children. This means that major efforts should be made in facilitating student voice, getting students more involved in their own learning, collaborating with students on making improvements, and treating students as persons rather than as objects to be moulded. There is the belief that *all* children can succeed, that all children should be supported through a positive school environment, and that schools can make a major difference in improving educational outcomes and closing the achievement gap.

Negative school cultures are much different. They have some or many of the following characteristics (Peterson & Deal, 2009; Deal & Peterson, 2009). First, rather than an emphasis on learning and a willingness to adopt new ideas to improve learning, there is distrust of new ideas and criticism of suggestions for reform. There is unwillingness to change and a preference for conformity and the status quo. Second, rather than a belief in collaboration, there is reluctance among teachers to cooperate and share information and a preference for individualized work and for traditional bureaucratic ways of doing things. Third, rather than a belief in results and in the application of research to improve results, there is the view that only so much can be done and that the school is doing the best it can. There is a distrust of outsiders and experts and the view that only the teachers inside the school understand the needs of the school. Fourth, rather than a belief that the school should be centred on children and that all children can succeed, there is distrust of student participation, a view that not all children can succeed, and a belief that it is not really possible to close the achievement gap. According to Peterson and Deal (2009), when these beliefs are pervasive in a school, the school culture is not only negative but toxic. New teachers and new students come into a school where there is constant complaining and criticism, resistance to anything new, and a regular focus on the failure of students, new ideas, and new programs. For new teachers, there is the danger of acculturation and the adoption of this negative outlook.

Traditionally, as pointed out by Fullan (2007), school cultures have been largely negative. They have been marked more by the values of authoritarianism, bureaucracy, and hierarchy than the ones of collaboration, collegiality, and shared leadership. Inside the classroom, they have been marked by a strong belief in the authority of teachers and the principle of "teacher knows best." The teacher is to set the rules in the classroom and the students are simply to obey them. There is little room for student input and participation. In regard to learning, the task of the teacher is to provide the students with the facts, and the task of the students is to memorize the facts and provide the correct answers on tests. There is little room for self-directed learning on the basis of discovery, experimentation, and problem solving. Finally, in traditional school cultures, there is the belief that if students fail to make progress, it is their fault or the fault of their parents or family backgrounds – not the fault of teachers or schools. If poverty is the problem, the problem is so profound and enduring that teachers and schools are unable to do anything about it.

As Fullan (2007) has noted, based on his review of the research literature, the outcomes from such cultures are highly negative for children. Many children come to hold very unfavourable views of their teachers and schools, and many feel alienated and disengaged from school. The outcome is that they drop out of school or they fail to achieve to their potential. Reculturing, therefore, is imperative.

The case for establishing positive school cultures is compelling. However, an important element remains missing in most descriptions of a positive school culture. The descriptions do make reference to the belief that schools should be centred on the well-being of children and improvement in their learning. The descriptions seldom refer to the rights of the child, however. To be fully centred on children, and to be consistent with the principle of the best interests of the child as enshrined in the Convention on the Rights of the Child, positive school cultures need to be infused with the values and beliefs of the Convention. It is important to recall that the best interests principle requires that schools pay close attention to the rights of children. In the words of the U.N. Committee on the Rights of the Child: "Children do not lose their human rights by virtue of passing through the school gates" (2001, p. 8). Education in the best interests of the child means that in schools, as elsewhere, children are provided with their protection, provision, and participation rights and with their right to education on the basis of equal opportunity. It also means that children – as well as adults – know and understand the rights of the child. Such a requirement for children's rights education is part of Article 29 of the Convention, which states that one of the aims of education is to develop respect for human rights, including the human rights of the child. The development of respect for rights requires knowledge, and it requires a positive school culture that highlights and embraces the rights of the child. Such a rights-based culture means the presence of a values framework that is shared not only by the adults in the school, but also by the children.

The U.N. Convention on the Rights of the Child as a Values Framework

A positive school culture is one in which the Convention on the Rights of the Child serves as the shared-values framework to guide school policies and practices. A rights-based framework has the benefit of relevance to every student as well as to their teachers and principals. Importantly, it has legitimacy.

Writing on the need for educational psychologists in the United Kingdom to take a more proactive role in implementing Every Child Matters, Joan Baxter and Norah Frederickson (2005) emphasize the importance of reforming schools to promote resilience among disadvantaged children. Schools, they suggest, need to adopt a new and legitimate values framework to direct that reform. They describe three criteria for selecting the appropriate values for reculturing schools: The values should stand the test of time, they should provide a yardstick against which the promotion of optimal child development and learning can be defined and assessed, and they should be usable as a framework and reference point for all members of the school learning community. The values must also be ones that can be shared by each member of the school community (Huffman, 2003).

The values identified are those enshrined in the Convention on the Rights of the Child. We agree. As described in chapter 2, the Convention expresses a global consensus, which has developed since the Second World War, on what childhood should be. As such, the values have stood the test of time. In articulating the specific rights children are entitled to for their healthy development, it provides a yardstick for progress. Finally, the overarching principles and provisions of the Convention provide a ready reference point for children and for all those working with or for children.

The Convention is a legally binding document that describes an international consensus on appropriate education. The aims of education, and the underlying pedagogy, actions, and interventions needed to achieve them, are clearly specified. The comprehensiveness of the articles relevant to education allows the Convention to be used as a values framework for all school teaching and practices. No country that has ratified the Convention has taken a reservation on the articles that describe obligations in education. Each is required to progressively implement the education provisions.

The unquestionable legitimacy of the Convention is important. With the exception of faith-based schools, historically it has been difficult for schools to adopt a values framework. Particularly in multicultural societies, it has been difficult obtaining consensus on what values should be given dominance (Howe & Covell, 2005). In response, and with the intent of enhancing respect for diversity, some educators have tried to operate values-free schools. This, they thought, would avoid having to select from a variety of values, and sometimes competing values, in a pluralistic society. Unfortunately, what happened was antithetical to their hopes. The values-free schools inadvertently encouraged judgmental attitudes and behaviours among the children (Howe & Covell, 2005). The Convention both avoids the difficulties associated with values-free schools and the difficulties of imposing values that may be culturally relative or at least not shared by all members of the community (Howe & Covell, 2005).

The legitimacy of the Convention is important also because, in addition to the rights of the child, it identifies the responsibilities of the duty-bearers. This avoids the perennial and ever-present problem of children's poor achievement being attributed to parents by schools and to schools by parents. States parties, and through them education authorities and schools, have primary responsibility for children's education (Lundy & McEvoy, 2009). This does not negate a role for parents. As described in chapter 2, parents are responsible for providing children appropriate direction and guidance in the exercise of their Convention rights, and for having the best interests of their children as their primary concern. The prevailing myth is that all parents want the best for their children and sacrifice their own lives to this end. The reality is different. The architects of the Convention took into account that not all parents can or do have the best interests of their children as their primary concern, and that even when they do, they may not be in a position to act accordingly. Where parents have difficulties fulfilling their responsibilities, Article 18(2) obligates state parties to "render appropriate assistance to parents." Children whose parents lack either the material or psychological resources to prepare them well for school, to be involved in their children's schooling, or to provide the nurturance their children need for healthy physical and psychological functioning are still children with all the rights of the Convention. They are not to be discounted and denied equal opportunity. They are, as it states in Article 2, not to be discriminated against because of their family circumstances.

Ideally, schools and parents would work cooperatively together to ensure education in the best interests of the child. In the case of disadvantaged children, however, the state – the school and its teachers – is expected to step in as necessary. Education departments, school administrators, teachers, and non-teaching staff, where necessitated by family circumstances, must assume full responsibility for the education of disadvantaged children to ensure their equal opportunity. They must do so first through providing well-funded and appropriate early school readiness interventions. Rights-consistent preschool enrichment programs that address the difficulties associated with early deprivation and neurodevelopmental delays should be available to any child. These would then be followed up with well-resourced and rights-consistent formal schooling.

Finally, the legitimacy of the Convention is important in that particular schools or school districts cannot opt out of their obligations under it. Every child *does* matter, and no child *should* be left behind. These are more than slogans. Every school in every neighbourhood in every country that has ratified the Convention has the obligation to provide rights-based education. Resources must be provided and reforms must be made to ensure that all children – including all disadvantaged children – have access to education that is in their best interests.

In addition to its legitimacy, there are other advantages of the Convention. Having a shared-values framework in schools promotes a sense of community among staff and students and is related to quality teaching (Amrein-Beardsley, 2007). There is a shared language – the discourse of rights – and a shared understanding of the importance of respecting rights. In teaching, the value of rights can be used to guide critical thinking by providing a standard against which to assess thought or action. In behaviour management, the value of rights can be used to determine appropriate behaviours and to define infractions. Moreover, when children's rights are the shared-values framework for the school, they can guide reforms that all school staff can agree on since the outcome goals will be common – those that are in the best interests of the child.

Implementing the Values Framework

Adopting the Convention as the basis of a positive school culture would stimulate four fundamental reforms. These are changes in attitudes towards educating children, learning outcome goals, curricula, and school management strategies.

A first reform would require a reorientation of focus to positive objectives and asset building and away from deficit models that focus on children's shortcomings, and away from the kind of crisis management that results in exclusions. This would entail three changes. One is providing students with systematic opportunities for participation in the classroom and in school functioning. This would involve such practices as self-directed learning and student representation on school committees. Second, rather than the current, almost exclusive, focus on how well the child has accumulated facts, progress in the child's overall wellbeing and social and emotional functioning would be monitored. Such monitoring would include the child's school attendance, self-esteem, engagement in school, participation in activities, and relationships with peers and teachers. Third, assessment strategies would be altered to incorporate a variety of techniques that allow for taking into consideration the diverse backgrounds, needs, and learning styles of individual students. Self-assessments can be particularly useful. These can include learning logs or journals (e.g., What I did, What I learned, What questions I still have), reflective writing, student-teacher interviews, and peer assessments. Such changes to assessment practices would benefit all children, but disadvantaged children in particular. There is considerable evidence that resilience among disadvantaged children can be developed through the identification of positive objectives, and progress in such areas as academic performance, participation in the classroom and in extracurricular activities, school attendance, and school completion (Masten et al., 2008).

A second reform would be the broadening of learning outcome goals to include life skills. With increasing emphasis in schools on technology and economic gain rather than human values, some have asked the question whether schools should focus on "education for life" or "education to make a living" (Howe & Covell, 2005). Article 29 of the Convention, which describes the aims of education, suggests this is a false dichotomy. Developing the whole child requires both. As the U.N. Committee on the Rights of the Child (2001) noted, basic skills do not just include literacy and numeracy. Literacy and numeracy are important. However, life skills also are important: "the ability to make well-balanced decisions; to resolve conflicts in a non-violent manner; and to develop a healthy lifestyle, good social relationships and responsibility, critical thinking, creative talents" (para. 9). A focus on life skills and on assets rather than deficits contributes significantly to the disadvantaged child's success in school (Cuthrell et al., 2010).

A change in curricula would be a third reform. The Convention requires that curricula be of direct relevance to the child and that children be explicitly taught their rights. Education, the Committee says, should be "inspiring and motivating" (U.N. Committee, 2001, para. 11). This is unlikely if the subjects and issues under discussion bear little relevance to the child's daily life. This does not mean that traditional subjects such as mathematics and science should be discarded. It *does* mean teaching them from a rights basis. For example, in mathematics, students could consider the right to food and the Millennium Development Goal of halving the population of malnourished people. Students could compare several countries' malnutrition percentages from 2000 to the present, and then graph or calculate the percentage increase or decrease of malnourishment in specified countries. They may end by comparing these statistics with those of their own country, and by discussing the progress made on attaining the Millennium Development Goal and what this means for children's rights to food and health. With the rights of the child embedded across curricula and in all aspects of pedagogy, what is being taught can have direct relevance and interest to every child.

Finally, the Convention requires that school management strategies respect the dignity and rights of every child. As the Committee on the Rights of the Child has stressed repeatedly, this means a full prohibition on the use of corporal punishment, verbal abuse, and emotional violence. The focus should be on clearly communicating and consistently reinforcing expected behaviours. Using rights as the justification for behaviours – for example, everyone has a right to play, and so no bullying is allowed – helps children understand and appreciate the need for appropriate behaviours. Disciplinary action must be positive. Appropriate use of time out is one such example. Collaborating with the students on the articulation of expected behaviours and sanctions for misbehaviours increases the likelihood that rules will be respected.

At the heart of a school with a culture of rights, all teaching and non-teaching staff and every student is knowledgeable of children's rights. Respect for those rights is evidenced in all school policies, teaching practices, and interpersonal interactions. In essence, the Convention requires the establishment of a school culture that is based on and reflects the shared value of the rights of the child. Such a culture can be expected to promote a positive school climate for learning, and in so doing, improve learning and reduce the achievement gap.

Positive School Climate

A positive school climate – one in which every child feels welcomed, supported, respected, and safe – is of undeniable importance to achievement for all children. Historically, there has been inadequate attention to the climate of the classroom or school. A narrow focus on academics has been preferred (Walker & Greene, 2009). With increasing evidence of the strong relation between school climate and academic performance, and between school climate and behaviour, the issue of how to create a positive school climate is gaining increasing attention.

In the United States, the importance of a positive school climate has come to the fore over the past decade in reaction to student deaths and injuries as a result of bullying. Efforts to alter school climates, however, have been reactive, inappropriate, and largely unsuccessful. The legislative efforts of the state of South Carolina are illustrative. The considerable public outcry that followed the suicide deaths of two preteen boys who had been bullied at school led to the 2006 South Carolina Safe School Climate Act (Terry, 2010). The intent of the Act was to limit all types of bullying. Each school district was required to adopt an anti-bullying policy, encouraged to adopt bullying prevention programs, and to articulate punishments for any student who harassed, intimidated, or bullied another. Subsequent evaluations show no change in either the incidence of bullying or school climate (Terry, 2010). Terry suggests that the lack of change largely results from indifference in the community. This may be. It also seems unlikely that a positive school climate can be developed through the addition of punishment. It is particularly unlikely that punishment will reduce student violence or improve the school climate in schools that permit teachers to use corporal punishment, as is the case in South Carolina.

A positive school climate affects students' satisfaction with school regardless of their family circumstances (Zullig, Huebner, & Patton, 2011). It affects student success (Konishi et al., 2010; Schaps, Battistich, & Solomon, 2004; Zins et al., 2004). A positive school climate is particularly important for children living in disadvantaged homes and neighbourhoods. The less physically and psychologically safe the home and neighbourhood are, and the less supportive the relationships in the child's family and community are, the more compensatory is the positive school climate. The research literature shows that a supportive school climate functions as a protective factor that mediates or suppresses the negative impact of poverty and promotes positive outcomes among disadvantaged children (Malecki & Demaray, 2006; Walker & Greene, 2009; Woolley & Bowen, 2007). It does so primarily through increasing engagement in school. Engagement describes the child's enjoyment in learning, academic effort, behaviours, relationships with peers and teachers, sense of belonging, and overall perception of the school (Appleton et al., 2006; Furlong et al., 2003; Jimerson et al., 2003).

High levels of school engagement are predictive of positive outcomes especially among disadvantaged children who are at risk of failure.

A large number of researchers across the developed world have examined the effects of school climate on students' engagement in school. The findings are consistent and unambiguous. Children who perceive their school climate positively show a wide range of associated positive attitudes and behaviours. In terms of attitudes, research in Norway shows a relation between children's satisfaction with, or engagement in school, and overall life satisfaction (Danielsen et al., 2009). Of particular importance to disadvantaged students, much research has found that students' career and educational aspirations are increased in positive school climates (Metheny, McWhirter, & O'Neil, 2008). For example, research conducted in Slovakia to identify how to improve the educational attainment of children from low-income families found the key to be an engaging school atmosphere; the adolescents in this study who reported a positive school climate were significantly more likely to plan further study than were their peers who found their schools to be either bearable or bad (Geckova et al., 2010). In turn, children who are engaged in school are less likely to drop out early (Klem & Connell, 2004).

Positive feelings towards school also improve the quality of relationships at school (McGrath & Noble, 2010). These positive attitudes and relationships are reflected in greater motivation, academic effort, attendance, and achievement (Anderman, 2002; Barber, Eccles, & Stone, 2001; Eccles & Barber, 1999; Jang et al., 2010; Martin & Marsh, 2006; Metheny et al., 2008). Since problem behaviours are incompatible with motivation to achieve and with high educational and career aspirations, it is not surprising that engagement is associated also with decreases in antisocial and health-risk behaviours. Bullying among children aged 8 through 13 years, for example, was found in a New Zealand study to be significantly lessened in a positive school climate in which children are engaged in learning (Raskauskas et al., 2010). Among adolescents, those who are engaged in their schools are less likely to use substances, engage in violence, or become involved in early sexual activity (Carter et al., 2007; McNeely, Nonnemaker, & Blum, 2002; Wang et al., 2010). Of particular interest is a large-scale recent study of students from elementary through high school in Taiwan. Despite cultural differences, the link between school violence and engagement was found to be essentially the same as that in Western countries (Chen & Astor, 2011).

The ingredients of a positive school climate that create engagement are threefold. Not surprisingly, one key ingredient is that teachers are supportive. A second is that instructional and administrative practices provide for meaningful participation and centre on issues of relevance to the students. Third is that all school discipline strategies respect the rights of the child to be treated with dignity. We stress that these three ingredients must be present across the school, in every classroom, and in all school activities.

Supportive Teachers. The overarching need for children to perceive a positive school climate is supportive teachers. These are the high-quality teachers described in chapter 5. These teachers do not show a preference for advantaged children, they do not dismiss difficult children as only the parents' problem, and they do not confuse deprivation with depravation. They respect the fundamental rights of every child with whom they come into contact, and they do their utmost to ensure that the child's best interests are their primary concern. All children, but especially disadvantaged children, need to feel that their teachers are fair and can be trusted (Brooks, 2006; Goddard, Salloum, & Berebitsky, 2009). They also need to feel that their teachers care about them, respect them, and have high expectations for their success (Klem & Connell, 2004; Wang et al., 2010). Each child needs to feel like a valued member of the classroom, and, of course, the school (Walker & Greene, 2009). When teachers are empathetic, consistent, and encourage self-management and meaningful participation, classroom climate improves (McNeely et al., 2002). In behavioural terms, this means teachers need to be autonomy-supportive, promoting meaningful participation (Klem & Connell, 2004), to treat every child with respect for the child's rights, and to provide learning materials and assignments of interest and relevance to the student (Walker & Greene, 2009).

Participation and Relevance. There is considerable evidence of the benefits of participatory pedagogies such as the project-based learning described in chapter 5. Participation in their own learning enhances children's engagement in school: their commitment to learning, achievement, academic aspirations, enjoyment in school, self-esteem, and optimism for the future (Fredricks & Eccles, 2006, 2008; Jennings, 2003; Martin & Marsh, 2006; Pancer et al., 2007; Peck et al., 2008).

Involving children in their learning has not been easy for teachers. The standard of the U.N. Convention on the Rights of the Child is actually quite demanding. It requires that educators collaborate with children to determine optimum teaching strategies and materials. Asking students for their views on teaching is a fairly new occurrence that has emerged, at least in part, as a result of the Convention (McIntyre,

Pedder, & Rudduck, 2005). However, it remains uncommon (Könings, Brand-Gruwel, & van Merrienboer, 2010). Even when teachers do consult with their students about classroom practices, they are reluctant to act on student recommendations (Bahou, 2011). Teachers cite pragmatic concerns such as time and organizational needs, and the need to deliver the full mandated curriculum (McIntyre et al., 2005). More likely reasons are suspicion of students, a conviction that teacher knows best, and concerns about disempowerment and de-professionalization (Hopkins, 2008; Koh et al., 2009; Könings et al., 2010). The evidence suggests such concerns are unfounded. Where children are consulted, they are quite capable of providing very useful input, and their recommendations show a remarkable consistency with the empirical evidence.

Across cultures and across ages, children are in agreement with Elvis Presley. What they want, to paraphrase Elvis, is a little less talk and a little more action. Young children, of course, may not be able to articulate their preferences in adultlike ways. However, they can express them. As called for in Article 13 of the Convention, children are encouraged to express their views through a variety of media. In an innovative study of 3- to 5-year-olds, children's conceptions of play were used to determine optimum classroom practices. The children were asked to categorize photographs representing options for learning conditions into those that depicted work and those that depicted play. They were then asked to justify their choices. Playful conditions were identified as those that allowed choice, self-direction, and little adult involvement. The researchers then presented the children with tasks in either the child-defined playful conditions or typical classroom conditions. Not surprisingly, those in the playful conditions demonstrated more on-task behaviour, more purposeful problem solving, and improved outcomes (McInnes et al., 2009).

Research in England with children from ages 7 to 11 (Hopkins, 2008) and young to mid-adolescents (McIntyre et al., 2005), and in Singapore with 12- to 15-year-olds (Koh et al., 2009), consistently has identified the importance that students place on self-direction and participation. Asked what classroom conditions would enable children to enjoy school and achieve better, the 7- to 11-year-olds in Elizabeth Hopkins' research (2008) stressed the need for less talk and more action. Teachers, they said, "talk too much" and "she tells us again and again and then we run out of time," said one child expressing her frustration (p. 397). Rather, they emphasized, it would be better to be more directly involved in their own learning. In the words of one child, "You learn loads when you do it yourself ... and don't copy up work" (p. 397). Similarly, in their study of older children, Donald McIntyre and his colleagues (2005) found that there was consensus among students that the most crucial component of teaching was lacking – participation: "I think it will be a little bit better if we do it ourselves more" and "she rambles on and that makes us lose concentration" (p. 153). These children also called for more collaborative learning with their peers. Students in Singapore, in an assessment of their perceptions of group work, expressed their satisfaction with group work that allowed autonomy. That, they said, was what increased their motivation and their achievement (Koh et al., 2009). What is truly remarkable with these research findings is the consistency of the children's opinions and preferences with the evidence on effective pedagogy.

The Convention requirements for participation go beyond instructional strategies and materials. Children have the right to participate in *all* matters that affect them. At school, this would include school design, hiring, expenditures, and discipline practices. Such participation is even rarer than is classroom participation. Nevertheless, it is beginning.

There has been growing realization recently of the benefits of involving children in the design of school renovation. The school's physical environment influences children's attitudes towards school, their engagement, and their achievement (Flutter, 2006). Noisy and crowded buildings and disrepair convey a message that children are of little worth. They became distracted from learning. Student involvement in planning and renovating school buildings has been identified as an important step to improving achievement. Norway, Sweden, Australia, and the United Kingdom, for example, have developed building and renovation programs that include student participation (Flutter, 2006). In the early 2000s, the U.K. government committed £18 billion for renovating its secondary schools under the Building Schools for the Future Programme. Student participation was a requirement of this initiative (Newman & Thomas, 2008).

Evaluations of this and similar programs have shown consistently positive outcomes. Participation promotes resilience by allowing children to develop skills, discipline, and motivation; to exercise developmentally appropriate autonomy; and to explore educational opportunities (Finn & Rock, 1997; Peck et al., 2008). Particularly for disadvantaged children, the experience builds self-worth and confidence (Lundy, 2007). Participating with architects and designers to create better school facilities builds on students' assets. The experience teaches the children the skills of problem solving, team working, communication, and negotiation (Flutter, 2006). The children feel empowered, and many report that it is the first time they have been listened to and had their thoughts taken seriously (Newman & Thomas, 2008). Julia Flutter (2006) provides exemplary quotes from students and teachers. From a student: "It made me more confident about getting a job ... it made me feel there was a point to the whole school experience" (p. 188). And from a teacher: "This project has strengthened my view that if you ask students their opinions and give them responsibility, they will often surpass your wildest dreams" (p. 188).

These kinds of projects require a genuine respect for the child's participation rights. Laura Lundy (2007) provides an excellent discussion of the importance of participation and how to provide it in schools. As she describes, too often participation in schools is limited to the establishment of student councils. Often these are controlled by teachers who set the agenda and limit the issues to be discussed. In fact, the reality is that student councils often constrain rather than promote participation. Typically their membership is restricted to "elite" students who are unlikely to challenge teachers or administration. Issues of real concern to students are often disallowed – their relationships with teachers, for example, or issues related to sexuality. Rarely is open expression or discussion of alternate viewpoints allowed in student councils, in school newspapers, or elsewhere in school (Howe & Covell, 2005). It is often difficult for students to express their thoughts on matters that are important to them without fear of reprisal. They are afraid of being shouted at and having their expression seen not as their fundamental human right, but as an attempt to undermine adult authority (Lundy, 2007). Yet there is so much evidence of the benefits to adults of listening to children.

Greg Mortenson (2009) describes the benefits of listening to children in his best-selling book *Stones into Schools*. For example, he could not understand why the children were not attending the post-earthquake tent-schools in Afghanistan. By asking and listening to a Grade 9 student he found out. The student explained that few children were attending school because there were no desks in the tents. Desks, she explained, "make children feel safe" and "the tents feel more like a real school" (p. 104). Even if school is to be outside, desks are needed. Desks were obtained, and the children returned to school. Recalling this and many other examples, Mortenson concluded: "When you take time to actually listen, with humility, to what people have to say, it's amazing what you can learn. Especially if the people who are doing the talking also happen to be children" (p. 191). Listening is something teachers need to learn how to do (Lundy, 2007). Rights-based schools may be able to help teachers learn to listen to children and to treat them as worthy of opinion.

Providing for meaningful participation in all aspects of schooling is easier when there is a children's rights–based shared-values framework or school culture. Respect for the rights of every child becomes the standard within which discussion can occur and against which possibilities can be assessed. In learning, children can use the standard of children's rights as a framework for understanding and for critical thinking. For example, children may learn about the effects of natural disasters such as the 2011 earthquake in Japan by considering how such events might affect the realization of the rights of children whose families were affected. They can discuss also such issues as whether inattention to rights can contribute to natural disasters and what remedial action is needed to provide for children's rights. Student councils and school newspapers can be run with rights as the overarching framework for issues. For example, since every child has the right to nutrition, students may consider whether the school needs a breakfast program.

Discipline with Dignity. When children participate in establishing school disciplinary strategies and consequences for infractions, there are two benefits. First, as described in chapter 5, children are more likely to adhere to rules in whose development they have participated. Second, if they are in line with the requirements of the Convention, discipline strategies are more likely to respect the dignity of the child. It is highly unlikely that children would suggest the use of corporal punishment or verbal abuse. The shared value of children's rights facilitates such participation. In discipline practices, staff and students can collaborate to determine expectations and infractions from a rights basis. They can jointly consider, for example, what rights must be respected so that every child can learn and play without fear of bullying. Standards for behaviour can be developed from these considerations. This approach is impossible unless children and all school staff are aware of and understand the importance of children's rights.

A school culture of rights also requires the explicit teaching of children's rights. There are three reasons for this. One is that the explicit teaching of rights increases the likelihood that the focus on rights as the shared-values framework will be sustained over time. There is a tendency for schools to adopt a "flavour of the month" approach to reform and to then "favour a new flavour." Second, there is some evidence that when teachers are required to educate their students about the U.N. Convention on the Rights of the Child, they become more supportive of children being independent bearers of inalienable human rights (Covell, O'Leary, & Howe, 2002). Since beliefs guide actions, it would be difficult for teachers to appreciate each child as a bearer of the same fundamental human rights and continue to behave differentially to children on the basis of their socioeconomic status. Third, rights-infused curricula would be of interest and relevance to children from preschool through school completion since it is their rights they are learning about. Currently, when children do learn about rights, they typically learn about the rights that they will enjoy as future adult citizens. The future, however, is far away. Children are most interested in their own rights in the here and now as expressed in the Convention. Curricula that allow for self-interest are inherently motivating. Moreover, contrary to common belief, self-interest is not synonymous with selfishness (Goodman, 2000). It is, however, engaging. When concepts such as rights are linked with children's daily realities, they are understood better and they are more engaging (Howe & Covell, 2005). When children's rights are explicitly taught and respected, children learn that they, and all children everywhere, have value. This can be particularly powerful for children, such as those living in poverty, whose daily experiences might be sending a very different message.

Initiatives in Children's Rights Education

Has children's rights education been put into effect? We first note that some analysts have suggested that the Reggio Emilia approach to schools can be understood as a rights-based system of education (e.g., Martin & Evaldsson, 2012). The Reggio Emilia approach is not a defined method or formal model of schooling, and teacher certification standards and accreditation processes are not defined (Edwards, 2002; Wien, 2008). However, the popularity of the approach appears to be increasing. Reggio Emilia schools, which had their beginnings in the 1940s in northern Italy with socially disadvantaged preschoolers, have been more widely and recently adopted into elementary schools (Edwards, 2002; Kennedy, 2010). Like Waldorf and Montessori schools, Reggio Emilia schools are consistent with children's participation rights. Since every child is assumed able to construct knowledge, the right to participate and opportunities to participate are fundamental features of the approach. Project-based learning with peers is common, and children collaborate with their teachers in the selection of learning materials and in the establishment of rules (Kennedy, 2010; Martin & Evaldsson, 2012; New, 2007). The schools also are consistent with the obligations described in Article 29 of the Convention to educate the whole child in ways that develop her or his skills and talents. Reggio Emilia schools stress the value of every child and the diversity of learning styles. Assuming a multi-dimensional model of intelligence, children are encouraged to learn through exploring their environments and to express their learning with symbolic representations in the medium of their choice – drama, painting, sculpting, drawing, or movement (Runswick-Cole & Hodge, 2009; Wien, 2008). However, whereas the pedagogy and underlying philosophy of the Reggio Emilia schools may be consistent with children's rights, overall consistency with the Convention is lacking. For a school to be fully rights-consistent, rights must not only be evidenced in the hidden curriculum, but also they must be explicitly taught.

We turn now to the evidence from early initiatives in Belgium and Canada to an example of rights-based school reform in England and its offspring in New Zealand. What is particularly compelling is that although each of these initiatives used different curricula, different target groups (individual classrooms or whole schools, primary or secondary schools), and different implementation techniques, the outcome data are consistent and they are positive. Despite their differences, each has as its core focus educating children on the U.N. Convention on the Rights of the Child through the use of relevant curricula materials, the provision of extensive participation, and the use of instructional styles such as role play and small group activities that allow for self-direction. Each has resulted in a more positive school climate. This commonality of positive findings is likely due to the fundamental consistency of rights-based practices with the research evidence on best practices described in earlier chapters.

Early Efforts. The earliest initiative in the literature is that undertaken in Bruges, Belgium. This was a comprehensive child rights education project that was introduced in the early 1990s at De Vrijdagmarkt Primary School (Decoene & De Cock, 1996). Involving children aged 3 to 12 years, the goal was to educate them about the contents of the Convention, using democratic pedagogy and ensuring child participation in the learning process. Children were taught about their rights through a variety of media including art and poetry. Art activities, for example,

included newspaper collages representing examples of rights viola-
tions. There was considerable provision for child-initiated and small
group activities, role play, and group discussion. The curriculum activities used issues of relevance and interest to the children. Younger
children, for example, learned about the right to food by creating a very
large doll with illustrations of food. Older children engaged in discussions and role play regarding rights to adoption, privacy, education,
and family.

Interviews with the children and their teachers formed the basis of
the evaluation of the project in Bruges (Decoene & De Cock, 1996). Some
teachers expressed concern that there was insufficient attention paid to
responsibilities and too much participation allowed. Overall, however,
the response was very positive from teachers and students alike. The
primary focus of the evaluation was on the students' social behaviour.
Gains in social understanding, respectful behaviours, concern for others, and prosocial action were the key observed changes. For example,
the children became more interested in social justice and rights-related
issues such as peace, war, injustice, and hunger. They wanted to discuss
the rights of marginalized children – those living with disabilities, in institutions, and of ethnic minority status. They requested that they be allowed to visit peers who were in medical or juvenile justice institutions;
they made an appointment with the mayor to discuss their concerns;
and they wrote letters to U.N. military personnel in the former Yugo-
slavia and to schoolchildren in Zimbabwe. The researchers concluded
that the children's rights education had, by increasing the children's
prosocial behaviours and empathy for others, decreased the common
school problems of truancy and disengagement. Changes in academic
performance were not assessed. However, it would seem a corollary of
the sort of action the children took that they would improve their critical thinking, research, communication, and writing skills.

Following on the success of the Bruges initiative, child rights education was introduced in Cape Breton, Canada, in the late 1990s. Rather
than being in one school like the Bruges project, however, specific classrooms in a number of Cape Breton schools agreed to implement education on the rights of the child. Taking into account developmental
issues, curriculum materials based on the Convention were developed
in collaboration with children and their teachers for three grade levels (Howe & Covell, 2005). At the Grade 6 level (children aged 11 to 13
years), the teaching focused on introducing the rights of the Convention in terms of their relevance to the individual child. Issues included

healthy living, personal safety, families and family life, discrimination, drug abuse, freedom of speech, and decision-making. For example, to learn about their Article 33 right to protection from narcotics, students role played children and drug dealers and examined ways of handling pressure to try or sell drugs. At the Grade 8 level (ages 13 to 15 years), the focus was on relationships of relevance to the child. The curriculum included units on sexuality, education, youth justice, abuse, and exploitation. For example, students analysed popular song lyrics to discuss how rights in sexuality are represented in music; they designed alternative advertising for alcohol and tobacco to consider rights to health and to protection from harmful substances; and they completed cartoons that involved the competing considerations of freedom of speech and rights against discrimination. The Grade 12 curriculum (for ages 17 to 19) expanded the sphere of children's rights knowledge with application to global issues. These issues included children affected by war, child labour, and the sexual exploitation of children. At this level, activities included holding a mock U.N. Conference on war-affected children in which small groups had responsibility for representing the players at the conference, and a sweatshop talk show in which groups researched child labour and then held a talk show to discuss their findings. Formal evaluations were conducted on the Grade 6 and Grade 8 projects. Only anecdotal information was obtained for the Grade 12 projects.

Because these projects were implemented only at the level of the classroom, they allowed for a group of students in the same schools, who had received their traditional curriculum, to be compared with those who received the rights curriculum. The formal evaluation showed that the classroom rights education projects resulted in improved classroom climate, engagement, and behaviour (Covell & Howe, 1999; 2001b). Using multiple evaluations, differences at the Grade 6 level were found between the two groups in their understanding of rights, their acceptance of minority children, and their perceived levels of peer and teacher support. Children who were appropriately taught about their rights understood rights to be entitlements that were different from wants or freedoms. They understood that the rights they owned were to be protected from harm and that they have a right to have their basic needs met. They also expressed concern about children whose rights were violated. When asked to describe what they had learned about rights, typical answers included the following: "How traumatic it is for kids who have their rights violated," "The hard truth about poverty," "Everyone deserves a future," "How to become better citizens and understand each other," and "To know when I am being disrespected and disrespectful." Such learning is consistent with Article 29 of the Convention. Moreover, it is empowering. The children in classes that did not participate in the rights initiative thought having a right meant you could do what you want, for example, to ride a motorbike without a helmet, or to stay up late. They also thought that only older children and good children had rights. The differences in perceived support and in acceptance of diversity were clearly reflected in improved behaviour and more positive classroom climates.

At the Grade 8 level, these findings generally were replicated. In addition, a measure of self-esteem that was added showed that the children who received the rights education had increases in their self-esteem.

It was interesting that the types of projects initiated by the students in Bruges were also undertaken by the adolescents in Cape Breton. Realizing that not every child in the area was assured their right to nutritious food (the schools were in low-income areas), the students from one school initiated a breakfast program for the school by obtaining co-operation and donations from the local community. To our knowledge, this program continues to date. In a different school, the class decided to work at a local food bank to help children whose families were unable to provide sufficient nutritious food. The dividends in skills learning and sense of efficacy are inestimable.

Anecdotal data from the teachers who used the Grade 12 curriculum described how engaged their students were in the activities, and they noted improvements in their students' appreciation of global problems and of the complexity and importance of respecting human rights. Students who had participated in the project completed a survey. The results showed them to be three times more likely than their peers to understand humanitarian assistance for children in difficult circumstances as a fundamental human right. Again there were no data on academic achievement, but the heightened engagement would indicate its likelihood.

The successes of the projects in Cape Breton led to curriculum activities becoming incorporated into the Nova Scotia primary school curriculum in health and social studies (kindergarten to Grade 6) and in personal development and relationships (Grade 8). To support their use, knowledge of the U.N. Convention on the Rights of the Child was identified as a required learning outcome. However, no effort has been made to reform schools to be rights-consistent. Teaching children about the Convention without modelling and respecting the rights that they are learning about cannot be expected to have any positive effect on children's behaviour or engagement in school. The opposite may even be the case. Being told you have rights while not being allowed to enjoy them can only be expected to increase the levels of disengagement as children perceive the hypocrisy and adult-centric nature of teaching and schools.

Nonetheless, the data from the Cape Breton classroom and Bruges school projects demonstrate that even when children's rights education is provided in a limited way, it can make a significant difference to how children feel about themselves, their schooling, their peers, and their teachers. Such improvements may be unsustainable if the reforms are limited. Sustainability requires a whole-school approach and a whole–school district approach. Fortunately, the findings from Cape Breton inspired such an approach in Hampshire County, England.

The Hampshire Reform: Rights, Respect, and Responsibility. Hampshire's initiative of Rights, Respect, and Responsibility (RRR) is the best known and most promising model of children's rights–consistent education to date (Covell, Howe, & McNeil, 2008; Covell & Howe, 2008). One of the largest counties in southern England with among the largest numbers of students in the country, Hampshire has had a long-standing interest in educational reform. In the early 2000s, senior administrators in the Hampshire Education Authority – the body responsible for matters of education in the county – had a particular interest in advancing reforms that would improve educational outcomes for children in Hampshire. They believed that a key to this end was the development of a new values framework for school functioning that would produce a more positive school climate for learning. Reading of the success of the rights education project in Cape Breton (most notably Covell & Howe, 2001b), they decided that children's rights education held promise in providing the values framework they were searching for. They organized a study leave for a group of administrators and teachers in Cape Breton. Returning to Hampshire, they decided to pilot test and then launch their own version of child rights education in Hampshire. After successful pilot testing in 2003, they officially launched RRR in 2004.

To put the objectives of RRR into effect, Hampshire authorities – with funding from the Department of Education – devised a 3-year strategic plan of implementation. This included provisions for teacher training, development of resources, and monitoring of developments. The plan was that the initiative would first be introduced in infant, primary, and junior schools, and then over time, as children went into higher grades, it would be introduced in secondary schools. Between 2004 and 2006, 360 schools took up offers of some introductory training on RRR. By 2011, over 400 Hampshire schools were involved at varying levels of implementation; this number is substantial since the total number of schools in Hampshire is 527.

The basic aim of RRR was to improve educational outcomes for children by transforming school cultures, building a shared-values framework based on the Convention, and promoting educational practices consistent with the Convention. Knowledge and understanding of rights, respect, and social responsibility were to provide the values framework for all school policies, classroom practices, codes of conduct, mission statements, school regulations, and school curricula. The framework was to be put into effect across the whole school – across classrooms, across grade levels, across curricula, and across school practices. Of particular importance, consistent with children's participation rights as described in Article 12 of the Convention, behaviour codes, rules, and regulations were to be developed in collaboration with the children, classroom teaching was to be democratic, and children were to be provided with numerous meaningful opportunities to participate in all aspects of school functioning. In essence, the design of the RRR embodies the evidence-based practices in education that are in the best interests of the child.

With funding from the Social Sciences and Humanities Research Council of Canada, we have been evaluating the implementation and outcomes of the Hampshire initiative since its inception. Prior to describing outcomes, we provide examples of the daily reality of RRR for the children. We start with our observations of RRR when it has been fully implemented in the classroom.

Teaching in the RRR classroom is participatory with the teacher playing the role of guide or facilitator. Student participation is evident in self-directed and cooperative group learning, critical thinking, discussion, role play, and project-based learning. Rights provide the framework for all learning. One example that is illustrative was reported in the Hampshire media (Lightfoot, 2009). After reading the classic fairy tale *Cinderella*, the children are asked to comment on her life. Daniel, aged 10, answers: "The stepmother and her sisters were horrible to Cinderella. They kept her in a cellar and made her work like a slave which infringed Article 19, the right to be protected from being hurt or badly treated." Grace, aged 11, adds: "Her stepmother was very cruel and denied her right to be protected from abuse and it infringed Article 31 when they didn't let her go to the ball, because children have a right to play." Such responses show that not only are the children engaged and thinking critically, but also they are able to apply what they have learned about their own rights to the lives of others. Rights are incorporated in all subjects; for instance, they are integrated into science (e.g., the right to water and health when learning about microorganisms), technology (e.g., researching and designing a power point presentation on some aspect of rights), English (e.g., analysis of stories as above), and mathematics (e.g., graphing of distances between food supply and access).

Importantly, rights are not taught as an add-on or separate subject, but are integrated into required learning. For example, to learn about the Second World War – a required curriculum outcome for social studies – one class decided to put together a war museum. The children (10- and 11-year-olds) decided which aspects were of interest to them and then formed into small groups. One group built replicas of battlefields, which a second group filmed. A third group was interested in fashions of the time; they researched, drew, and found examples for display. Another group role played children separated from their parents and wrote diaries and letters about how they felt (some noting how their right to family was being compromised). One child brought in his grandfather's uniform and medals, while others contributed information about what soldiers wore and what kinds of medals they received. We visited the class as the final preparations were being made for the museum. The background work had been done to present the contextual information, and the classroom displays were almost ready. The next day an official from a local museum was coming to judge the children's efforts. The excitement was palpable. This, we thought, was the "inspiring and motivating" learning that the U.N. Committee on the Rights of the Child had called for. There is no doubt, also, that these children learned far more about the Second World War than the thousands of others who have copied dates and battles from endless blackboards or whiteboards, or memorized data from computer screens. Importantly, each child was able to develop his or her skills, talents, and interests, consistent with the Convention's Article 29.

Participation in skills learning in RRR schools begins at the infant school level with 4- and 5-year-olds. For example, to learn how to use scissors the children are asked what they would like to cut. In traditional schools, children typically are provided sheets of paper and required to cut on lines drawn to depict some object or animal. In one

RRR infants' class, we observed that some children were cutting animal shapes or flowers from coloured paper, and one little boy had some fabric from which, he told us, he was cutting out a dress for his sister. All were learning how to use scissors. To learn how to think critically and research questions of interest, the children were shown paintings from a major art gallery. Each child was encouraged to ask a question of interest, and the questions raised were pursued. Some were not easily answered – "What material is her hat made out of?" or "Is the lady the baby's mother?" – but the underlying skills were developing well. Another class at an infants' school was learning about invitations. They decided to invite their local member of Parliament to ask him questions about children's rights in their community. He came, and found the experience more daunting, he said, than being in the House of Commons.

All aspects of behaviour management in RRR schools are developed collaboratively between staff and students and all refer to children's rights. Most codes of behaviour are developed as charters that articulate rights-based expectations for behaviour. At the beginning of the school year, each class with their homeroom teacher develops a classroom charter of rights and corresponding responsibilities. For example, "we have the right to be heard and the responsibility to listen to and respect other people's ideas"; "we all have the right to learn, so we will help each other." And in a school with a high preponderance of children with serious behavioural disorders, "we all have the right to be safe at school and the responsibility to have kind hands and feet." Similar charters are across the school. In the playground, for example, the charter may state: "We all have the right to play so we will not bully anyone." And in the library: "We have the right to get information, so we will be careful with books and share computers." These charters are used throughout the year as reminders of expected behaviours. Interestingly, they are used not only by school staff but also by the children. In one class, an 8-year-old girl stopped another child who was being very noisy and said: "Excuse me, but you are interfering with my right to an education and I think you need a time-out." "Oops," said the offender and sat down quietly. Signs around the school provide a constant reminder of rights and responsibilities.

Participation across school functioning is characteristic of RRR schools. There are student councils, as in many schools; however, the members are democratically elected within each classroom and the framework for their work is the Convention. Teachers play subsidiary roles only, and councils are not limited in their choice of issues for discussion. Similarly with school newspapers, the children who run them are provided full autonomy but with support as requested. In addition, children are elected to represent the student body on issues of budgetary allocations, spending, and hiring. Students have requested and obtained funding for things such as an aquarium for a hallway, and for an outdoor classroom. When student requests are not funded, full explanations are provided to the children. Participation is not tokenistic. Even in hiring decisions, the children's perspectives are taken seriously. One noteworthy example is seen in the hiring of a "dinner lady." Many schools in the United Kingdom provide a hot lunch. Community adults – usually women – are hired to prepare and serve the lunch. These are the "dinner ladies." A new one was needed at an infants' school, and the student representative on the committee was a 4-year-old girl. When asked for her interview questions, she provided the following cogent three: "Are you a good cook? Do you like children? Do you shout?"

In addition to the explicit teaching of the Convention and the provisions for meaningful participation, there is an emphasis in RRR schools on asset building. Self-directed learning provides a means by which children's interests, strengths, and talents can be identified and encouraged. Children's accomplishments are celebrated. When children are less academically inclined, their artwork may be on display in the school foyer or principal's office. Where children do well in writing, their stories are displayed in hallways; when they do well in sports, their trophies are displayed, and so forth. The message is clear. Every child does matter.

A preliminary assessment over the first 2 years of the implementation of RRR provided the same pattern of data found in the Cape Breton classrooms. Teachers reported a number of improvements in children's behaviours and attitudes to learning. We then conducted a 3-year study (2005–6 to 2007–8) with 18 schools (5 infant, 5 primary, and 8 junior schools) representing a variety of geographical and socioeconomic contexts.

Although each of these schools was eager to implement the RRR, not all were successful. This allowed the identification of factors that facilitated the extensive school reform that was necessitated by the RRR. The key factor differentiating successful implementation was the extent to which the school principal showed leadership, commitment, and planning in so doing (Covell et al., 2008). In turn, this was facilitated by an understanding that RRR was at the core of the school culture providing an overarching framework into which school functioning, teaching practices, and other related school programs and policies fit, which included Healthy Schools, Social and Emotional Aspects of Learning (SEAL), and the national policy of Every Child Matters. Successful school leaders saw RRR as an important way to bolster these other activities and not simply to be an add-on to existing school responsibilities. In contrast, in schools where implementation was less successful, school leaders were more likely to see RRR as an add-on and the latest in a series of new programs. Nonetheless, all schools were successful to some extent. This allowed assessment of the effect of the full reform with appropriate comparison groups.

Evaluation of RRR

The findings of the 3-year evaluation indicated improvements in schools that were successful in fully implementing RRR in children's understanding of rights, achievement, school engagement, behaviour, and participation (Covell, 2010; Covell & Howe, 2007, 2008; Covell et al., 2008; Covell, McNeil, & Howe, 2009). We summarize the findings below. We use the term RRR schools to denote those schools in which the RRR was fully implemented.

Understanding of Rights and Responsibilities. One of the ironic outcomes of explicitly teaching children about their rights is that contrary to concerns that they will run amuck and chaos will ensue, they come to be increasingly respectful of rights and understand the inextricable link between rights and responsibilities. Surprisingly, even young children understand this. Prior to our experiences with the RRR, we, like many other constructivists, had assumed that children would be unlikely to understand abstract concepts such as rights prior to late childhood. It appears they can. Researchers have demonstrated that children as young as 5 or 6 years of age can think critically about the fairness of laws, can make distinctions between unjust and socially beneficial laws (Helwig & Jasiobedzka, 2001), and can even understand that there can be legitimate reasons for non-compliance with authority (Dawson & Gabrielian, 2003). Rowe (2006) believes that children as young as 3 years of age have the capacity to understand abstract concepts such as fairness and rights but will only demonstrate this understanding in a teaching environment that models the concepts in its pedagogy. That very young children can understand rights in a rights-respecting teaching environment was supported in the data.

As part of the RRR evaluation, 96 children aged 4 to 10 (with an average age of 7 years) were interviewed individually to see how they understood the concepts of rights and responsibilities. Children whose schools had not fully implemented the RRR had difficulty describing the concept of rights and were most likely to say they did not know. Those in RRR schools provided descriptions of rights in concrete terms. They did not talk, like older children, about abstract concepts such as equality and justice, but their answers indicated that they had grasped the fundamental meanings. Rights, they said, mean you "have clean water and healthy food," "play nicely," "stay safe," and get "treated properly." Further understanding was reflected in answers to why rights might be important for children and whether all children should have rights. "It [rights] allows children to have a good life and not be hurt," "if they don't have water, they will dehydrate," and "my friend was very naughty before we learned about rights and responsibilities but now he behaves." All children were able to describe what it meant to have a responsibility. Interestingly, however, there were qualitative differences here. Children in the less rights-consistent schools talked about responsibility towards objects – looking after toys, being careful with books, and so forth. Only children in RRR schools talked about their responsibilities in terms of people. Examples include: "The most important responsibility is to make sure everyone has their rights"; "You have a responsibility not to hurt others and if someone's hurt to help them"; and – our favourite description of the responsibility to do the right thing even if it is unpleasant – "If there's a dead rat, don't leave it." Understanding rights this way indicates a greater empathy and sense of connection with all other children. In turn, bullying of the disadvantaged is less common.

Achievement. In follow-up interviews with the teachers and head teachers, those in RRR schools described the improved learning styles they had observed among the children. They commented in particular on increased levels of self-regulation, confidence, effort, and motivation. An illustration of this was provided in the following anecdote from one teacher. She had struggled, she told us, with one little boy who was just too fidgety to get his work done. He was always the last child in the class to finish any task. One day, much to everyone's astonishment, he finished first (finishing was indicated by raising a hand). The class, she said, erupted in spontaneous applause. She asked him what had changed. "Well miss," came the reply, "it was knowing that I had a *right* to education – I thought I'd better take it." Teachers provided many examples of children's increased use of critical thinking, persuasive argument, decision-making, and collaborative learning. The changes were described by one as a change from passive thinking to active questioning. These changes were reflected in marked and steady increases in children's achievement scores on the standardized assessment tests (SATs) since the implementation of the RRR. This was particularly noteworthy since in some of the schools that did not fully implement the RRR, the head teacher explained their reluctance as their need to focus on academic achievement and find a way of increasing SAT scores.

School Engagement. Engagement was defined broadly to include its cognitive, behavioural, and affective dimensions: children's academic effort, enjoyment in school, positive behaviours, participation, peer and teacher relationships, and perception of overall school climate. Engagement was assessed both with teacher reports of students' levels of engagement, and with student self-report among those aged 9 to 12 years. Both reported increased levels of engagement. To confirm these findings, we undertook a larger scale study using the self-report measure with almost 1,300 students across the district. The findings from this study showed that compared with their peers, those in the RRR schools perceived a more respectful and fair and safe school climate, had more positive relationships at school, and participated more in learning and school committees and activities. In addition, more positive comments were made about their school. An interesting difference emerged in the type of comments children added to their surveys. Positive comments from the children in RRR schools focused on the school climate and the good relationships among peers, teachers, and administrators. Positive comments from children in the comparison schools centred on the physical resources of their school, for example, their sports equipment.

Behaviours. Teachers in RRR schools reported significant improvements in behaviours. As suggested above, the understanding of rights that the children evidenced was reflected in improved behaviour. The students were reported to be more cooperative with each other, more inclusive, more sensitive to the needs of children with learning difficulties, and more respectful in general. Incidents of bullying and other inappropriate behaviours decreased over time. It was noted that when the children had disagreements, they often used rights discourse to settle them. In consequence, most schools demonstrated a decrease in exclusions. As well as showing increased prosocial behaviours with each other, the children were reported to show more respect for school property, for example, books and gym equipment. It is not the case that every school that fully implemented the RRR became the perfect place with no problems at all. It is the case, however, that changes in children's behaviour, achievement, and participation were positive enough to affect teachers.

Participation. From the perspective of the school administrators, the most significant changes in teachers were in their use of democratic teaching and positive classroom management, and in less confrontational dealings with their students. Teachers were listening to children and taking their views into account. In interviews, many teachers explained their initial reluctance to listen to children and to allow participation, followed by their surprise at the improvements that ensued. Rather than evoking disrespect, the promotion of participation increased respect. "It's amazing," one teacher told us, "the more you let them participate in the classroom, the more they respect you." Rather than increasing demands for attention, listening to children decreased demands for attention. The children knew that they were being heard. That teachers were finding student participation to be positive was demonstrated in survey data. Teachers in RRR schools reported significant reductions in job-related burnout over time.

Teacher burnout is important because it has negative effects on teaching quality. High levels of teacher burnout are common in the industrialized world, and are strongly associated with student disengagement and misbehaviour (e.g., Betoret, 2006; Hastings & Bham, 2003; Kokkinos, 2007; Santavirta, Solovieva, & Theorell, 2007). Some interesting patterns emerged over 3 years of the RRR with regard to student engagement, participation, and teacher burnout. Burnout was measured using the Maslach Burnout Inventory (Evers, Brouwers, & Tomic, 2002). This measure assumes burnout to comprise emotional exhaustion (the stressful effects of teaching on energy levels), depersonalization (feeling detached and unable to empathize with the children), and personal achievement (sense of accomplishment gained from teaching). Where schools had fully implemented the RRR, there was a decrease in teacher burnout that accompanied the increase in student engagement. Teachers showed considerable gains in a sense of personal achievement over the 3 years, and significant decreases in emotional exhaustion and depersonalization. The decrease in burnout was especially strong among teachers in schools that had fully embraced the reform in the first year of implementation. They were sustained and strengthened over time. Of particular interest was how reduced teacher burnout was predicted by student participation. The more the children participated in the classroom and school, the greater the teachers' sense of personal achievement, and the more likely they were to empathize with and feel connected to their students. The importance of these data is in their implications for high-quality teachers. In effect, the teachers in the RRR schools were, over time, incrementally improving their quality of teaching and looking increasingly like the high-quality teachers described by Farr (2010), in chapter 5. It was participation – a core requirement of the Convention and component of RRR – that accounted for the improvement.

RRR and the Achievement Gap. Among all the positive findings of the evaluation of the RRR, the most intriguing was that at each time of measure the most disadvantaged school showed the greatest positive changes (Covell et al., 2011). To protect the privacy of the students and their families, we refer to the school as Woodview. Woodview Elementary School was among the first to participate in the RRR. From the beginning in 2002, the principal and all her staff saw the possibilities for school improvement in the adoption of rights-consistent schooling, and embraced the reform as a means of improving outcomes for their disadvantaged students. The students at Woodview primarily are from families who are living with the aid of social assistance and public housing. Single-parenthood, drug addiction, and criminal involvement among the families is significantly higher than average. At the time of launching of the RRR, the school was being considered for closure. Absentee rates were very high, behavioural problems endemic, and school failure was common. Following the successful implementation of RRR, there were marked improvements in behaviour and in academic achievement.

Between 2002 and 2008, the number of exclusions dropped from 101 days (2002–3) to 31 days (2005–6) to 2 days in 2007–8. (Exclusions are counted in days rather than individual students; for example, 2 days may indicate two students each of whom is excluded for one day, or one student who is excluded for 2 days.) The principal reported that she threw away her behaviour incidence record book in 2007 since she believed it would no longer be needed. Over the same period, test scores were steadily rising. Students' aggregate SAT scores increased from 133 in 2002–3, to 231 in 2005–6, and to 243 in 2007–8. There is general agreement that it was the transformed school culture and the children's rights education that accounted for these remarkable improvements. Interview data demonstrate that school officials firmly believe that the improvements in children's behaviour and achievement were brought about by the RRR whose components altered their educational experiences and, in turn, their motivations and aspirations. The principal at Woodview noted that for many children this was the first time they were experiencing respect, success, and hope for their futures. As she said, "they know now that they don't need drugs and can see their way out of their parental problems." That the RRR could account for the changes is indicated also in the stability of the principal, classroom teachers, and family profiles over time. In fact, the changes were so dramatic that they attracted the attention of a number of British government officials including the Minister of Children and Families who after visiting the school called it "inspirational." Rather than closing Woodview, the school was renovated and expanded.

By the time the school was slated for expansion, the children were used to being involved in all school matters. They had a history of active classroom participation and involvement in school governance, often interacting with adults in the community. Being involved in the planning of the renovation and expansion was a natural next step. They worked with adult members of the school's board of governors, community business owners, local community leaders and politicians, and during the reconstruction, the various professionals and workers involved – architects, landscapers, and others. Committees of students also designed and selected the new school logo, uniform, and colours. We note here that this is the only English school we have visited in which the children have been proud of their uniforms; others complain. The respect and empowerment the children of Woodview experienced, together with their increased academic success and enjoyment of school, appears to have done much to increase their intrinsic motivation (Ryan & Deci, 2000), and to overcome the poverty of aspiration that so often accompanies socioeconomic disadvantage and so often leads to school disengagement and failure. Had it, however, reduced the achievement gap?

We assessed whether the RRR had any effect on reducing the achievement gap among disadvantaged students by comparing the students at Woodview with two other schools – one that was similarly disadvantaged but had not adopted the RRR (pseudonym: Riverview School), and one that was a well-resourced school, in a socioeconomically advantaged neighbourhood, and had adopted the RRR (pseudonym: Knob Hill). Our assessment focused on self-reported levels of school engagement, optimism about the future, self-concept, school social

problems, and SAT scores (Covell et al., 2011). The comparisons indicated the following. Compared with their peers at Riverview and Knob
Hill, the disadvantaged children at Woodview reported significantly
higher levels of engagement in school. This meant that compared with
the children at both other schools, they perceived their teachers to be
more supportive and they rated their school climate as more positive
and respectful. It meant also that their levels of participation, academic
motivation, and effort were higher than those of the children in the
other two schools, and that the relationships among students and staff
were more positive. These findings are quite astonishing given the advantaged nature of both the school and the families of Knob Hill. We
also made comparisons between the two disadvantaged schools. Here
we found that compared with Riverview students, Woodview students
reported more positive self-concepts, fewer social problems such as
bullying and fighting at school, more optimism about their futures, and
more commitment to stay in school longer.

And, yes, the achievement gap was profoundly lessened. The SAT
scores between the advantaged Knob Hill students and the disadvantaged students at Woodview were almost indistinguishable. The
percentage of students who achieved expected or better scores (the
standard comparison) in math, science, reading, and writing respectively was Woodview: 83, 88, 84, and 50; Knob Hill: 82, 92, 94, and 49;
and Riverview: 43, 50, 46, and 29. In summary, Woodview showed a
student socio-demographic profile that largely paralleled that of Riverview, and an achievement profile that paralleled that of Knob Hill.

The children from Woodview are now in secondary school. Our continued monitoring of these students shows that they have maintained
their engagement and enthusiasm through the difficult transition period. This is very important. The most significant transition in schooling occurs between childhood and early adolescence (11 to 13 years).
Adjustment difficulties at this time are common, but they are particularly pronounced among students from disadvantaged backgrounds
(Cauley & Javanovich, 2006; Humphrey & Ainscow, 2006; Plunkett et
al., 2008; Reyes et al., 2000), and especially those who are disengaged
from school (Crosnoe & Elder, 2004). During the first few years of secondary schooling, a substantial number of disadvantaged students
show declines in school engagement and achievement, and increases in
problem behaviours such as substance abuse, criminal offending, early
pregnancy, and early school leaving (Roeser et al., 2008; Stone et al.,
2008). The students from Woodview have not to date. This suggests

that the RRR might have the capacity to function as a protective factor – an inoculation against future adversity. Had the outcomes been short-lived, a band-aid rather than an inoculation, with the challenges that accompany the transition to secondary school, these at-risk disadvantaged students would be expected to revert to the more common pattern of underachievement, disengagement, and behavioural problems.

Finally, it should be noted also that parental involvement has increased at Woodview. This, in part, stems from the improved child outcomes. Parents have been invited to the school to see the expansion and new furnishings, and to see how well their children are doing, rather than to face difficult discussions about disciplinary infractions and exclusions. Perhaps more importantly, the school staff has made a concerted effort to gain the trust of the parents and to encourage their attendance at school functions by incorporating space and programs for parents in the renovated school. One room has been set aside. Here parents are provided nutrition and cooking classes and knowledge about the importance of children's rights being respected. They also are provided the opportunity to improve their literacy and employment-related skills with access to the school computers and library collection. The school has become a welcoming place for these parents and their children. This is a very new experience for many, and it is one to which they are responding very well. There seems no question that rights-consistent education is, in its apparent capacity to build assets and resilience, in the best interests of the child.

Post-RRR Developments

The success of the Hampshire reform has impelled similar efforts in many other education jurisdictions. Children's rights education has been introduced in a number of schools in other parts of the United Kingdom, Canada, and New Zealand. We summarize two of these initiatives here. One is in Canada where rights education was introduced with very young children, and one is in New Zealand where efforts are underway for widespread rights-based school reform.

Canadian educators Pamela Wallberg and Maria Kahn (2011) introduced rights education to an early childhood program group of 3- and 4-year-old children over a 3-month period. The introduction of 'The Rights Project' was motivated in large part by observations of the children's self-focus and disregard for the feelings of their peers. Using a colouring book designed to teach very young children about their rights (available from the Cape Breton University Children's Rights Centre), the teachers hoped to shift the children's focus from individual wants to community needs – to increase levels of cooperation, altruism, and empathy. They were successful. Rights education was found to "transform the classroom into a new learning environment based on equity, inter-dependence and group accountability" (p. 31). As classroom rules were replaced with rights, less adult control was needed and group conversations changed from chaotic chatter to the respectful exchange of ideas. The children's behaviour towards each other changed markedly. Their interactions reflected an understanding of the universality of rights and the importance of protecting the rights of others. Even at this very young age, rights discourse replaced arguing; for example, "you are hurting my right to play" became an effective problem solver that replaced tears and fighting. Wallberg and Kahn conclude that the children's recognition of the relationship between rights and responsibilities shifted their focus "from 'me' to 'we'" (p. 31). "The Rights Project" illustrates the power of rights education to create an optimum early learning environment for every child.

Among the more ambitious developments is seen in New Zealand where efforts are underway to make rights-consistent schooling a nationwide initiative. The context for the initiative is favourable. A strong human rights theme runs through New Zealand's Education Act, national education goals, curriculum, and national administrative guidelines. Initial discussions between 2002 and 2004 about incorporating children's rights education into the New Zealand curriculum were given momentum by the evidence provided from the Cape Breton and Hampshire County initiatives (HRiE, 2009).

Like elsewhere, educators and human rights advocates in New Zealand had been concerned with poor achievement levels, bullying, and violent behaviours observed among a significant minority of children in schools. Also like elsewhere, teachers and administrators were frustrated by the range of difficult demands in schools, the fragmentation of efforts to address common problems, and the disappointing results of those efforts. Learning about the successes of the Cape Breton and the Hampshire County initiatives, the collaborative initiative Human Rights in Education/Mana Tika Tangata (HRiE) was formed (HRiE, 2009). Its goal was to develop positive school cultures on the basis of the rights of the child and to improve achievement for all children through having schools and early childhood education centres become learning communities that know, promote, and live human rights and responsibilities.

To achieve this goal, HRiE has been following the Hampshire model in using children's rights as an overarching and integrating values framework for teaching, learning, and school management and organization. All members of the school community – school leadership, teachers and other staff, students, boards of trustees, and parents – learn about children's rights and the responsibilities that go with them. They recognize that *every* member of the school community has the right to be treated with dignity and fairness, and to participate in effective education. Students are formally recognized as contemporaneous citizens of the school and country with explicit rights and responsibilities. They participate in decision-making across the school, and rights are embedded across the curriculum, school practices, and policies.

At the end of the first 2 years of the initiative, in 2009, 12 schools were fully involved. Although no formal evaluation has yet been published, anecdotal evidence suggests the outcomes are comparable to those reported from Hampshire (HRiE, 2009). Teachers report improved learning environments and decreased stress. Highlighted in their responses are comments on the unexpected and extensive benefits of starting the school year with a classroom charter of rights and responsibilities developed collaboratively between teachers and children. "Makes me think critically about some of the things I do in my classroom," a teacher reported, "especially some of the aspects of my behaviour management." And another stressed that she has "had fabulous response from the children." It seems likely that if this initiative is sustained, it too will have the capacity to improve the academic outcomes of disadvantaged children.

Obstacles to Reform

The initiatives and reforms described above demonstrate the capacity of children's rights education to improve school climate, improve educational outcomes, and reduce the achievement gap. That seems clear. Whether such reforms will be expanded to other jurisdictions or even sustained is less clear. School reform is neither easy to implement nor to sustain. Fullan (2007) has identified a number of obstacles that stand in the way of success. One is the lack of sustained commitment, leadership, and planning among education officials and new program leaders.

Officials often get sidetracked by problems that periodically flare up such as budgetary issues and school staffing concerns. Another obstacle is the lack of cooperation from teachers and staff. Teachers need to perceive a new program as necessary, practical, and easy to implement. This presents a major challenge for education on the rights of the child. Like other people, most teachers lack knowledge and understanding of children's rights. Many are suspicious of the concept of children's rights and so are hesitant to agree to teach the subject matter. Many also see children's rights as a threat to the authority of teachers and to the ability of teachers to control their classroom. A further obstacle is the decentralized nature of many education systems. In England, as in many education jurisdictions, there is considerable local autonomy in education decision-making. Local boards of governors and head teachers have a significant amount of power in deciding whether or not to cooperate and support new initiatives such as RRR. They would have to approve of the initiative, and they would have to see it as fitting in with school priorities and other programs.

No obstacle is greater than a lack of knowledge of the existence of the U.N. Convention on the Rights of the Child, a lack of understanding of the importance of its provisions for optimal child development, and a lack of appropriate teacher training. Teachers lack knowledge of the democratic pedagogy necessary for rights-consistent education, they lack specific training on how to listen to children, and they lack awareness of how to respect the participation rights of the child. It is difficult to imagine widespread implementation of any school reform in the absence of the training needed to promote understanding of its nature and value, and to promote the confidence needed to effect its instructional demands.

Since the mid-1990s, we have observed many efforts to implement and sustain children's rights education. We have seen the obstacles described by Fullan (2007), and we have seen how difficult it can be to transform school cultures and to sustain school reform. This has been the case even with the RRR initiative. In terms of its implementation, the most common problem we have observed is a conviction that RRR can be put in place one R at a time (Howe & Covell, 2010b). The first R (rights) is postponed for 2 years while children are taught the other two (respect and responsibility) Whether this results from underlying concerns about teaching children's rights or from an absence of understanding that holistic reform is needed, we do not know. However, interview data do suggest a lack of appreciation that it is through learning about their rights that children come to understand their responsibility to respect the rights of others. Implementation in such circumstances has been unsuccessful.

Difficulty in sustaining rights-consistent school reform primarily has come from three sources. First, changes in school leadership often have led to decreases in commitment to RRR. When new principals, or head teachers, are appointed, they seem reluctant to adopt and sustain existing approaches, however successful. They want instead to implement, and perhaps to take credit for, their own ideas and reforms. A rights-consistent school, then, may move away from its original design or purpose to a particular favourite approach of the new school principal. Second, and perhaps a more insidious source of difficulty, is complacency. Principals in some RRR schools, after some time, decided that the rights of the child were so firmly embedded in curricula, policies, and practices, that they no longer needed to explicitly teach them. A gradual erosion of respect for rights and for children's knowledge of rights has occurred in consequence. Rights may still be prominently displayed in school mission statements, but teacher interactions with students and classroom teaching practices no longer put that mission statement into action. The third source of difficulty in sustainability seems to have been an unintended by-product of a UNICEF U.K. award certificate program.

Schools proudly display their awards. Among the myriad of possible certificates are the Healthy Schools Award, the Eco School Award, the Community Partnership Award, the Green School Award, and now the UNICEF Rights Respecting School Award. This latter award was developed to acknowledge and reward those schools where the RRR was fully implemented and to encourage more schools to adopt children's rights as their framework. Criteria were developed to assess the level of rights-consistency and schools are awarded a Level 1 or a Level 2 Rights Respecting School Award certificate. Schools gain status through their awards. Certainly, a certificate announcing that the school is rights respecting is something to be proud of. Moreover, there is a certain level of competition to be among the first to obtain new award certificates. The problem is that the focus of reform can easily move away from the principles of the program to the achievement of criteria for the award. The danger is that the reform itself can take second place to the certificate. Then, having achieved the certificate, it is time to move on to the newest award available.

It has been our experience that the award certificate approach has created a bandwagon effect. We see two serious implications for rights-consistent schooling. One is that schools are attempting to adopt a rights approach very quickly in order to obtain the certificate. The successes at Woodview, described above, were gained over a 6-year period. The extent of professional development, teaching resources, and organizational changes required to fully implement children's rights as the school's overarching framework precludes speed. The second is that providing an award certificate for school reform puts that reform on the same platform as the endless "add-ons" that are normally associated with certificates. In turn, there is a real danger that the understanding of rights-consistent schooling is moved away from that of a new framework to yet another initiative. Finally, and importantly, certificates, once achieved, are neither reviewed nor rescinded. We, unfortunately, visited a number of schools that proudly displayed their Rights Respecting School Award, while teachers shouted at students or even humiliated them in front of us. "Awards," as stated by Rogers and colleagues (1998) after evaluating the Healthy Schools Award Scheme, "may be little more than promotional gimmicks" (p. 40). They can be useful, but their credibility and effectiveness depend on rigorous external evaluation, standard methods of assessment, and highly stringent monitoring. Furthermore, they can be counter-productive. A school that displays an award for being rights-respecting when it is not is a school that is teaching the children that adults are hypocritical and cannot be trusted.

In the Final Analysis

The positive outcomes associated with children's rights education will not be accomplished if, for whatever reason, the school does not fully implement the necessary changes and then sustain them. Institutional memory can be long and obstruct change. Reforms that are ill-effected or not sustained may well lead to future efforts being abandoned on the basis that they were tried but they failed. Reform is not accomplished quickly and cannot be sustained without concerted effort. It is not something that is *achieved*. Rather, it is a new approach to schooling that must be carefully and systematically implemented and must be reflected in all practices and policies.

Children's rights education is not a magic bullet. There will still be children with behavioural disorders and developmental delays whose difficulties cannot easily be overcome. However, what the evidence has shown is that children's rights education has many benefits. As the key ingredient of a positive school culture, children's rights education contributes significantly to building a positive climate, improving learning, and reducing the achievement gap. As such, it clearly is in the best interests of the child to have rights-consistent schooling. We discuss the prospects of bringing this about in the final chapter.

Chapter Seven

Moving Forward

If education were truly in the best interests of the child, children with backgrounds of social disadvantage would enjoy their right to education on the basis of equal opportunity. But such is not the case. Across the developed world, to greater or lesser degrees, there continues to be an achievement gap. As in the past, disadvantaged children are more likely than other children to be disengaged from school, experience school failure, and drop out of school. As a result, in later life, their health and economic outcomes are less positive. Early inequality brings later inequality. This need not occur. The evidence provided in the preceding chapters has shown that the achievement gap can be reduced significantly through implementing early childhood education, improving school practices, and transforming school cultures. Children who attend schools such as the RRR schools in Hampshire, England, or the Met in Rhode Island do well despite their histories that place them at risk of failure. These are, however, exceptions. Three questions remain which we address here. Can the achievement gap be fully closed through educational reform alone? Why has there been so little progress in closing the achievement gap? What are the prospects for change?

Closing the Achievement Gap

Can educational reform itself close the achievement gap? In addressing this question, we emphasize that the issue is not eliminating differences in educational achievement. Differences based on natural abilities, talents, and interests will remain. Rather, the question is whether educational reform can remove differences based on social background.

The continued existence of an achievement gap has led some scholars to conclude that the adversities associated with being reared in poverty are simply too great for schools to overcome. Since the 1960s (e.g., Coleman et al., 1966), doubters of the capacity of educational reform to close the achievement gap argue that educators are hindered by issues that originate in the child's family and community. The achievement gap, they believe, starts at home and is robust (e.g., Fryer & Levitt, 2004). Schools alone, say the doubters, cannot compensate for social environments and the chronic underachievement of poor children. Some analysts go further and suggest that the source of the problem is in social structures and in unequal power relations in society. From this perspective – which Carlo Raffo and his colleagues (2010) refer to as the "socially critical" position – educational reform is incapable of closing the achievement gap because of the powerful effects of existing social arrangements and inequalities. Real progress in achieving educational equity requires tackling social inequality.

Education researcher and commentator Ben Levin (2006) is among those who believe that schools can have only a limited effect in countering the early adversities associated with family poverty. There is, he suggests, a ceiling on improvement effects. This ceiling is partly due to problems within high-poverty schools such as fewer resources, higher staff turnover, and lower likelihood of quality teachers. It is due also, Levin contends, to the magnitude of the challenges outside the school in the form of family and community disadvantage. Citing evidence from the United States and elsewhere, Levin asserts that because of the challenges, school reforms alone are unlikely to result in sustained improvement in schools in high-poverty areas. Closing the achievement gap would require strong efforts not only in schools but also in broader social policy. Levin illustrates this with an example from northern Canada where disadvantaged children miss a great deal of school because of tooth decay arising from poor diets. Milk and fresh food are very expensive in the far north. Improving educational outcomes in such a context, says Levin, requires more than high-quality teachers and schools. It also requires social policy measures.

Other scholars and commentators argue that the achievement gap could be closed in the absence of social policy and community interventions if only schools adopted appropriate practices. Karin Chenoweth (2007), for example, reports on her visits to eight U.S. schools that received the Education Trust's Dispelling the Myth Award. The myth being dispelled is that not all students can be educated to high levels.

The award is given to high-poverty and high-minority schools that are also high-achieving schools. In describing these exceptional schools, Chenoweth demonstrates well the capacity of schools to fully close the achievement gap. The evaluations of the RRR initiative in Hampshire and of the Met also show that schools alone *can* close the gap. However, it is hard to generalize from a few exceptional schools, and so our stance is somewhat more cautious. Whereas we are confident that schools alone can do much to significantly reduce the achievement gap and in some cases actually close it, we believe also that the full closing of the gap is more likely in the presence of strong family policies and supports. With increasing evidence of the importance of the early years to subsequent learning and achievement, school reform needs to be supported and reinforced with broader social reforms. It perhaps is not a question of whether schools can close the achievement gap, but one of how families and communities can support schools in closing the achievement gap.

The Harlem Children's Zone (HCZ) project provides an interesting example of a holistic approach. The intent of the HCZ project is to create and sustain positive school cultures and supportive communities in order to level the playing field. The project, as founder Geoffrey Canada describes, has community building at its foundation, one neighbourhood, or zone, at a time. The project started in 1997 with a 24-block zone of central Harlem; by 2007, a 97-block zone was covered (Dobbie & Fryer, 2009). Social and health services for families are provided as well as education programs that start in early childhood and continue through college. In addition to offering high-quality formal schooling, the project provides Head Start programs, parenting education programs and supports, drug and alcohol counselling, supports for tenant associations, financial and legal counselling, health initiatives, and recreational and educational programs for all ages. Early childhood education programs are designed to bolster school readiness and to promote parental involvement. As part of the project, the Promise Academy Charter Schools emphasize the recruitment and retention of high-quality teachers. They also have an extended school day and year; provide medical, dental, and mental health services; and offer after-school programs and Saturday programs. As noted in the introduction to this book, the HCZ project has been shown to be highly effective in increasing the achievement of very poor, and in this case, minority students. Will Dobbie and Roland Fryer (2009), who conducted an extensive evaluation of the project, concluded that the closed achievement gap they observed was the result either of the high quality of the schools or of a combination of the school reforms and the community interventions. What was clear in the data was that community interventions alone did not lessen the achievement gap. Schools, on the other hand, did make a huge difference.

Overall, then, we conclude that schools alone can greatly reduce and even close the achievement gap. To ensure and sustain equality of opportunity, however, family and community supports should also be provided. The full closing of the achievement gap is more likely when family- and child-friendly policies and supports are put into place to counteract the difficulties, pressures, and stresses that result from poverty. It is in children's best interests not only to have supportive teachers and positive school cultures, but also supportive social and family environments. Social and family policies that are in place to build such environments and reduce deprivation are of fundamental importance.

It is instructive to compare countries with lower and higher achievement gaps, as measured by PISA results in reading, mathematics, and scientific literacy (UNICEF, 2007, 2010; Wilkinson & Pickett, 2010). Finland, with a consistently low achievement gap, not only provides a system of high-quality teacher education and schools, but also it has strong social policies in place to provide income support for poor families, universal and accessible health care, generous programs of parental leave and child care, and evidence-based programs of early intervention such as home visitation and parenting education (Covell & Howe, 2009; Olsen, 2002). As a result of such policies, there is less social inequality and poverty in Finland (and other Nordic countries), and there are more supports for poor children and their families, which bolsters school improvements. In contrast, a country such as the United States, with a consistently high achievement gap, also has policies that provide less income support for poor families, less coverage for health care, less generous parental leave, and less overall support for low-income families. This spells more social inequality and more children living in poverty. These comparisons illustrate the point that educational inequality is related not only to differences in schools and education systems but also to social inequality and differences in the strength and comprehensiveness of social policies and family supports.

Furthermore, it may be important to note that greater gaps in achievement are related to lower average student achievement. As pointed out by Wilkinson and Pickett (2010), social inequality pulls down the average or median. When social inequality is greater – or the social gradient is steeper – average student achievement, as measured by PISA results, tends to be lower. And when social equality is greater – or the social gradient is flatter – average achievement tends to be higher. In short, larger socioeconomic differences at the bottom bring down average achievement. So in a country like Finland, average achievement is higher. In a country like the United States, it is lower. A conclusion to be drawn from these comparisons is that there is no evidence of a trade-off between equity and average levels of achievement. As noted by UNICEF (2010), it sometimes has been argued that efforts to equalize educational opportunity result in a country's lower educational performance. International evidence shows the opposite, however. The most unequal of developed countries tend to have the lowest average achievement scores and the most equal countries have the highest. Children born in Finland, for example, have a lower chance of falling behind their peers in school and a higher chance of achieving above the average. The point is that with greater social equality and strong social policies, not only is the achievement gap more likely to be lower but average student achievement is more likely to be higher.

Closing the achievement gap, then, is more likely when strong social and family policies are in place. However, educational reform can make a significant contribution. As reported in this book, educational outcomes for disadvantaged children are greatly improved through high-quality early childhood education, high-quality teachers and school leaders, evidence-based practices, and school cultures that embrace the rights of the child. Nevertheless, despite our knowledge of how educational reform can make a difference, it remains amazing how little progress has been made. Despite the variations from country to country and the relative success of countries such as Finland, the overall achievement gap across the developed world has not been reduced significantly in recent decades. This begs the question of why.

Lack of Commitment

In the United States, the national policy of No Child Left Behind was designed not only to raise achievement but also to close the achievement gap. In the United Kingdom, the policy of Every Child Matters was intended, among other things, to equalize educational achievement. In both countries, despite the intentions, there has *not* been substantial progress in reducing the gap in achievement. Disadvantaged children continue to be left behind, Every Child Matters is seldom mentioned anymore in the United Kingdom, and the policy of No Child Left Behind is repeatedly criticized in the United States for its failures. Although more progress has been made in some other countries, the results of international tests over the years indicate that the overall advance in equalizing opportunity has not been significant. There are, no doubt, many reasons to account for such lack of progress. A full explanation would require an extensive analysis that is beyond the scope of this book. Among the reasons, and important ones, we suggest, have been a general lack of public commitment and political will. If there were full and unwavering public commitment to equity in education and the best interests of every child, and if this commitment were clearly expressed to political and education authorities through public pressure, these authorities would have responded to the pressure by taking strong measures to close the achievement gap. This has not been the case. Although there have been very positive developments in some countries, some school districts, and some schools, there has been an overall lack of progress because there has not been the public and political will.

This is not because citizens and policy-makers do not care about children. Across countries and across the ideological spectrum, most people value children, most place high value on education, most believe in equal educational opportunity, most sympathize with the plight of disadvantaged children, and most believe in the principle of the best interests of the child. Support for something in the abstract, however, is not the same thing as full commitment. Support for children is not the same thing as commitment to acting on behalf of disadvantaged children. Political authorities and education policy-makers may know the research, and they may be aware of evidence-based measures to reduce the achievement gap. They themselves may want to act. Nevertheless, in a context of political demands from powerful and conflicting interests, competing priorities, and limited resources, their willingness to act often will depend on the strength of public opinion and public pressure. With strong and undivided public opinion and with sustained public pressure, they may decide to act even when there is opposition from interest groups. It may be in their electoral and political interests to do so. The problem, however, is that strong public pressure has been lacking because firm public commitment has been lacking.

Such lack of public commitment is reflected in the views of many teachers, school leaders, parents, and citizens at large. As found in the research and as discussed in previous chapters, although high-quality teachers believe that the achievement gap can be closed and that they can make a difference, other teachers do not. A reason they give is that disadvantaged children simply lack the capacity for significant educational improvement (Auwarter & Aruguete, 2008; Beswick et al., 2005, 2008). In their view, the lower educational performance of poor children is inherent in the children themselves and their family situation. Because poor parents do not encourage their children in school and because they may not value education, their children lack the motivation and capacity to achieve at the same level as other children. The effects are profound and enduring. Because this is so, conclude these teachers, there is very little that schools can do for disadvantaged children. Thus, the teachers have lower expectations of the children, which alters their behaviours to the children and makes the problem worse. These teachers fail to see that through their teaching styles, practices, and expectations, they may serve as a protective factor for the children. These teachers are not aware that through their efforts, they may provide the children with the resilience required to overcome their challenging circumstances and improve their achievement.

Moreover, many teachers do not believe that it is their responsibility, or the responsibility of schools, to make special efforts to level the playing field. On the one hand, they do believe in the principle of equal educational opportunity. But on the other, they conceive equal opportunity in the traditional sense of meritocracy that already exists (Ullucci, 2007). This means that they believe that all students already have equality of opportunity. Some students may come to school with certain disadvantages. But if they work hard and apply themselves, they *can* succeed in school and in life. Schools are neutral places that provide students with a fair chance. That disadvantaged children tend to underachieve does not take away from the fact that they had a fair chance. Their failure is their responsibility and the responsibility of their families. It is not the responsibility of schools to make special efforts beyond their normal educational activities to close gaps in achievement. It is the job of schools simply to provide education and deliver the curriculum, not to equalize opportunities or advance equity.

Similarly, many principals and school leaders lack commitment to equalizing opportunity. Although some leaders strongly believe in equity and make efforts to mobilize schools to close the achievement gap, many others engage in what Lyman and Villani (2004) call *deficit thinking*. Such deficit thinkers do not believe that schools are responsible for tackling the problem of disadvantage and, if schools do take on this responsibility, they would make little difference. They believe that poor children, because of their social circumstances and family upbringing, lack the fundamental capacity needed to achieve in school. Because of their lack of role models, lack of encouragement by their parents, and lack of educational stimulation in the home, these children are destined for failure. So like many teachers, these school leaders conclude that there is little that schools can accomplish. Thus, they do not inspire and mobilize teachers for the task of reducing the achievement gap, they do not make special attempts to involve parents in their children's education, and they do not seek to create positive school cultures for equity and improved learning.

They also make little effort to examine research on best practices, preferring instead the path of least resistance and traditional methods of school management. Thus, they do not pass along to their teachers and staff knowledge of evidence-based practices. A result is that many or most teachers remain uninformed of practices and interventions that could otherwise provide help and support for disadvantaged children (Stormont, Reinke, & Herman, 2011). Moreover, even if school leaders and teachers do become aware of research findings on best practices, many ignore the evidence and resist new guidelines based on research evidence, believing instead that each school has unique circumstances and that the new guidelines are an infringement on the professional autonomy of teachers and educational administrators (Levin, 2010b).

Many parents lack commitment to the goal of closing the achievement gap. This applies to both low-income and high-income parents. Among many low-income parents, commitment is lacking because they do not put high value on education (Cooper et al., 2010; Fan & Williams, 2010; Hill & Tyson, 2009). It may be the case that they did not receive much education themselves and so do not see its value. Or they may have doubts about the ability of their children to do well in school. Whatever the reason, these parents are less likely to encourage their children in education and less likely to be involved in their children's school, which contributes further to the achievement gap. At the same time, among many higher-income parents, firm commitment also is lacking. This is reflected in their behaviour. For example, under policies that give parents the choice of which schools to send their children to, many middle-class and affluent parents will send their children to schools where the social mix is more on the side of families with higher incomes and educationally advanced children (Field et al., 2007). They do this in the knowledge that children learn not only from their teachers but also from their peers and out of fear that their children's progress will be compromised by association with less-advantaged peers. So if they are able to do so, despite any belief in equal opportunity, these parents will send their own children to schools where the children are more advantaged. This speaks volumes about their actual commitment to equity and is at odds with the goal of equalizing opportunity.

Parents may support equal opportunity in theory, and be sympathetic to the difficulties of disadvantaged children. However, when they see a conflict between efforts to remedy disadvantage and their own children's educational advancement, many parents give priority to the progress of their own children. This point is illustrated in a troublesome case in Florida in March 2011. To accommodate a child with a severe peanut allergy, authorities at Edgewater Elementary School in Volusia County required students to wash their hands and rinse their mouths twice a day and not bring to school peanuts or peanut butter sandwiches. Many parents became alarmed, organized a large-scale protest, and threatened to remove their children from the school. Their reason was that – through the extra washing – valuable educational time was being taken away from their own children. Their children's education, they said, was being compromised in order to accommodate one particular disadvantaged student. Although this was a case of disability rather than poverty, it reveals the ultimate priorities of many parents.

Finally, apart from parents and teachers, many citizens lack commitment to equalizing opportunities for children. Some may not be aware of or concerned about the achievement gap. Others may not believe that there actually is an achievement gap. Others, even though they know that there is an achievement gap, may think that the achievement gap is the result of factors outside the school and that closing the gap is not the responsibility of schools. These points are confirmed, for example, in surveys of public opinion in the United States (Hess, 2006, 2007; Rose & Gallup, 2007; Teaching for America, 2005). The surveys show that a significant minority of the American public is not even aware of an achievement gap, and among those who say they are aware, a significant number are not concerned. Moreover, concern has been lessening over time. Whereas concern about the gap was 80 per cent in 2002, it was 67 per cent by 2006 (Hess, 2007). The surveys also show that many believe that equal educational opportunity has largely been accomplished. In one survey, almost 80 per cent of respondents said that white students and students of colour (disproportionately poor) have similar educational opportunities within their communities (Teaching for America, 2005).

Furthermore, the surveys show that a majority of people believe that if there is an achievement gap, it is due to factors outside the school – lack of parental involvement, a negative home life, and lack of interest and motivation on the part of the low-achieving students themselves. The surveys also show that although most Americans believe that schools should assume responsibility for closing the achievement gap (even though they are not responsible for it) a significant minority – over 40 per cent in one survey – do not approve of schools taking on this responsibility (Hess, 2007). In their view, as in the view of many teachers and school leaders, schools should focus simply on academic matters. Thus, although there is broad public support for equality of educational opportunity, there is not overwhelming commitment to action. Moreover, many Americans and many citizens in other countries do not see teaching as a profession that requires much skill and expertise (Levin, 2010b). They are reluctant, then, to support efforts and resources to expand the numbers of high-quality teachers, programs, and initiatives that would benefit disadvantaged children.

These same mixed views among citizens are present across the developed world. There are exceptions. In the Nordic countries, for example, there is stronger public support for advancing equity because of long-standing political and educational cultures in which access to quality education is considered to be a right (OECD, 2010a). But overall, in most countries, public attitudes are more mixed. This is reflected in the fact that the achievement gap is seldom an issue during election campaigns. It is true that in most developed countries, the public does support high levels of funding for education and for the goal of improving the educational performance of students and schools. However, this is often for instrumental rather than principled reasons. In the United States, for example, studies show that most Americans support the goal of improving education so that the United States can be more competitive in the global marketplace and that students can be better prepared for the workplace (Budig, 2011). A belief in equity is less of a consideration. Although most citizens in the United States and elsewhere value education, and although they support the goal of raising educational achievement, many do not see quality education as a right, they do not see equality of educational opportunity as a right, and they do not see equity in education as being in the best interests of the child.

Such lack of commitment among citizens and within the education community helps to account for the lack of strong political will to close the achievement gap. In the context of divided or ambivalent public opinion, politicians and policy-makers are less inclined to take decisive action. Or if they do take action, it is often motivated more by their own beliefs, simplistic ideology, or partisan politics, than by research evidence (Levin, 2010b). This has been the case with the U.S. policy of No Child Left Behind, with its faulty assumptions about the benefits of high-stakes testing, school accountability, competition, and market solutions to issues in education. It is not surprising that with such faulty assumptions, an outcome has been failure to reduce the achievement gap. Future progress will require a much different approach and direction. It will require thoughtful policies and practices that are informed by the careful application of research evidence. Moreover, it will require much stronger and unambiguous public commitment to educational equity and the best interests of the child.

Prospects for Progress

When viewed from a short-term perspective, we see that little progress has been made in levelling the educational playing field. If, however, we view change from a longer-term perspective, especially since the 1950s, we see that there has been progress in advancing educational equity for disadvantaged children. Strong programs of early childhood education have been established in Europe, especially in the Nordic countries, standards have been raised significantly for teachers and the teaching profession in countries such as Finland, educational priority zones have been created and revitalized in France and Belgium, and policies have been developed such as Every Child Matters in the United Kingdom and No Child Left Behind in the United States. Many advances also have been made in individual schools and school districts. Among them have been creation of the Met in Rhode Island, the Harlem Children's Zone in New York, and the initiative of *Rights, Respect, and Responsibility* in Hampshire, England. The very language of *every child matters* and *no child left behind* is reflective of serious and ongoing efforts to level the playing field and improve outcomes for *all* children.

There is also little doubt that from a longer-term perspective, political cultures across the developed world have become more receptive and more supportive of the rights of children and the principle of equal educational opportunity. Political scientist Ronald Inglehart (1990) has developed a persuasive theory of the recent evolution of political cultures in advanced industrial countries that is relevant to the best interests of children. According to the theory, which is based on a massive body of survey data over time, materialist values are gradually giving way to what he calls *post-materialist* values. When people are more secure in their own basic needs, and when they are socialized into believing in the greater good of other people and society, they are more likely to subscribe to higher-order post-materialist values such as basic human rights, environmental protection, social equality, democracy, gender equality, inclusion, freedom of expression, and individual autonomy. The development of these values may be uneven over time and across countries because of varying economic conditions and cultural traditions. But this shift of values, which occurs with generational change, is a central part of long-term change in political cultures across the developed world. Post-materialist values, says Inglehart, are increasingly being embraced by citizens, affecting political agendas, laws, and public policies, including policies in education.

Inglehart himself makes little reference to children apart from noting a belief that children's rights are part of the shift to post-materialist values (Inglehart & Welzel, 2005). It is logical to assume, then, that within this shift is growing cultural support for the higher-order values of the best interests of the child; the rights of children to protection, provision, and participation; and the child's right to education on the basis of equal opportunity. Few people would say that values such as human rights, participation, freedom of expression, and equality of opportunity apply only to adults. Most would agree that although these values might apply to children in different ways than they do to adults, they still apply in a fundamentally important way. Moreover, most people would agree that children are persons deserving of respect and that their best interests ought to be given primary consideration in decision-making. The signing and ratification of the U.N. Convention on the Rights of the Child and the steady expansion of laws to protect and provide for children is a reflection of the broad international support for these values.

Inglehart and Welzel (2005) suggest that the recent shift to post-materialist values is part of a human development sequence in which long-term socioeconomic development produces a culture of humanism that emphasizes the values of individual autonomy, self-expression, and the development of human potential. It would be odd to think that such a culture would not include children. The development of auton-omy, self-expression, and potential are all vitally important for chil-dren and are core features of the Convention. It also would be odd to think that the culture of humanism would not apply to schools and education systems. If *all* children are to develop their potential, express themselves, and become autonomous persons, they require education that promotes their well-rounded development, equalizes their oppor-tunities, and provides for their best interests. Such reasoning is to be expected among citizens in a culture of humanism. Furthermore, as this culture grows, we can expect a growth of public commitment to the goal of closing the achievement gap, generating the political will to make it happen.

For a variety of reasons, the impetus to equalize educational oppor-tunity has been stalled in recent years. Recurring economic difficulties, austerity measures by governments, public preoccupation with other issues, and a political environment of public worry and insecurity have conspired to slow down or push back reform efforts in education. But the values and principles that inform long-term efforts to increase eq-uity in education remain unchanged. Few would challenge the view – at least in principle – that every child matters and no child should be left behind. Because this is so, with the support of the continuing shift to post-materialist values, principled arguments can be made by reform-ers and used in public education efforts to effect change. Among the arguments are these. First, like adults, all children have value. Children are persons in their own right and deserve fair and equitable treatment, including in the area of education. Second, education is important and in the best interests of children. Apart from its inherent value, educa-tion increases the likelihood that children – as they become adults – have better long-term economic, social, and health outcomes. Third, children have the need for and the right to equal educational opportu-nity, which has been denied. This is evident from the continuing reality of the achievement gap. Disadvantaged children come to school behind other children and they are likely to leave school behind other children. Such an achievement gap is in contradiction of the basic principles and values that most citizens support. By hammering home on this contra-diction, reformers can help build more public pressure for change.

Principled arguments are very important. But they are often more effective when they are backed by pragmatic arguments. Among the pragmatic arguments are the following. Education and equal oppor-tunity are not only in the best interests of the child but also in the best interests of the economy. Successful modern economies require highly educated people, high-quality teachers, and effective schools and education systems. School failure, low rates of school completion, and low levels of achievement are costly both for government and the economy. Thus, the raising of achievement levels and of average student achievement is in the interests of moving the economy forward. This is to be expected. If a country invests in improving educational outcomes for disadvantaged children, average student achievement will be higher and with this, the prospects for a more productive economy will be greater. Contrary to what is sometimes suggested, there is no trade-off between educational equity and economic efficiency. Experience shows that they are complementary in economic development. Skills are needed – critical thinking, problem solving, innovation, initiative, effective communication – for building national economies and for competing in the global economy and the more people who have these skills the better. In short, putting into place measures to increase skills and to reduce the achievement gap is in the best interests not only of the child but also the economy.

So a combination of principled and pragmatic arguments can be used to advance the goal of equal educational opportunity. But this is not all. Effective arguments also can be made about the policy means and reforms needed for realizing the goal, which has been the subject of this book. Because the required reforms are evidence based, they are compelling. It hardly needs to be said that effective policy should be based not on what policy-makers think is best but on what actually has been shown to work. Research evidence is increasingly called for and used in many fields of public policy (Levin, 2010b). For example, reforms in the areas of environmental regulations, public health regulations, and bans or restrictions on the corporal punishment of children have been put into place because research evidence helped prod political action. Research findings are increasingly seen as an important component of sound public policy. There is no reason, then, why research should not also be applied to education.

A decade ago, Bryan Cook, professor of special education and Hubert Everly Scholar at the University of Hawaii, described the gap between research evidence and educational practice as a crisis in education (Cook et al., 2012; 2003). The effects of this gap, as Cook and colleagues note, are particularly pronounced for children who are at risk for poor outcomes, those with learning or behavioural challenges. Such children are disproportionately those in poverty. Little has changed. There continues to be a lack of systematic adoption of effective practices for instruction and management despite extensive research evidence identifying them. Identification of evidence-based practices is, as Cook and his colleagues say, useful only to the extent that they are implemented (Cook et al., 2009). In the ensuing decade, Cook and his colleagues (Cook et al., 2002, 2003, 2009, 2012; Cook, Tankersley, & Harjusola-Webb, 2008) have provided detailed analyses of how to get widespread use of evidence-based practices. The solutions they propose include the following. First, and importantly, they call for researchers to involve teachers in research and to make their findings accessible. Teacher educators, teachers, and parents should be able to understand research findings and why they are important to student outcomes. Second, they stress the importance not only of more relevant teacher training but also of training teacher educators to critically assess and use research findings. Without this, Cook et al. point out, teachers cannot be expected to use effective strategies. In addition, Cook and his colleagues provide excellent guidelines for assessing and interpreting research findings. Third, they call for the provision of systemic support in schools for the use and evaluation of efforts at implementing evidence-based practices. Fourth, they emphasize the need for teachers to collaborate with parents. The systemic adoption of these research-based suggestions would certainly help make effective education more widespread.

In summary, a first policy reform for equalizing opportunity is establishing quality and comprehensive early childhood education and care. This should include strong and intensive programs of preschool enrichment for disadvantaged children that are part of the formal school system. A second reform is taking the following measures to improve school practices: providing high-quality programs of teacher training, ensuring high-quality teachers, using evidence-based pedagogical and management practices, promoting social integration, providing special assistance to disadvantaged children, and providing appropriate resources. Finally, a third reform is developing positive school cultures for learning. This includes establishing a shared-values framework in which the school community learns about the U.N. Convention on the Rights of the Child, develops an understanding of the rights and responsibilities of children, and develops classroom and school practices that are consistent with the Convention. With children's rights education, disadvantaged children are more able to learn in a school environment that provides them with respect and a sense of their own value.

These reforms would serve the best interests of the child. But there is one additional reform item. It would be in the best interests of the child if the aims and purposes of education, as expressed in education laws and policies, were explicitly to include advancing the best interests of the child. This would be in keeping with international law and with the Convention. Moreover, and importantly, if best interests were a declared principle and purpose of education, this would add to the pressure for equalizing educational opportunity. Reformers would be better positioned to criticize decision-makers if educational practices were out of alignment with the principle of best interests. Decision-makers, in turn, would be more under pressure to bring educational practice into alignment with best interests, including increasing school engagement and closing the achievement gap. These reforms, together with supportive social and family policies, are critical to the best interests of children.

Some months after we saw the t-shirt we described at the beginning of this book, we held small focus groups with over 140 children aged 12 and 13 years to assess their experiences at secondary schools in England. Their responses indicated an acute awareness that there was not equality of opportunity or treatment among the children. Those who participated in the groups represented a range of family situations and income levels, but they had all experienced elementary schools that embraced a culture of rights. When asked about their concerns, there was agreement on the need for equitable treatment at school. They noted that although they did not like their school uniforms, they appreciated that they were all dressed the same so that no child would be bullied for having poor clothing. They expressed their concern over the price of food in the school cafeteria and school trips, pointing out that many of their peers could not afford to participate in outings, or eat the food they wanted. This, they said, was most unfair. They also expressed the wish that their teachers would treat everyone the same. Teachers should not have favourites, they told us, but should understand that some children have problems at home, and teachers should be kind and fair to all. Furthermore, one child added, teachers should know that kids learn differently, so they should help everybody learn. We agree.

If the voices of these children were heard, and the reforms we have described were put into effect, education would be in the best interests of the child.

References

Ackerman, B.P., Brown, E.D., & Izard, C.E. (2004). The relations between contextual risk, earned income, and the school adjustment of children from economically disadvantaged families. *Developmental Psychology, 40*(2), 204–216. http://dx.doi.org/10.1037/0012-1649.40.2.204 Medline:14979761

Aguiar, A., Eubig, P.A., & Schantz, S.L. (2010). Attention deficit/hyperactivity disorder: A focused overview for children's environmental health researchers. *Environmental Health Perspectives, 118*(12), 1646–1653. http://dx.doi.org/10.1289/ehp.1002326 Medline:20829148

Aikens, N.L., & Barbarin, O. (2008). Socioeconomic differences in reading trajectories: The contribution of family, neighborhood, and school contexts. *Journal of Educational Psychology, 100*(2), 235–251. http://dx.doi.org/10.1037/0022-0663.100.2.235

Akyol, G., Sungur, S., & Tekkaya, C. (2010). The contribution of cognitive and metacognitive strategy use to students' science achievement. *Educational Research and Evaluation, 16*(1), 1–21. http://dx.doi.org/10.1080/13803611003672348

Alexander, K.L., Entwisle, D.R., & Dauber, S.L. (2003). *On the success of failure: A reassessment of the effects of retention in the primary grades*. Cambridge: Cambridge University Press.

Allington, R.L., McGill-Franzen, A., Camilli, G., Williams, L., Graff, J., Zeig, J., Zmach, C ., & Nowak, R. (2010). Addressing summer reading setback among economically disadvantaged elementary students. *Reading Psychology, 31*(5), 411–427. http://dx.doi.org/10.1080/02702711.2010.505165

Alloway, T.P., Gathercole, S.E., Kirkwood, H., & Elliott, J. (2009). The cognitive and behavioral characteristics of children with low working memory. *Child Development, 80*(2), 606–621. http://dx.doi.org/10.1111/j.1467-8624.2009.01282.x Medline:19467014

Alston, P. (1994). The best interests principle: Towards a reconciliation of culture and human rights. *International Journal of Law and the Family, 8*(1), 1–25. http://dx.doi.org/10.1093/lawfam/8.1.1

Amrein-Beardsley, A. (2007). Recruiting expert teachers into hard-to-staff schools. *Phi Delta Kappan, 89*(1), 64–67.

Anderman, E.M. (2002). School effects on psychological outcomes during adolescence. *Journal of Educational Psychology, 94*(4), 795–809. http://dx.doi.org/10.1037/0022-0663.94.4.795

Andersson, U. (2006). The contribution of working memory to children's mathematical word problem solving. *Applied Cognitive Psychology, 21*(9), 1201–1216. http://dx.doi.org/10.1002/acp.1317

Appleton, J.J., Christenson, S.L., Kim, D., & Reschly, A.L. (2006). Measuring cognitive and psychological engagement: Validation of the Student Engagement Instrument. *Journal of School Psychology, 44*(5), 427–445. http://dx.doi.org/10.1016/j.jsp.2006.04.002

Armstead, C.L., Bessell, A.G., Sembiante, S., & Plaza, M.P. (2010). What students need, what students say they want: Student perspectives on the promise of Smaller Learning Communities. *Peabody Journal of Education, 85*(3), 365–374. http://dx.doi.org/10.1080/0161956X.2010.491706

Arcia, E. (2006). Achievement and enrolment status of suspended students: Outcomes in a large, multicultural school district. *Education and Urban Society, 38*(3), 359–369. http://dx.doi.org/10.1177/0013124506286947

Arnove, R.F. (2010). Extraordinary teachers, exceptional students. *Kappan Magazine, 92*(2), 46–50.

Arnsten, A.F.T. (2009). Toward a new understanding of attention-deficit hyperactivity disorder pathophysiology: An important role for prefrontal cortex dysfunction. *CNS Drugs, 23*(Suppl 1), 33–41. http://dx.doi.org/10.2165/00023210-200923000-00005 Medline:19621976

Aronen, E.T., Vuontela, V., Steenari, M.R., Salmi, J., & Carlson, S. (2005). Working memory, psychiatric symptoms, and academic performance at school. *Neurobiology of Learning and Memory, 83*(1), 33–42. http://dx.doi.org/10.1016/j.nlm.2004.06.010 Medline:15607686

Aunola, K., Nurmi, J.E., Onatsu-Arvilommi, T., & Pulkkinen, L. (1999). The role of parents' self-esteem, mastery-orientation and social background in their parenting styles. *Scandinavian Journal of Psychology, 40*(4), 307–317. http://dx.doi.org/10.1111/1467-9450.404131 Medline:10658515

Auwarter, A.E., & Aruguete, M.S. (2008). Effects of student gender and socioeconomic status on teacher perceptions. *Journal of Educational Research, 101*(4), 242–246. http://dx.doi.org/10.3200/JOER.101.4.243-246

Bahou, L. (2011). Rethinking the challenges and possibilities of student voice and agency. *Educate – Special Issue*, 2–14.

Baker, J.A., Kamphaus, R.W., Home, A.M., & Winsor, A.P. (2006). Evidence for population-based perspectives on children's behavioral adjustment and needs for service delivery in schools. *School Psychology Review*, 35(1), 31–46.

Baker-Henningham, H., Meeks-Gardner, J., Chang, S., & Walker, S. (2009). Experiences of violence and deficits in academic achievement among urban primary school children in Jamaica. *Child Abuse and Neglect*, 33(5), 296–306. http://dx.doi.org/10.1016/j.chiabu.2008.05.011 Medline:19481803

Bandura, A. (1993). Perceived self-efficacy in cognitive development and functioning. *Educational Psychologist*, 28(2), 117–148. http://dx.doi.org/10.1207/s15326985ep2802_3

Barbarin, O., Bryant, D., McCandies, T., Burchinal, M., Early, D., Clifford, R., Pianta R, & Howes, C. (2006). Children enrolled in public pre-K: The relation of family life, neighborhood quality, and socioeconomic resources to early competence. *American Journal of Orthopsychiatry*, 76(2), 265–276. http://dx.doi.org/10.1037/0002-9432.76.2.265 Medline:16719646

Barber, B.L., Eccles, J.S., & Stone, M. (2001). Whatever happened to the jock, the brain, and the princess? Young adult pathways linked to adolescent activity involvement and social identity. *Journal of Adolescent Research*, 16(5), 429–455. http://dx.doi.org/10.1177/0743558401165002

Barnett, W.S. (2008). *Preschool education and its lasting effects: Research and policy implications*. Boulder and Tempe: Education and the Public Interest Centre and Education Policy Research. http://epicpolicy.org/publication/preschool-education Retrieved 12 Nov. 2010.

Barnett, W.S., & Frede, E. (2010). The promise of preschool: Why we need early education for all. *American Educator*, 34, 21–29.

Baum, A.C., & Swick, K.J. (2008). Dispositions toward families and family involvement: Supporting preservice teacher development. *Early Childhood Education Journal*, 35(6), 579–584. http://dx.doi.org/10.1007/s10643-007-0229-9

Baxter, J., & Frederickson, N. (2005). Every Child Matters: Can educational psychology contribute to radical reform? *Educational Psychology in Practice*, 21(2), 87–102. http://dx.doi.org/10.1080/02667360500128697

Becker, M. (1992). Maternal feelings: Myth, taboo, and child custody. *Southern California Review of Law and Women's Studies*, 1, 133–172.

Beebe-Frankenberger, M., Bocian, K.M., MacMillan, D.L., & Gresham, F.M. (2004). Sorting second-grade students: Differentiating those retained from those promoted. *Journal of Educational Psychology*, 96(2), 204–215. http://dx.doi.org/10.1037/0022-0663.96.2.204

Beers, S.R., & De Bellis, M.D. (2002). Neuropsychological function in children with maltreatment-related posttraumatic stress disorder. *American Journal of Psychiatry, 159*(3), 483–486. http://dx.doi.org/10.1176/appi.ajp.159.3.483 Medline:11870018

Behlmer, G. (1982). *Child abuse and moral reform in England, 1870–1908*. Stanford, CA: Stanford University Press.

Bell, S. (2010). Project-based learning for the 21st century: Skills for the future. *Clearing House (Menasha, Wis.), 83*(2), 39–43. http://dx.doi.org/10.1080/00098650903505415

Ben-Arieh, A. (2008). Indicators and indices of children's well-being: Towards a more policy-oriented perspective. *European Journal of Education, 43*(1), 37–50. http://dx.doi.org/10.1111/j.1465-3435.2007.00332.x

Ben-Arieh, A., & Goerge, R. (2005). Measuring and monitoring children's well-being: The policy process. In A. Ben-Arieh & R. Goerge (Eds.), *Indicators of children's well-being: Understanding their role, usage and policy influence* (pp. 21–30). Dordrecht: Springer-Verlag.

Benner, A.D., & Mistry, R.S. (2007). Congruence of mother and teacher educational expectations and low-income youth's academic competence. *Journal of Educational Psychology, 99*(1), 140–153. http://dx.doi.org/10.1037/0022-0663.99.1.140

Bennett, J. (2008). *Early childhood services in the OECD countries: Review of the literature and current policy in the early childhood field*. Florence: UNICEF Innocenti Research Centre.

Berger, K.S. (2007). Update on bullying at school: Science forgotten? *Developmental Review, 27*(1), 90–126. http://dx.doi.org/10.1016/j.dr.2006.08.002

Beswick, J.F., Sloat, E.A., & Willms, J.D. (2008). Four educational myths that stymie social justice. *Educational Forum, 72*(2), 115–128. http://dx.doi.org/10.1080/00131720701804960

Beswick, J.F., Willms, J.D., & Sloat, E.A. (2005). A comparative study of teacher ratings of emergent literacy skills and student performance on a standardized measure. *Education, 136*(1), 116–137.

Betoret, F.D. (2006). Stressors, self-efficacy, coping resources and burnout among secondary school teachers in Spain. *Educational Psychology, 26*(4), 519–539. http://dx.doi.org/10.1080/01443410500342492

Biancarosa, G., & Snow, C.E. (2006). *Reading next: A vision for action and research in middle and high school literacy – A report to Carnegie Corporation of New York* (2nd ed.). Washington, DC: Alliance for Excellent Education.

Bielick, S., & Chapman, C. (2003). *Trends in the use of school choice, 1993–1999*. Washington, DC: Institute of Education Sciences, U.S. Department of Education.

Blair, C., & Razza, R.P. (2007). Relating effortful control, executive function, and false belief understanding to emerging math and literacy ability in kindergarten. *Child Development*, 78(2), 647–663. http://dx.doi.org/10.1111/j.1467-8624.2007.01019.x Medline:17381795

Blank, M. (2004). How community schools make a difference. *Educational Leadership*, 61(8), 62–65.

Bolam, R., & Weindling, D. (2006). *Synthesis of research and evaluation projects concerned with capacity-building through teachers' professional development*. London: General Teaching Council for England.

Bonvin, P., Bless, G., & Schuepbach, M. (2008). Grade retention: Decision-making and effects on learning as well as social and emotional development. *School Effectiveness and School Improvement*, 19(1), 1–19. http://dx.doi.org/10.1080/09243450701856499

Boon, H.J. (2008). Risk or resilience? What makes a difference? *Australian Educational Researcher*, 35(1), 81–102. http://dx.doi.org/10.1007/BF03216876

Bowers, A.J. (2010). Grades and graduation: A longitudinal risk perspective to identify student dropouts. *Journal of Educational Research*, 103(3), 191–207. http://dx.doi.org/10.1080/00220670903382970

Bowman-Perrott, L.J., Herrera, S., & Murry, K. (2010). Reading difficulties and grade retention: What's the connection for English Language Learners? *Reading and Writing Quarterly*, 26(1), 91–107. http://dx.doi.org/10.1080/10573560903397064

Bramley, G., & Karley, N.K. (2007). Home ownership, poverty and educational achievement: School effects as neighbourhood effects. *Housing Studies*, 22(5), 693–721. http://dx.doi.org/10.1080/02673030701474644

Breen, C. (2002). *The standard of the best interests of the child: A western tradition in international and comparative law*. The Hague: Martinus Nijhoff.

Britto, P.A., Fuligni, A., & Brooks-Gunn, J. (2006). Reading ahead: Effective interventions for young children's early literacy development. In D. Dickinson & S. Neuman (Eds.), *Handbook of early literacy research* (Vol. 2, pp. 311–332). New York: Guilford Press.

Broidy, L.M., Nagin, D.S., Tremblay, R.E., Bates, J.E., Brame, B., Dodge, K.A., et al. (2003). Developmental trajectories of childhood disruptive behaviors and adolescent delinquency: A six-site, cross-national study. *Developmental Psychology*, 39(2), 222–245. http://dx.doi.org/10.1037/0012-1649.39.2.222 Medline:12661883

Bronfenbrenner, U. (1979). *The ecology of human development*. Cambridge, MA: Harvard University Press.

Brooks, J.E. (2006). Strengthening resilience in children and youths: Maximizing opportunities through the schools. *Children and Schools, 28*(2), 69–76. http://dx.doi.org/10.1093/cs/28.2.69

Brunello, G., & Checchi, D. (2007). Does school tracking affect equality of opportunity? New international evidence. *Economic Policy, 22*(52), 781–861. http://dx.doi.org/10.1111/j.1468-0327.2007.00189.x

Buchanan, A., Brock, D., Daniels, N., & Wikler, D. (2000). *From chance to choice: Genetics and justice.* Cambridge: Cambridge University Press.

Buckner, J.C., Mezzacappa, E., & Beardslee, W.R. (2009). Self-regulation and its relations to adaptive functioning in low income youths. *American Journal of Orthopsychiatry, 79*(1), 19–30. http://dx.doi.org/10.1037/a0014796 Medline:19290722

Budig, G. (2011). Thoughtful change. *Phi Delta Kappan, 92*(5), 80.

Burnett, K., & Farkas, G. (2009). Poverty and family structure effects on children's mathematics achievement: Estimates from random and fixed effect models. *Social Science Journal, 46*(2), 297–318. http://dx.doi.org/10.1016/j.soscij.2008.12.009

Butler, H., Bond, L., Drew, S., Krelle, A., & Seal, I. (2005). *Doing it differently: Improving young people's engagement with school.* Melbourne, Australia: Brotherhood of St. Lawrence.

Cadima, J., McWilliam, R.A., & Leal, T. (2010). Environmental risk factors and children's literacy skills during the transition to elementary school. *International Journal of Behavioral Development, 34*(1), 24–33. http://dx.doi.org/10.1177/0165025409345045

Camilli, G., Vargas, S., Ryan, S., & Barnett, W.S. (2010). Meta-analysis of the effects of early education interventions on cognitive and social development. *Teachers College Record, 112*(3), 579–620.

Campaign 2000. (2010). *2009 report card on child and family poverty in Canada.* http://www.campaign2000.ca/reportCards/national/2009EnglishC2000NationalReportCard.pdf Retrieved 2 Nov. 2010.

Campbell, D.L. (2009). Student input is the key to effective classroom management. *Leadership for Educational and Organizational Advancement, 1*(7). http://www.leadershipadvancement.com/Student%20Input%20is%20the%20Key%20to%20Effective%20Classroom%20Management.pdf Retrieved 13 June 2012.

Caputo, R.K. (2005). The GED as a predictor of mid-life health and economic well-being. *Journal of Poverty, 9*(4), 73–97. http://dx.doi.org/10.1300/J134v09n04_05

Caro, D., & Lehmann, R. (2009). Achievement inequalities in Hamburg schools: How do they change as students get older? *School*

Effectiveness and School Improvement, 20(4), 407–431. http://dx.doi.
org/10.1080/09243450902920599

Carolina Abecedarian Project (2010). The Abecedarian Project. http://projects.
fpg.unc.edu/~abc/ Retrieved 13 June 2012.

Carter, M., McGee, R., Taylor, B., & Williams, S. (2007). Health outcomes in
adolescence: Associations with family, friends and school engagement.
Journal of Adolescence, 30(1), 51–62. http://dx.doi.org/10.1016/j.adoles-
cence.2005.04.002 Medline:16808970

Casella, R. (2003). Zero-tolerance policy in schools: Rationale, consequences,
and alternatives. *Teachers College Record, 105*(5), 872–892. http://dx.doi.
org/10.1111/1467-9620.00271

Cauley, K.M., & Javanovich, D. (2006). Developing an effective transition program for students entering middle school or high school. *Clearing House
(Menasha, Wis.), 80*(1), 15–25. http://dx.doi.org/10.3200/TCHS.80.1.15-25

Causa, O., & Chapuis, C. (2009). *Equity in student achievement across OECD
countries: An investigation of the role of policies.* Paris: OECD.

Celano, D., & Neuman, S.B. (2010). A matter of computer time. *Kappan, 92*(2),
68–71.

Chen, J.K., & Astor, R.A. (2011). School engagement, risky peers, and student-
teacher relationships as mediators of school violence: Taiwanese vocational
versus academically oriented high schools. *Journal of Community Psychology,
39*(1), 10–30. http://dx.doi.org/10.1002/jcop.20413

Cheng, R.W., Lam, S.F., & Chan, J.C. (2008). When high achievers and
low achievers work in the same group: The roles of group heterogene-
ity and processes in project-based learning. *British Journal of Educational
Psychology, 78*(2), 205–221. http://dx.doi.org/10.1348/000709907X218160
Medline:17588293

Chenoweth, K. (2007). *"It's being done": Academic success in unexpected schools.*
Cambridge, MA: Harvard Education Publishing.

Children's Defense Fund (2010). The state of America's children 2010. http://
www.childrensdefense.org/child-research-data-publications/data/state-of-
americas-children-2010-report.html Retrieved 3 Nov. 2010.

Cicchetti, D. (2002). The impact of social experience on neurobiological
systems: Illustration from a constructivist view of child maltreatment.
Cognitive Development, 17(3–4), 1407–1428. http://dx.doi.org/10.1016/
S0885-2014(02)00121-1

Clegg, J., Stackhouse, J., Finch, K., Murphy, C., & Nicholls, S. (2009). Language
abilities of secondary age pupils at risk of school exclusion: A preliminary
report. *Child Language Teaching and Therapy, 25*(1), 123–139. http://dx.doi.
org/10.1177/0265659008098664

Cohen, J., McCabe, L., Michelli, N.M., & Pickeral, T. (2009). School climate: Research, policy, practice and teacher education. *Teachers College Record*. www. tcrecord.org Retrieved 10 Oct. 2010.

Cohrs, C., Maes, J., Moschner, B., & Kielmann, S. (2007). Determinants of human rights attitudes and behavior: A comparison and integration of psychological perspectives. *Political Psychology, 28*(4), 441–469. http://dx.doi. org/10.1111/j.1467-9221.2007.00581.x

Coleman, J., Campbell, E., Hobson, C., McPartland, J., Mood, A., Weinfeld, F., & York, R. (1966). *Equality of educational opportunity*. Washington, DC: U.S. Government Printing Office.

Cook, B.G., Landrum, T.J., Tankersley, M., & Kauffman, J.M. (2003). Bringing research to bear on practice: Effecting evidence-based instruction for students with emotional or behavioral disorders. *Education and Treatment of Children, 26*(4), 345–361.

Cook, B.G., Shepherd, K.G., Cook, S.C., & Cook, L. (2012). Facilitating the effective implementation of evidence-based practices through teacher-parent collaboration. *Teaching Exceptional Children, 44*(3), 22–30.

Cook, B.G., Tankersley, M., & Harjusola-Webb, S. (2008). Evidence-based special education and professional wisdom: Putting it all together. *Intervention in School and Clinic, 44*(2), 105–111. http://dx.doi. org/10.1177/1053451208321566

Cook, B.G., Tankersley, M., & Landrum, T.J. (2009). Determining evidence-based practices in special education. *Exceptional Children, 75*(3), 365–383.

Cooper, C.E. (2010). Family poverty, school-based parental involvement, and policy-focused protective factors in kindergarten. *Early Childhood Research Quarterly, 25*(4), 480–492. http://dx.doi.org/10.1016/j.ecresq.2010.03.005

Cooper, C.E., Crosnoe, R., Suizzo, M.A., & Pituch, K. (2010). Poverty, race, and parental involvement during the transition to elementary school. *Journal of Family Issues, 31*(7), 859–883. http://dx.doi.org/10.1177/0192513X09351515

Corter, C., & Peters, R. (2011). *Integrated early childhood services in Canada: Evidence for the Better Beginnings, Better Futures (BBBF) and Toronto First Duty (TFD) Projects*. Encyclopedia on Early Childhood Development. http:// www.child-encyclopedia.com/documents/Corter-PetersANGxp1.pdf Retrieved March 2011

Coulton, C., & Irwin, M. (2009). Parental and community level of correlates of participation in out-of-school activities among children living in low-income neighborhoods. *Children and Youth Services Review, 31*(3), 300–308. http://dx.doi.org/10.1016/j.childyouth.2008.08.003

Covell, K. (2010). School engagement and rights-respecting schools. *Cambridge Journal of Education, 40*(1), 39–51. http://dx.doi. org/10.1080/03057640903567021

Covell, K., & Becker, J. (2011). *Five Years On: A global update on violence against children*. New York: NGO Advisory Council for the U.N. Secretary General's Study on Violence Against Children.

Covell, K., & Howe, R.B. (2009). *Children, families and violence: Challenges for children's rights*. London: Jessica Kingsley Press.

Covell, K., & Howe, R.B. (2008). *Rights, Respect and Responsibility: Final report on the County of Hampshire rights education initiative*. http://www3.hants.gov.uk/education/childrensrights/.

Covell, K., & Howe, R.B. (2007). *Rights, Respect and Responsibility: Report on the Hampshire County initiative*. www.hants.gov.uk/education/childrensrights/ Retrieved 13 June 2012.

Covell, K., & Howe, R.B. (2001a). *The challenge of children's rights in Canada*. Waterloo, ON: Wilfrid Laurier University Press.

Covell, K., & Howe, R.B. (2001b). Moral education through the 3 Rs: Rights, Respect and Responsibility. *Journal of Moral Education, 30*(1), 29–42. http://dx.doi.org/10.1080/03057240120033794

Covell, K., & Howe, R.B. (1999). The impact of children's rights education: A Canadian study. *International Journal of Children's Rights, 7*(2), 171–183. http://dx.doi.org/10.1163/15718189920494327

Covell, K., Howe, R.B., & McNeil, J.K. (2008). "If there's a dead rat, don't leave it": Young children's understanding of their citizenship rights and responsibilities. *Cambridge Journal of Education, 38*(3), 321–339. http://dx.doi.org/10.1080/03057640802286889

Covell, K., Howe, R.B., & Polegato, J.L. (2011). Children's human rights education as a counter to social disadvantage: A case study from England. *Educational Research, 53*(2), 193–206. http://dx.doi.org/10.1080/00131881.2011.5723 67

Covell, K., & MacLean, R. (2012). Fighting hunger the rights way: Using videogames and children's human rights education as a means of promoting global citizenship. In C. Wankel & S. Malleck (Eds.), *Ethical models and applications of globalization: Cultural, socio-political, and economic perspectives* (pp. 141–159). Hershey, PA: IGI Global.

Covell, K., McNeil, J.K., & Howe, R.B. (2009). Reducing teacher burnout by increasing student engagement: A children's rights approach. *School Psychology International, 30*(3), 282–290. http://dx.doi.org/10.1177/0143034309106496

Covell, K., O'Leary, J., & Howe, R.B. (2002). Introducing a new Grade 8 curriculum in children's rights. *Alberta Journal of Educational Research, 48*(4), 302–313.

Crosnoe, R., & Elder, G.H., Jr. (2004). Family dynamics, supportive relationships, and educational resilience during adolescence. *Journal of Family Issues, 25*(5), 571–602. http://dx.doi.org/10.1177/0192513X03258307

Crosnoe, R., & Huston, A.C. (2007). Socioeconomic status, schooling, and the developmental trajectories of adolescents. *Developmental Psychology, 43*(5), 1097–1110. http://dx.doi.org/10.1037/0012-1649.43.5.1097 Medline:17723038

Crosnoe, R., Leventhal, T., Wirth, R.J., Pierce, K.M., Pianta, R.C., & NICHD Early Child Care Research Network. (2010). Family socioeconomic status and consistent environmental stimulation in early childhood. *Child Development, 81*(3), 972–987. http://dx.doi.org/10.1111/j.1467-8624.2010.01446.x Medline:20573117

Crosnoe, R., Mistry, R.S., & Elder, G.H., Jr. (2002). Economic disadvantage, family dynamics, and adolescent enrolment in higher education. *Journal of Marriage and the Family, 64*(3), 690–702. http://dx.doi.org/10.1111/j.1741-3737.2002.00690.x

Crowder, K., & South, S.J. (2003). Neighborhood distress and school dropout: The variable significance of community context. *Social Science Research, 32*(4), 659–698. http://dx.doi.org/10.1016/S0049-089X(03)00035-8

Cullen, J.B., Jacob, B.A., & Levitt, S. (2003). *The effect of school choice on student outcomes: Evidence from randomized lotteries.* Cambridge MA: National Bureau of Economic Research. www.nber.org/papers/w10113. Retrieved 11 May 2011.

Cuthrell, K., Stapleton, J., & Ledford, C. (2009). Examining the culture of poverty: Promising practices. *Preventing School Failure, 54*(2), 104–110. http://dx.doi.org/10.1080/10459880903217689

Cutler, D., & Lleras-Muney, A. (2008). Education and health: Evaluating theories and evidence. In R. Schoeni, J. House, G. Kaplan, & H. Pollack (Eds.), *Making Americans healthier* (pp. 29–61). New York: Russell Sage.

Danielsen, A.G., Samdal, O., Hetland, J., & Wold, B. (2009). School-related social support and students' perceived life satisfaction. *Journal of Educational Research, 102*(4), 303–318. http://dx.doi.org/10.3200/JOER.102.4.303-320

Darling-Hammond, L. (2010). *The flat world and education: How America's commitment to equity will determine our future.* New York: Teachers College Press.

Darling-Hammond, L. (2006). Securing the right to learn: Policy and practice for powerful teaching and learning. *Educational Researcher, 35*(7), 13–24. http://dx.doi.org/10.3102/0013189X035007013

Davis-Kean, P.E. (2005). The influence of parent education and family income on child achievement: The indirect role of parental expectations and the home environment. *Journal of Family Psychology, 19*(2), 294–304. http://dx.doi.org/10.1037/0893-3200.19.2.294 Medline:15982107

Dawson, T.L., & Gabrielian, S. (2003). Developing conceptions of authority and contract across the lifespan: Two perspectives. *Developmental Review, 23*(2), 162–218. http://dx.doi.org/10.1016/S0273-2297(03)00011-X

DCFS (2009*). Deprivation and education: The evidence on pupils in England, Foundation Stage to Key Stage 4*. http://publications.education.gov.uk/ (DCFS-RTP-09-01.pdf) Retrieved 13 June 2012.

Deal, T., & Peterson, K. (2009). *Shaping school culture: Pitfalls, paradoxes and promises*. San Francisco, CA: Jossey-Bass.

Dearing, E., Kreider, H., Simpkins, S., & Weiss, H.B. (2006). Family involvement in school and low-income children's literacy: Longitudinal association between and within families. *Journal of Educational Psychology, 98*(4), 653–664. http://dx.doi.org/10.1037/0022-0663.98.4.653

De Bellis, M.D. (2005). The psychobiology of neglect. *Child Maltreatment, 10*(2), 150–172. http://dx.doi.org/10.1177/1077559505275116 Medline:15798010

Decoene, J., & De Cock, R. (1996). The children's rights project in the primary school "De vrijdagmarkt" in Bruges. In E. Verhellen (Ed.), *Monitoring children's rights* (pp. 627–636). The Hague: Martinus Nijhoff.

Dee, T.S. (2004). Are there civic returns to education? *Journal of Public Economics, 88*(9–10), 1697–1720. http://dx.doi.org/10.1016/j.jpubeco.2003.11.002

DePlanty, J., Coulter-Kern, R., & Duchane, K.A. (2007). Perceptions of parent involvement in academic achievement. *Journal of Educational Research, 100*(6), 361–368. http://dx.doi.org/10.3200/JOER.100.6.361-368

Detrick, S. (1999). *A commentary on the United Nations Convention on the Rights of the Child*. The Hague: Martinus Nifhoff.

Dewey, J. (1933). *How we think: Restatement of the relation of reflective thinking to the educative process*. Lexington, MA: D.C.Heath.

Dewey, J. (1916). *Democracy and education*. New York: Free Press.

Dickinson, D., McCabe, A., & Essex, M. (2006). A window of opportunity we must open to all. In D. Dickinson & S. Neuman (Eds.), *Handbook of early literacy research* (Vol. 2, pp. 11–28). New York: Guilford Press.

Dietel, R. (2009). After-school programs: Finding the right dose. *Phi Delta Kappan, 91*(3), 62–64.

Dishion, T.J., & Patterson, G.R. (2006). The development and ecology of antisocial behavior in children and adolescents. In D. Cicchetti & D.J. Cohen (Eds.) *Developmental psychopathology: Risk, disorder and adaptation*. (Vol. 3, pp. 503–541). NewYork: Wiley.

Dobbie, W., & Fryer, R.G. (2009). Are high quality schools enough to close the achievement gap? Evidence from a bold social experiment in Harlem. Harvard University. http://www.economics.harvard.edu/faculty/fryer/files/hcz%204.15.2009.pdf Retrieved 2 Aug. 2011.

Downer, J.T., Rimm-Kaufman, S.E., & Pianta, R.C. (2007). How do classroom conditions and children's risk for school problems contribute to children's behavioral engagement in learning? *School Psychology Review, 36*, 413–432.

Driessen, G., Smit, F., & Sleegers, P. (2005). Parental involvement and educational achievement. *British Educational Research Journal, 31*(4), 509–532. http://dx.doi.org/10.1080/01411920500148713

Dryfoos, J.G. (2010). Centers of hope. In M. Scherer (Ed.), *Keeping the whole child healthy and safe* (pp. 213–221). Alexandria, VA: ASCD.

Dubow, E.F., Boxer, P., & Huesmann, L.R. (2009, Jul). long-term effects of parents' education on children's educational and occupational success: Mediation by family interactions, child aggression, and teenage aspirations. *Merrill-Palmer quarterly (Wayne State University. Press), 55*(3), 224–249

Dufour, R., Dufour, R., Eaker, R., & Many, T. (2006). *Learning by doing*. Bloomington, IN: Solution Tree.

Dumais, S. (2006). Elementary school students' extracurricular activities: The effects of participation on achievement and teachers' evaluations. *Sociological Spectrum, 26*(2), 117–147. http://dx.doi.org/10.1080/02732170500444593

Duncan, G.J., Dowsett, C.J., Claessens, A., Magnuson, K., Huston, A.C., Klebanov, P., et al. (2007). School readiness and later achievement. *Developmental Psychology, 43*(6), 1428–1446. http://dx.doi.org/10.1037/0012-1649.43.6.1428 Medline:18020822

Duncan, S.C., Duncan, T.E., & Strycker, L.A. (2002). A multilevel analysis of neighborhood context and youth alcohol and drug problems. *Prevention Science, 3*(2), 125–133. http://dx.doi.org/10.1023/A:1015483317310 Medline:12088137

Duncan, G.J., & Magnuson, K.A. (2005). Can family socioeconomic resources account for racial and ethnic test score gaps? *Future of Children, 15*(1), 35–54. http://dx.doi.org/10.1353/foc.2005.0004 Medline:16130540

Duncan, G.J., Yeung, W.J., Brooks-Gunn, J., & Smith, J.R. (1998). How much does childhood poverty affect the life chances of children? *American Sociological Review, 63*(3), 406–423. http://dx.doi.org/10.2307/2657556

Dupper, D.R., & Dingus, A.E.M. (2008). Corporal punishment in U.S. public schools: A continuing challenge for school social workers. *National Association of Social Workers, 30*(4), 243–250.

Dwyer, J. (2006). *The relationship rights of children*. Cambridge: Cambridge University Press. http://dx.doi.org/10.1017/CBO9780511511097

Dyson, A., & Todd, L. (2010). Dealing with complexity: Theory of change evaluation and the full service extended schools initiative. *International Journal of Research and Method in Education, 33*(2), 119–134. http://dx.doi.org/10.1080/1743727X.2010.484606

Eamon, M.K. (2002). Effects of poverty on mathematics and reading achievement of young adolescents. *Journal of Early Adolescence, 22*(1), 49–74. http://dx.doi.org/10.1177/0272431602022001003

Eccles, J.S. (2004). Schools, academic motivation and stage-environment fit. In R.M. Lerner & L. Steinberg (Eds.), *Handbook of Adolescent Psychology.* (2nd ed., pp. 125–153). Hoboken, NJ: Wiley.

Eccles, J.S., & Barber, B.L. (1999). Student council, volunteering, basketball, or marching band: What kind of extracurricular involvement matters? *Journal of Adolescent Research, 14*(1), 10–43. http://dx.doi.org/10.1177/0743558499141003

Edwards, C.P. (2002). Three approaches from Europe: Waldorf, Montessori and Reggio Emilia. *Early Childhood Research and Practice, 4*(1), 1–24.

Elliston, S. (2007). *The best interests of the child in healthcare.* London: Routledge-Cavendish.

Elwood, J., & Lundy, L. (2010). Revisioning assessment through a children's rights approach: Implications for policy, process and practice. *Research Papers in Education, 25*(3), 335–353. http://dx.doi.org/10.1080/02671522.2010.498150

Erickson, C.L., Mattaini, M.A., & McGuire, M.S. (2004). Constructing nonviolent cultures in schools: The state of the science. *Children and Schools, 26*(2), 102–116. http://dx.doi.org/10.1093/cs/26.2.102

Evers, W.J., Brouwers, A., & Tomic, W. (2002). Burnout and self-efficacy: A study on teachers' beliefs when implementing an innovative educational system in the Netherlands. *British Journal of Educational Psychology, 72*(2), 227–243. http://dx.doi.org/10.1348/000709902158865 Medline:12028610

Fan, W., & Williams, C.M. (2010). The effects of parent involvement on students' academic self-efficacy, engagement, and intrinsic motivation. *Educational Psychology, 30*(1), 53–74. http://dx.doi.org/10.1080/01443410903353302

Fantuzzo, J.W., Rouse, H.L., McDermott, P.A., Sekino, Y., Childs, S., & Weiss, A. (2005). Early childhood experiences and kindergarten success: A population-based study of a large urban setting. *School Psychology Review, 34*(4), 571–588.

Farah, M.J., Shera, D.M., Savage, J.H., Betancourt, L., Giannetta, J.M., Brodsky, N.L., et al. (2006). Childhood poverty: Specific associations with neurocognitive development. *Brain Research, 1110*(1), 166–174. http://dx.doi.org/10.1016/j.brainres.2006.06.072 Medline:16879809

Farr, S. (2010). *Teaching as leadership: The highly effective teacher's guide to closing the achievement gap.* San Francisco, CA: Jossey-Bass.

Farrington, D.P., & Loeber, R. (2000). Epidemiology of juvenile violence. *Child and Adolescent Psychiatric Clinics of North America, 9*(4), 733–748. Medline:11005003

Feinberg, J. (1973). *Social philosophy.* Englewood Cliffs, NJ: Prentice-Hall.

Feinberg, J., & Narveson, J. (1970). The nature and value of rights. *Journal of Value Inquiry, 4*(4), 243–260. http://dx.doi.org/10.1007/BF00137935

220 References

Field, S., Kuczera, M., & Pont, B. (2007). *No more failures: Ten steps to equity in education*. Paris: OECD.

Fineman, M. (1995). *The neutered mother, the sexual family and other twentieth-century tragedies*. New York: Routledge.

Finn, J.D., & Rock, D.A. (1997). Academic success among students at risk for school failure. *Journal of Applied Psychology, 82*(2), 221–234. http://dx.doi.org/10.1037/0021-9010.82.2.221 Medline:9109280

Flekkoy, M., & Kaufman, N. (1997). *The participation rights of the child: Rights and responsibilities in family and society*. London: Jessica Kingsley.

Flutter, J. (2006). "This place could help you learn": Student participation in creating better school environments. *Educational Review, 58*(2), 183–193. http://dx.doi.org/10.1080/00131910600584116

Forget-Dubois, N., Dionne, G., Lemelin, J.-P., Pérusse, D., Tremblay, R.E., & Boivin, M. (2009). Early child language mediates the relation between home environment and school readiness. *Child Development, 80*(3), 736–749. http://dx.doi.org/10.1111/j.1467-8624.2009.01294.x Medline:19489900

Frankel, S., & Daley, G. (2007). *An evaluation of after school programs provided by Beyond the Bell's partner agencies: Executive summary and synopsis of methodology and findings*. New York: Partnership for After School Education.

Fredricks, J., & Eccles, J. (2008). Participation in extracurricular activities in the middle school years: Are there developmental benefits for African American and European American Youth? *Journal of Youth and Adolescence, 37*(9), 1029–1043. http://dx.doi.org/10.1007/s10964-008-9309-4

Fredricks, J.A., & Eccles, J.S. (2006). Is extracurricular participation associated with beneficial outcomes? Concurrent and longitudinal relations. *Developmental Psychology, 42*(4), 698–713. http://dx.doi.org/10.1037/0012-1649.42.4.698 Medline:16802902

Freeman, M. (2007). Article 3: The best interests of the child. In A. Alen, J. Lanotte, E. Verhellen, F. Ang, E. Berghmans, & M. Verheyde (Eds.), *A commentary on the United Nations Convention on the Rights of the Child* (pp. 1–79). Leiden: Martinus Nijhoff.

Freeman, M. (1997). *The moral status of children*. The Hague: Kluwer Law.

Freeman, M. (1983). *The rights and wrongs of children*. London: Frances Pinter.

Friendly, M. (2007). Early learning and child care: Is Canada on track? In R.B. Howe and K. Covell (Eds.), *A question of commitment: Children's rights in Canada* (pp. 45–72). Waterloo, ON: Wilfrid Laurier University Press.

Fryer, R., Jr., & Levitt, S. (2004). Understanding the black-white test score gap in the first two years of school. *Review of Economics and Statistics, 86*(2), 447–464. http://dx.doi.org/10.1162/003465304323031049

Fullan, M. (2007). *The new meaning of educational change*. New York: Teachers College Press.

Fullan, M. (2001). *Leading in a culture of change*. San Francisco, CA: Jossey-Bass.

Fuller, B. (2007). *Standardized childhood: The political and cultural struggle over early education*. Stanford, CA: Stanford University Press.

Furlong, M.J., Whipple, A.D., St Jean, G., Simental, J., Soliz, A., & Punthuna, S. (2003). Multiple contexts of school engagement: Moving toward a unifying framework for educational research and practice. *California School Psychologist, 8*, 99–113.

Furrer, C., Skinner, E., Marchand, G., & Kindermann, T.A. (2006). Engagement vs. disaffection as central constructs in the dynamics of motivational development. Paper presented at the Society for Research on Adolescence, San Francisco.

Futernick, K. (2010). Incompetent teachers or dysfunctional systems? *Kappan Magazine, 92*(2), 59–64.

Gakidou, E., Cowling, K., Lozano, R., & Murray, C.J. (2010). Increased educational attainment and its effect on child mortality in 175 countries between 1970 and 2009: A systematic analysis. *Lancet, 376*(9745), 959–974. http://dx.doi.org/10.1016/S0140-6736(10)61257-3 Medline:20851260

Gardinier, M. (2010). Why should the United States ratify the Convention on the Rights of the Child? *Child Welfare, 89*(5), 7–13. Medline:21361153

Gassman-Pines, A., & Yoshikawa, H. (2006). The effects of antipoverty programs on children's cumulative level of poverty-related risk. *Developmental Psychology, 42*(6), 981–999. http://dx.doi.org/10.1037/0012-1649.42.6.981 Medline:17087535

Gathercole, S.E., Alloway, T.P., Kirkwood, H.J., Elliott, J.G., Holmes, J., & Hilton, K.A. (2008). Attentional and executive function behaviours in children with poor working memory. *Learning and Individual Differences, 18*(2), 214–223. http://dx.doi.org/10.1016/j.lindif.2007.10.003

Gathercole, S.E., Tiffany, C., Briscoe, J., Thorn, A., & ALSPAC team. (2005). Developmental consequences of poor phonological short-term memory function in childhood: A longitudinal study. *Journal of Child Psychology and Psychiatry, and Allied Disciplines, 46*(6), 598–611. http://dx.doi.org/10.1111/j.1469-7610.2004.00379.x Medline:15877766

Gazeley, L. (2010). The role of school exclusion processes in the re-production of social and educational disadvantage. *British Journal of Educational Studies, 58*(3), 293–309. http://dx.doi.org/10.1080/00071000903520843

Geary, D.C., Hoard, M.K., Byrd-Craven, J., Nugent, L., & Numtee, C. (2007). Cognitive mechanisms underlying achievement deficits in children with mathematical learning disability. *Child Development, 78*(4), 1343–1359. http://dx.doi.org/10.1111/j.1467-8624.2007.01069.x Medline:17650142

Geckova, A.M., Tavel, P., van Dijk, J.P., Abel, T., & Reijneveld, S.A. (2010). Factors associated with educational aspirations among adolescents: Cues to counteract socioeconomic differences? *BMC Public Health, 10*(1), 154–163. http://dx.doi.org/10.1186/1471-2458-10-154 Medline:20334644

Gershoff, E.T. (2002). Corporal punishment by parents and associated child behaviors and experiences: A meta-analytic and theoretical review. *Psychological Bulletin, 128,* 539–579.

Gersten, R., Jordan, N.C., & Flojo, J.R. (2005). Early identification and interventions for students with mathematics difficulties. *Journal of Learning Disabilities, 38,* 293–304.

Gilbert, J., & Graham, S. (2010). Teaching writing to elementary students in grades 4–6: A national survey. *Elementary School Journal, 110*(4), 494–518. http://dx.doi.org/10.1086/651193

Gillies, R. (2003). The behaviors, interactions, and perceptions of junior high school students during small group learning. *Journal of Educational Psychology, 95*(1), 137–147. http://dx.doi.org/10.1037/0022-0663.95.1.137

Glaeser, E., Ponzetto, G., & Shleifer, A. (2007). Why does democracy need education? *Journal of Economic Growth, 12*(2), 77–99. http://dx.doi.org/10.1007/s10887-007-9015-1

Glennerster, H. (2002). United Kingdom education 1997–2001. *Oxford Review of Economic Policy, 18*(2), 120–136. http://dx.doi.org/10.1093/oxrep/18.2.120

Goddard, R.D., Salloum, S.J., & Berebitsky, D. (2009). Trust as a mediator of the relationships between poverty, racial composition, and academic achievement: Evidence from Michigan's public elementary schools. *Educational Administration Quarterly, 45*(2), 292–311. http://dx.doi.org/10.1177/0013161X08330503

Goldhaber, D., & Anthony, E. (2007). Can teacher quality be effectively assessed? National Board Certification as a signal of effective teaching. *Review of Economics and Statistics, 89*(1), 134–150. http://dx.doi.org/10.1162/rest.89.1.134

Goldstein, J., Solnit, A., Goldstein, S., & Freud, A. (1986). *The best interests of the child: The least detrimental alternative.* New York: The Free Press.

Gonzales-DeHass, A.R., Willems, P.P., & Holbein, M.F.D. (2005). Examining the relationship between parental involvement and student motivation. *Educational Psychology Review, 17*(2), 99–123. http://dx.doi.org/10.1007/s10648-005-3949-7

Good, T., & McCaslin, M. (2008). What we learned about research on school reform: Considerations for practice and policy. *Teachers College Record, 110*(11), 2475–2495.

Goodman, D. (2000). Motivating people from privileged groups to support social justice. *Teachers College Record, 102*(6), 1061–1085. http://dx.doi.org/10.1111/0161-4681.00092

Grieve, A.M. (2010). Exploring the characteristics of "teachers for excellence": Teachers' own perceptions. *European Journal of Teacher Education, 33,*(3), 265–277. http://dx.doi.org/10.1080/02619768.2010.492854

Griffith, C.A., Lloyd, J.W., Lane, K.L., & Tankersley, M. (2010). Grade retention of students during grades K-8 predicts reading achievement and progress during secondary schooling. *Reading and Writing Quarterly, 26*(1), 51–66. http://dx.doi.org/10.1080/10573560903396967

Grissmer, D., Grimm, K.J., Aiyer, S.M., Murrah, W.M., & Steele, J.S. (2010). Fine motor skills and early comprehension of the world: Two new school readiness indicators. *Developmental Psychology, 46*(5), 1008–1017. http://dx.doi.org/10.1037/a0020104 Medline:20822219

Gruwell, E. (1999). *The Freedom Writers diary.* New York: Random House.

Gurr, D., Drysdale, L., & Mulford, B. (2006). Models of successful principal leadership. *School Leadership and Management, 26*(4), 371–395. http://dx.doi.org/10.1080/13632430600886921

Gutman, L.M., Sameroff, A.J., & Cole, R. (2003). Academic growth curve trajectories from 1st grade to 12th grade: Effects of multiple social risk factors and preschool child factors. *Developmental Psychology, 39*(4), 777–790. http://dx.doi.org/10.1037/0012-1649.39.4.777 Medline:12859129

Haberman, M. (2010). 11 consequences of failing to address the "pedagogy of poverty." *Phi Delta Kappan, 92*(2), 45.

Hair, E., Halle, T., Terry-Humen, E., Lavelle, B., & Calkins, J. (2006). Children's school readiness in the ECLS-K: Predictions to academic health, and social outcomes in first grade. *Early Childhood Research Quarterly, 21*(4), 431–454. http://dx.doi.org/10.1016/j.ecresq.2006.09.005

Hallahan, D.P., & Kauffman, J.M. (2003). *Exceptional learners: Introduction to special education* (9th ed.). Boston, MA: Allyn and Bacon.

Halvorsen, A., Lee, V.E., & Andrade, F.H. (2009). A mixed-method study of teachers' attitudes about teaching in urban and low-income schools. *Urban Education, 44*(2), 181–224. http://dx.doi.org/10.1177/0042085908318696

Hammarberg, T. (2008). The principle of the best interests of the child: What it means and what it demands from adults. Strasbourg: Council of Europe. https://wcd.coe.int/wcd/ViewDoc.jsp?id=1304019 Retrieved 13 Oct. 2010.

Hammarberg, T. (1990). The U.N. Convention on the Rights of the Child – and how to make it work. *Human Rights Quarterly, 12*(1), 97–105. http://dx.doi.org/10.2307/762167

Hammond, C., Linton, D., Smink, J., & Drew, S. (2007). *Dropout risk factors and exemplary programs.* Clemson University, SC: National Dropout Prevention Center.

Hanushek, E., & Woessmann, L. (2006). *Does educational tracking affect performance and inequality? Differences-in-differences evidence across countries.* Working Paper No. 1415. Cambridge, MA: National Bureau of Economic Research.

Harding, D.J. (2003). Counterfactual models of neighborhood effects: The effect of neighborhood poverty on dropping out and teenage pregnancy. *American Journal of Sociology, 109*(3), 676–719. http://dx.doi.org/10.1086/379217

Hargreaves, D. (1995). School culture, school effectiveness and school improvement. *School Effectiveness and School Improvement, 6*(1), 23–46. http://dx.doi.org/10.1080/0924345950060102

Harris, A. (2008). Distributed leadership: What we know. *Journal of Educational Administration, 46*(2), 172–188. http://dx.doi.org/10.1108/09578230810863253

Harris, A., & Allen, T. (2009). Ensuring every child matters: Issues and implications for school leadership. *School Leadership and Management, 29*(4), 337–352. http://dx.doi.org/10.1080/13632430903152021

Harrison, J., Lawson, T., & Wortley, A. (2005). Facilitating the professional learning of new teachers through critical reflection on practice during mentoring meetings. *European Journal of Teacher Education, 28*(3), 267–292. http://dx.doi.org/10.1080/02619760500269392

Hart, S.N. (1991). From property to person status: Historical perspective on children's rights. *American Psychologist, 46*(1), 53–59. http://dx.doi.org/10.1037/0003-066X.46.1.53

Hastings, R.P., & Bham, M.S. (2003). The relationship between student behavior patterns and teacher burnout. *School Psychology International, 24*(1), 115–127. http://dx.doi.org/10.1177/0143034303024001905

Haughey, M., Snart, F., & Da Costa, J. (2003). Teachers' instructional practices in small classes. *Alberta Journal of Educational Research, 49*(2), 181–197.

Hauser-Cram, P., Sirin, S.R., & Stipek, D. (2003). When teachers' and parents' values differ: Teachers' ratings of academic competence in children from low-income families. *Journal of Educational Psychology, 95*(4), 813–820. http://dx.doi.org/10.1037/0022-0663.95.4.813

Hayward, D., Das, J.P., & Janzen, T. (2007). Innovative programs for improvement in reading through cognitive enhancement: A remediation study of Canadian First Nations children. *Journal of Learning Disabilities, 40*(5), 443–457. http://dx.doi.org/10.1177/00222194070400050801 Medline:17915499

Helwig, C.C., Arnold, M.L., Tan, D., & Boyd, D. (2003). Chinese adolescents' reasoning about democratic and authority-based decision making in peer, family, and school contexts. *Child Development, 74*(3), 783–800. http://dx.doi.org/10.1111/1467-8624.00568 Medline:12795390

Helwig, C., & Jasiobedzka, U. (2001). The relation between law and morality: Children's reasoning about socially beneficial and unjust laws. *Child Development, 72* (5), 1382–1393. http://dx.doi.org/10.1016/j.cogdev.2007.06.003

Hemphill, S.A., McMorris, B.J., Toumbourou, J.W., Herrenkohl, T.I., Catalano, R.F., & Mathers, M. (2007). Rates of student-reported antisocial behavior, school suspensions, and arrests in Victoria, Australia, and Washington State, United States. *Journal of School Health, 77*(6), 303–311. http://dx.doi.org/10.1111/j.1746-1561.2007.00211.x Medline:17600587

Hemphill, S.A., Smith, R., Toumbourou, J.W., Herrenkohl, T.I., Catalano, R.F., McMorris, B.J., & Romaniuk, H. (2009). Modifiable determinants of youth violence in Australia and the United States: A longitudinal study. *Australian and New Zealand Journal of Criminology, 42*(3), 289–309. http://dx.doi.org/10.1375/acri.42.3.289 Medline:20204170

Hemphill, S.A., Toumbourou, J.W., Herrenkohl, T.I., McMorris, B.J., & Catalano, R.F. (2006). The effect of school suspensions and arrests on subsequent adolescent antisocial behavior in Australia and the United States. *Journal of Adolescent Health, 39*(5), 736–744. http://dx.doi.org/10.1016/j.jadohealth.2006.05.010 Medline:17046511

Herring, J. (2005). Farewell welfare? *Journal of Social Welfare and Family Law, 27*(2), 159–171. http://dx.doi.org/10.1080/09649060500195989

Hertzman, C., Siddiqi, A., Hertzman, E., Irwin, L.G., Vaghri, Z., Houweling, T., et al. (2010). Bucking the inequality gradient through early child development. *British Medical Journal.* www.bmj.com/content/340/bmj.c468.short?rss=1 Retrieved 6 Feb. 2011.

Hertzman, C., & Williams, R. (2009). Making early childhood count. *Canadian Medical Association Journal, 180*(1), 68–71. http://dx.doi.org/10.1503/cmaj.080512 Medline:19124792

Hess, F.M. (2007). No Child Left Behind: What the public thinks. American Enterprise Institute for Public Policy Research. http://www.aei.org/article/education/no-child-left-behind-what-the-public-thinks/ Retrieved 13 June 2012.

Hess, F.M. (2006). Accountability without angst? Public opinion and No Child Left Behind. *Harvard Educational Review, 76*(4), 587–610.

Heymann, S., Penrose, K., & Earle, A. (2006). Meeting children's needs: How does the United States measure up? *Merrill-Palmer Quarterly, 52*(2), 189–215. http://dx.doi.org/10.1353/mpq.2006.0014

Hill, N.E. (2001). Parenting and academic socialization as they relate to school readiness: The roles of ethnicity and family income. *Journal of Educational Psychology, 93*(4), 686–697. http://dx.doi.org/10.1037/0022-0663.93.4.686

Hill, N.E., & Tyson, D.F. (2009). Parental involvement in middle school: A meta-analytic assessment of the strategies that promote achievement. *Developmental Psychology*, 45(3), 740–763. http://dx.doi.org/10.1037/a0015362 Medline:19413429

Hodgkin, R., & Newell, P. (2007). *Implementation handbook for the Convention on the Rights of the Child*. New York: UNICEF.

Hodgson, D. (1996). The international human right to education and education concerning human rights. *International Journal of Children's Rights*, 4(3), 237–262. http://dx.doi.org/10.1163/157181896X00158

Hoglund, W.L., & Leadbeater, B.J. (2004). The effects of family, school, and classroom ecologies on changes in children's social competence and emotional and behavioral problems in first grade. *Developmental Psychology*, 40(4), 533–544. http://dx.doi.org/10.1037/0012-1649.40.4.533 Medline:15238041

Holt, M.K., Finkelhor, D., & Kaufman-Kantor, G.K. (2007). Multiple victimization experiences of urban elementary school students: Associations with psychosocial functioning and academic performance. *Child Abuse and Neglect*, 31(5), 503–515. http://dx.doi.org/10.1016/j.chiabu.2006.12.006 Medline:17537507

Hong, G., & Raudenbush, S.W. (2005). Effects of kindergarten retention policy on children's cognitive growth in reading and mathematics. *Educational Evaluation and Policy Analysis*, 27(3), 205–224. http://dx.doi.org/10.3102/01623737027003205

Hopkins, E.E. (2008). Classroom conditions to secure enjoyment and achievement: The pupils' voice – Listening to the voice of *Every Child Matters*. *Education*, 36, 3–13.

Howe, R.B., & Covell, K. (2010a). Toward the best interests of the child in education. *Education and Law Journal*, 20, 17–33.

Howe, R.B., & Covell, K. (2010b). Miseducating children about their rights. *Education. Citizenship and Social Justice*, 5(2), 91–102. http://dx.doi.org/10.1177/1746197910370724

Howe, R.B., & Covell, K. (2005). *Empowering children: Children's rights education as a pathway to citizenship*. Toronto: University of Toronto Press.

Howse, R.B., Lange, G., Farran, D.C., & Boyles, C.D. (2003). Motivation and self-regulation as predictors of achievement in economically disadvantaged young children. *Journal of Experimental Education*, 71(2), 151–174. http://dx.doi.org/10.1080/00220970309602061

HRiE (2009). Human Rights in Education, 2009 Report. www.rightsined.org.nz Retrieved 1 March 2011.

Huang, D., Leon, S., La Torre, D., & Mostafavi, S. (2008). *Examining the relationship between LA's BEST program attendance and academic achievement on LA's BEST students.* Technical Report No. 749, Los Angeles, CA: National Center for Research on Evaluation, Standards and Student Testing.

Huffman, J. (2003). The role of shared values and vision in creating professional learning communities. *NASSP Bulletin, 87*(637), 21–34. http://dx.doi.org/10.1177/019263650308763703

Human Rights Watch & American Civil Liberties Union (2009). *Impairing education: Corporal punishment of students with disabilities in US public schools.* www.hrw.org Retrieved 8 Feb. 2011.

Humphrey, N., & Ainscow, M. (2006). Transition club: Facilitating learning, participation and psychological adjustment during the transition to secondary school. *European Journal of Psychology of Education, 21*(3), 319–331. http://dx.doi.org/10.1007/BF03173419

Inglehart, R. (1990). *Culture shift in advanced industrial society.* Princeton, NJ: Princeton University Press.

Inglehart, R., & Welzel, C. (2005). *Modernization, cultural change, and democracy: The human development.* Cambridge: Cambridge University Press.

Jackson, A.P., Choi, J.K., & Bentler, P.M. (2009). Parenting efficacy and the early school adjustment of poor and near-poor black children. *Journal of Family Issues, 30*(10), 1339–1355. http://dx.doi.org/10.1177/0192513X09334603 Medline:19774203

Jang, H., Reeve, J., & Deci, E.L. (2010). Engaging students in learning activities: It is not autonomy support or structure, but autonomy support and structure. *Journal of Educational Psychology, 102*(3), 588–600. http://dx.doi.org/10.1037/a0019682

Janosz, M., Archambault, I., Morizot, J., & Pagani, L.S. (2008). School engagement trajectories and their differential predictive relations to dropout. *Journal of Social Issues, 64*(1), 21–40. http://dx.doi.org/10.1111/j.1540-4560.2008.00546.x

Jennings, G. (2003). An exploration of meaningful participation and caring relationships as contexts for school engagement. *California School Psychologist, 8,* 43–52.

Jeynes, W.H. (2007). The relationship between parental involvement and urban secondary school student academic achievement: A meta-analysis. *Urban Education, 42*(1), 82–110. http://dx.doi.org/10.1177/0042085906293818

Jimerson, S.R. (2001). Meta-analysis of grade retention research: Implications for practice in the 21st century. *School Psychology Review, 30*(3), 420–437.

Jimerson, S.R., Anderson, G.E., & Whipple, A.D. (2002). Winning the battle and losing the war: Examining the relationship between grade retention and dropping out of high school. *Psychology in the Schools, 39*(4), 441–457. http://dx.doi.org/10.1002/pits.10046

Jimerson, S.R., Campos, E., & Greif, J.L. (2003). Toward an understanding of definitions and measures of school engagement. *California School Psychologist, 8*, 43–52.

Jimerson, S.R., & Kauffman, A.M. (2003). Reading, writing, and retention: A primer on grade retention research. *Reading Teacher, 56*(7), 622–635.

Johnson, M.K., Crosnoe, R., & Elder, G.H. (2001). Students' attachment and academic engagement: The role of ethnicity. *Sociology of Education, 74*(4), 318–340. http://dx.doi.org/10.2307/2673138

Jones, H.A., & Chronis-Tuscano, A. (2008). Efficacy of teacher in-service training for attention-deficit/hyperactivity disorder. *Psychology in the Schools, 45*(10), 918–929. http://dx.doi.org/10.1002/pits.20342

Joseph, R. (1999). Environmental influences on neural plasticity, the limbic system, emotional development and attachment: A review. *Child Psychiatry and Human Development, 29*(3), 189–208. http://dx.doi.org/10.1023/A:1022660923605 Medline:10080962

Jussim, L., & Harber, K.D. (2005). Teacher expectations and self-fulfilling prophecies: Knowns and unknowns, resolved and unresolved controversies. *Personality and Social Psychology Review, 9*(2), 131–155. http://dx.doi.org/10.1207/s15327957pspr0902_3 Medline:15869379

Kalil, A., & Ziol-Guest, K.M. (2008). Teacher support, school goal structures, and teenage mothers' school engagement. *Youth and Society, 39*(4), 524–548. http://dx.doi.org/10.1177/0044118X07301001

Kaplan, D., & Walpole, S. (2005). A stage-sequential model of reading transitions: Evidence from the early childhood longitudinal study. *Journal of Educational Psychology, 97*(4), 551–563. http://dx.doi.org/10.1037/0022-0663.97.4.551

Karoly, L., Kilburn, M.R., & Cannon, J. (2005). *Early childhood interventions: Proven results, future promise.* Santa Monica, CA: Rand Corporation.

Katz, M. (1996). *In the shadow of the poor house: A social history of welfare in America.* New York: Basic Books.

Keltikangas-Järvinen, L., Jokela, M., Hintsanen, M., Salo, J., Hintsa, T., Alatupa, S., & Lehtimäki, T. (2010). Does genetic background moderate the association between parental education and school achievement? *Genes, Brain and Behavior, 9*(3), 318–324. http://dx.doi.org/10.1111/j.1601-183X.2009.00561.x Medline:20039947

Kennedy, R.K. (2010). Comparison of Montessori, Waldorf and Reggio Emilia. *Private School Review.* www.privateschoolreview Retrieved 29 Jan. 2012.

Kim-Cohen, J., Arseneault, L., Caspi, A., Tomás, M.P., Taylor, A., & Moffitt, T.E. (2005). Validity of DSM-IV conduct disorder in 4½–5-year-old children: A longitudinal epidemiological study. *American Journal of Psychiatry*, *162*(6), 1108–1117. http://dx.doi.org/10.1176/appi.ajp.162.6.1108 Medline:15930059

Kishiyama, M.M., Boyce, W.T., Jimenez, A.M., Perry, L.M., & Knight, R.T. (2009). Socioeconomic disparities affect prefrontal function in children. *Journal of Cognitive Neuroscience*, *21*(6), 1106–1115. http://dx.doi.org/10.1162/jocn.2009.21101 Medline:18752394

Kiuhara, S.A., Graham, S., & Hawken, L.S. (2009). Teaching writing to high school students: A national survey. *Journal of Educational Psychology*, *101*(1), 136–160. http://dx.doi.org/10.1037/a0013097

Klassen, R.M., & Chiu, M.M. (2010). Effects on teachers' self-efficacy and job satisfaction: Teacher gender, years of experience, and job stress. *Journal of Educational Psychology*, *102*(3), 741–756. http://dx.doi.org/10.1037/a0019237

Klem, A.M., & Connell, J.P. (2004). Relationships matter: Linking teacher support to student engagement and achievement. *Journal of School Health*, *74*(7), 262–273. http://dx.doi.org/10.1111/j.1746-1561.2004.tb08283.x Medline:15493703

Klibanoff, R.S., Levine, S.C., Huttenlocher, J., Vasilyeva, M., & Hedges, L.V. (2006). Preschool children's mathematical knowledge: The effect of teacher "math talk." *Developmental Psychology*, *42*(1), 59–69. http://dx.doi.org/10.1037/0012-1649.42.1.59 Medline:16420118

Koh, C., Wang, C.K.J., Tan, O.S., Liu, W.C., & Ee, J. (2009). Bridging the gaps between students' perceptions of group project work and their teachers' expectations. *Journal of Educational Research*, *102*(5), 333–348. http://dx.doi.org/10.3200/JOER.102.5.333-348

Kokkinos, C.M. (2007). Job stressors, personality and burnout in primary school teachers. *British Journal of Educational Psychology*, *77*(1), 229–243. http://dx.doi.org/10.1348/000709905X90344 Medline:17411497

Kokko, K., Tremblay, R.E., Lacourse, E., Nagin, D.S., & Vitaro, F. (2006). Trajectories of prosocial behavior and physical aggression in middle childhood: Links to adolescent school dropout and physical violence. *Journal of Research on Adolescence*, *16*(3), 403–428. http://dx.doi.org/10.1111/j.1532-7795.2006.00500.x

Könings, K.D., Brand-Gruwel, S., & van Merrienboer, J.J.G. (2010). An approach to participatory instructional design in secondary education: An exploratory study. *Educational Research*, *52*(1), 45–59. http://dx.doi.org/10.1080/00131881003588204

Konishi, C., Hymel, S., Zumbo, B.D., & Li, Z. (2010). Do school bullying and student-teacher relationships matter for academic achievement? *Canadian Journal of School Psychology, 25*(1), 19–39.

Konstantopoulos, S. (2009). Effects of teachers on minority and disadvantaged students' achievement in the early grades. *Elementary School Journal, 110*(1), 92–113. http://dx.doi.org/10.1086/598845

Koponen, T., Aunola, K., Ahonen, T., & Nurmi, J.E. (2007). Cognitive predictors of single-digit and procedural calculation skills and their covariation with reading skill. *Journal of Experimental Child Psychology, 97*(3), 220–241. http://dx.doi.org/10.1016/j.jecp.2007.03.001 Medline:17560969

Krajewski, K., & Schneider, W. (2009). Early development of quantity to number-work linkages as a precursor of mathematical school achievement and mathematical difficulties: Findings from a four-year longitudinal study. *Learning and Instruction, 19*(6), 513–526. http://dx.doi.org/10.1016/j.learninstruc.2008.10.002

Kucharski, G.A., Rust, J.O., & Ring, T.R. (2005). Evaluation of the Ecological, Futures, and Global (EFG) curriculum: A project-based approach. *Education, 125*(4), 652–668.

Kuklinski, M.R., & Weinstein, R.S. (2001). Classroom and developmental differences in a path model of teacher expectancy effects. *Child Development, 72*(5), 1554–1578. http://dx.doi.org/10.1111/1467-8624.00365 Medline:11699687

LaFave, L. (1989). Origins of the evolution of the "best interests of the child" standard. *South Dakota Law Review, 34*, 459–470.

Lagana-Riordan, C., & Aguilar, J. (2009). What's missing from No Child Left Behind? A policy analysis from a social work perspective. *Children and Schools, 31*(3), 135–144. http://dx.doi.org/10.1093/cs/31.3.135

Lantz, P.M., Lynch, J.W., House, J.S., Lepkowski, J.M., Mero, R.P., Musick, M.A., & Williams, D.R. (2001). Socioeconomic disparities in health change in a longitudinal study of U.S. adults: The role of health-risk behaviors. *Social Science and Medicine, 53*(1), 29–40. http://dx.doi.org/10.1016/S0277-9536(00)00319-1 Medline:11380160

Lareau, A. (2003). *Unequal childhoods: Class, race, and family life.* Berkeley, CA: University of California Press.

Lauen, D.L. (2007). Contextual explanations of school choice. *Sociology of Education, 80*(3), 179–209. http://dx.doi.org/10.1177/003804070708000301

Lee, S.M., Brescia, W., & Kissinger, D. (2009). Computer use and academic development in secondary schools. *Computers in the Schools, 26*(3), 224–235. http://dx.doi.org/10.1080/07380560903095204

Lee, V.E., & Burkham, D.T. (2002). *Inequality at the starting gate: Social background differences in achievement as children begin school.* Washington, DC: Economic Policy Institute.

Lee, M., & Friedrich, T. (2007). The "smaller" the school, the better? The Smaller Learning Communities (SLC) program in the U.S. high schools. *Improving Schools, 10* (3), 261–282.

Lee, V.E., & Loeb, S. (2000). School size in Chicago elementary schools: Effects on teachers' attitudes and student achievement. *American Educational Research Journal, 37*(1), 3–32.

Leithwood, K., Harris, A., & Hopkins, D. (2008). Seven strong claims about successful school leadership. *School Leadership and Management, 28*(1), 27–42. http://dx.doi.org/10.1080/13632430701800060

Lengua, L.J., Honorado, E., & Bush, N.R. (2007). Contextual risk and parenting as predictors of effortful control and social competence in preschool children. *Journal of Applied Developmental Psychology, 28*(1), 40–55. http://dx.doi.org/10.1016/j.appdev.2006.10.001 Medline:21687825

Leventhal, T., Fauth, R.C., & Brooks-Gunn, J. (2005). Neighborhood poverty and public policy: A 5-year follow-up of children's educational outcomes in the New York City moving to opportunity demonstration. *Developmental Psychology, 41*(6), 933–952. http://dx.doi.org/10.1037/0012-1649.41.6.933 Medline:16351338

Levin, B. (2010a). International comparisons. *Phi Delta Kappan, 92*(4), 95–96.

Levin, B. (2010b). Governments and education reform: Some lessons from the last 50 years. *Journal of Education Policy, 25*(6), 739–747. http://dx.doi.org/10.1080/02680939.2010.523793

Levin, B. (2007). Schools, poverty and the achievement gap. *Phi Delta Kappan, 89*(1), 75–76.

Levin, B. (2006). Schools in challenging circumstances: A reflection on what we know and what we need to know. *School Effectiveness and School Improvement, 17*(4), 399–407. http://dx.doi.org/10.1080/09243450600743459

Levin, B. (2003). *Approaches to equity in policy for lifelong learning.* Paris: OECD.

Levine, T. (2010). What research tells us about the impact and challenges of Smaller Learning Communities. *Peabody Journal of Education, 85*(3), 276–289. http://dx.doi.org/10.1080/0161956X.2010.491431

Li, Y., & Lerner, R.M. (2011). Trajectories of school engagement during adolescence: Implications for grades, depression, delinquency, and substance use. *Developmental Psychology, 47*(1), 233–247. http://dx.doi.org/10.1037/a0021307 Medline:21244162

Lieberman, A., Falk, B., & Alexander, L. (1995). A culture in the making: Leadership in learner-centered schools. In J. Oakes & K. Huner Quartz (Eds.), *Creating new educational communities* (pp. 108–129). Chicago, IL: University of Chicago Press.

Liew, J., Chen, Q., & Hughes, J.N. (2010). Child effortful control, teacher-student relationships, and achievement in academically at-risk children:

Additive and interactive effects. *Early Childhood Research Quarterly*, 25(1), 51–64. http://dx.doi.org/10.1016/j.ecresq.2009.07.005 Medline:20161421

Lightfoot, L. (2009). Cinderella gets the politically correct treatment as pupils learn about their rights. www.telegraph.co.uk/education Retrieved 17 Aug. 2009.

Li-Grining, C.P. (2007). Effortful control among low-income preschoolers in three cities: Stability, change, and individual differences. *Developmental Psychology*, 43(1), 208–221. http://dx.doi.org/10.1037/0012-1649.43.1.208 Medline:17201520

Lindsay, G., Dockrell, J.E., & Strand, S. (2007). Longitudinal patterns of behaviour problems in children with specific speech and language difficulties: Child and contextual factors. *British Journal of Educational Psychology*, 77(4), 811–828. http://dx.doi.org/10.1348/000709906X171127 Medline:17173708

Lloyd, J.E.V., & Hertzman, C. (2009). From Kindergarten readiness to fourth-grade assessment: Longitudinal analysis with linked population data. *Social Science and Medicine*, 68(1), 111–123. http://dx.doi.org/10.1016/j.socscimed.2008.09.063 Medline:18986743

Lochner, L., & Moretti, E. (2004). The effect of education on crime. *American Economic Review*, 94(1), 155–189. http://dx.doi.org/10.1257/000282804322970751

Lombaerts, K., & Engels, N. (2009). Determinants of teachers' recognitions of self-regulated learning practices in elementary education. *Journal of Educational Research*, 102(3), 163–173.

Looney, M. (2011). Developing high-quality teachers: Teacher evaluation for improvement. *European Journal of Teacher Education*, 46(4), 440–455.

Lou, Y., Abrami, P.C., Spence, J.C., Poulsen, C., Chambers, B., & d'Apolonia, S. (1996). Within-class grouping: A meta-analysis. *Review of Educational Research*, 66, 423–458.

Low, M.D., Low, B.J., Baumler, E.R., & Huynh, P.T. (2005). Can education policy be health policy? Implications of research on the social determinants of health. *Journal of Health Politics, Policy and Law*, 30(6), 1131–1162. http://dx.doi.org/10.1215/03616878-30-6-1131 Medline:16481310

Lundy, L. (2007). Voice is not enough: Conceptualizing article 12 of the United Nations Convention on the Rights of the Child. *British Educational Research Journal*, 33(6), 927–942. http://dx.doi.org/10.1080/01411920701657033

Lundy, L. (2006). Mainstreaming children's rights in, to and through education in a society emerging from conflict. *International Journal of Children's Rights*, 14(4), 339–362. http://dx.doi.org/10.1163/157181806779050186

Lundy, L., & McEvoy, L. (2009). Developing outcomes for educational services: A children's rights-based approach. *Effective Education, 1*(1), 43–60. http://dx.doi.org/10.1080/19415530903044050

Lyman, L., & Villani, C. (2004). *Best leadership practices for high-poverty schools*. Lanham, MD: Scarecrow.

Maag, J.W. (2002). Rewarded by punishment: Reflections on the disuse of positive reinforcement in school. *Exceptional Children, 67*, 173–186.

Magnuson, K.A., Meyers, M.K., Ruhm, C.J., & Waldfogel, J. (2004). Inequality in preschool education and school readiness. *American Educational Research Journal, 41*(1), 115–157. http://dx.doi.org/10.3102/00028312041001115

Malecki, C.K., & Demaray, M.K. (2006). Social support as a buffer in the relationship between socioeconomic status and academic performance. *School Psychology Quarterly, 21*(4), 375–395. http://dx.doi.org/10.1037/h0084129

Marks, A.K., & Coll, C.G. (2007). Psychological and demographic correlates of early academic skill development among American Indian and Alaska Native youth: A growth modeling study. *Developmental Psychology, 43*(3), 663–674. http://dx.doi.org/10.1037/0012-1649.43.3.663 Medline:17484578

Marmot, M. (2004). *The status syndrome: How social standing affects our health and longevity*. New York: Henry Holt.

Marmot, M., & Wilkinson, R. (2006). *Social determinants of health*. Oxford: Oxford University Press.

Marshall, K. (1997). *Children's rights in the balance: The participation-protection debate*. Edinburgh: Stationery Office.

Martin, A.J., & Marsh, H.W. (2006). Academic resilience and its psychological and educational correlates: A construct validity approach. *Psychology in the Schools, 43*(3), 267–281. http://dx.doi.org/10.1002/pits.20149

Martin, C., & Evaldsson, A.C. (2012). Affordances for participation: Children's appropriation of rules in a Reggio Emilia school. *Mind, Culture, and Activity, 19*(1), 51–74. http://dx.doi.org/10.1080/10749039.2011.632049

Mason, E. (2006). The best interests of the child. In J. Todres, M. Wojcik, & C. Revaz (Eds.), *The U.N. Convention on the Rights of the Child: An analysis of treaty provisions and implications of U.S. ratification* (pp. 121–126). Ardsley, NY: Transnational Publishers. http://dx.doi.org/10.1163/ej.9781571053633.i-376.45

Masten, A.S., Herbers, J.E., Cutuli, J.J., & Lafavor, T.L. (2008). Promoting competence and resilience in the school context. *Professional School Counseling, 12*(2), 76–84. http://dx.doi.org/10.5330/PSC.n.2010-12.76

Mayer, G.R. (2001). Antisocial behavior: Its causes and prevention within our schools. *Education and Treatment of Children, 24*, 467–478.

Mayer, G.R., & Butterworth, T. (1979). A preventive approach to school violence and vandalism: An experimental study. *Personnel and Guidance Journal, 57*(9), 436–441. http://dx.doi.org/10.1002/j.2164-4918.1979.tb05431.x

Mayer, G.R., Butterworth, T., Nafpaktitis, M., & Sulzer-Azaroff, B. (1983). Preventing school vandalism and improving discipline: A three-year study. *Journal of Applied Behavior Analysis, 16*(4), 355–369. http://dx.doi.org/10.1901/jaba.1983.16-355 Medline:6654768

McCain, M., Mustard, J.F., & Shankar, S. (2007). *Early years study 2: Putting science into action.* Toronto: Council for Early Child Development.

McCartney, K., Dearing, E., Taylor, B.A., & Bub, K.L. (2007). Quality child care supports the achievement of low-income children: Direct and indirect pathways through caregiving and the home environment. *Journal of Applied Developmental Psychology, 28*(5–6), 411–426. http://dx.doi.org/10.1016/j.appdev.2007.06.010 Medline:19578561

McClelland, M.M., Cameron, C.E., Connor, C.M., Farris, C.L., Jewkes, A.M., & Morrison, F.J. (2007). Links between behavioral regulation and preschoolers' literacy, vocabulary, and math skills. *Developmental Psychology, 43*(4), 947–959. http://dx.doi.org/10.1037/0012-1649.43.4.947 Medline:17605527

McCoy, E. (1988). Childhood through the ages. In K. Finsterbusch (Ed.), *Sociology 88/89* (pp. 44–47). Guildford, CT: Dushkin.

McCrory, E., De Brito, S.A., & Viding, E. (2010). Research review: The neurobiology and genetics of maltreatment and adversity. *Journal of Child Psychology and Psychiatry, and Allied Disciplines, 51*(10), 1079–1095. http://dx.doi.org/10.1111/j.1469-7610.2010.02271.x Medline:20546078

McCrystal, P., Higgins, K., Percy, A., & Thornton, M. (2005). Adolescent substance abuse among young people excluded from school in Belfast. *Drugs: Education Policy and Prevention, 12*(2), 101–112. http://dx.doi.org/10.1080/09687630512331323503

McCrystal, P., Percy, A., & Higgins, K. (2007). Exclusion and marginalization in adolescence: The experience of school exclusion on drug use and antisocial behavior. *Journal of Youth Studies, 10*(1), 35–54. http://dx.doi.org/10.1080/13676260701196103

McFarland, S., & Mathews, M. (2005). Who cares about human rights? *Political Psychology, 26*(3), 365–385. http://dx.doi.org/10.1111/j.1467-9221.2005.00422.x

McGill-Franzen, A., Zmach, C., Solic, K., & Zeig, J.L. (2006). The confluence of two policy mandates: Core reading programs and third-grade retention in Florida. *Elementary School Journal, 107*(1), 67–91. http://dx.doi.org/10.1086/509527

McGrath, H., & Noble, T. (2010). Supporting positive pupil relationships: Research to practice. *Educational and Child Psychology, 27*(6), 79–90.

McInnes, K., Howard, J., Miles, G.E., & Crowley, K. (2009). Behavioral differences exhibited by children when practicing a task under formal and playful conditions. *Educational and Child Psychology, 26*(2), 31–39.

McIntyre, D., Pedder, D., & Rudduck, J. (2005). Pupil voice: Comfortable and uncomfortable learnings for teachers. *Research Papers in Education, 20*(2), 149–168. http://dx.doi.org/10.1080/02671520500077970

McKay, M.M., Gonzales, J., Quintana, E., Kim, L., & Abdul-Adil, J. (1999). Multiple family groups: An alternative for reducing disruptive behavioral difficulties of urban children. *Research on Social Work Practice, 9*(5), 593–607. http://dx.doi.org/10.1177/104973159900900505

McLeskey, J., & Billingsley, B.S. (2008). How does the quality and stability of the teaching force influence the research-to-practice gap? *Remedial and Special Education, 29*(5), 293–305. http://dx.doi.org/10.1177/0741932507312010

McNeely, C.A., Nonnemaker, J.M., & Blum, R.W. (2002). Promoting school connectedness: Evidence from the National Longitudinal Study of adolescent health. *Journal of School Health, 72*(4), 138–146. http://dx.doi.org/10.1111/j.1746-1561.2002.tb06533.x Medline:12029810

McPartland, E. (2010). *The best interests of the child: Interpreting Irish child legislation.* Dublin: Gil and Macmillan.

Melton, G. (2002). Starting a new generation of research. In B. Bottoms, M. Kovera, & B. McAuliff (Eds.), *Children, social science and the law* (pp. 449–453). Cambridge: Cambridge University Press. http://dx.doi.org/10.1017/CBO9780511500114.017

Melton, G.B. (1996). The child's right to a family environment: Why children's rights and family values are compatible. *American Psychologist, 51*(12), 1234–1238. http://dx.doi.org/10.1037/0003-066X.51.12.1234 Medline:8962531

Merton, R.K. (1948). The self-fulfilling prophecy. *Antioch Review, 8*(2), 193–210. http://dx.doi.org/10.2307/4609267

Metheny, J., McWhirter, E.H., & O'Neil, M.E. (2008). Measuring perceived teacher support and its influence on adolescent career development. *Journal of Career Assessment, 16*(2), 218–237. http://dx.doi.org/10.1177/1069072707313198

Ministry of Children and Youth Services. (Ontario). (2008). Full-day kindergarten and child care integration: A look at promising practices in Ontario. http://eyeonkids.ca/docs/files/promisingpractices_finalreport_14july08.pdf Retrieved 2 Feb. 2012.

Mirowsky, J., & Ross, C. (2003). *Education, social status, and health.* New York: Aldine de Gruyter.

Mistry, R.E., Benner, A.D., Biesanz, J.C., Clark, S.L., & Howes, C. (2010). Family and social risk, and parental investments during the early childhood years as predictors of low-income children's school readiness outcomes. *Early Childhood Research Quarterly, 25*(4), 432–449. http://dx.doi.org/10.1016/j.ecresq.2010.01.002

Mistry, R.S., White, E.S., Benner, A.D., & Huynh, V.W. (2009). A longitudinal study of the simultaneous influence of mothers' and teachers' educational expectations on low-income youth's academic achievement. *Journal of Youth and Adolescence, 38*(6), 826–838. http://dx.doi.org/10.1007/s10964-008-9300-0 Medline:19636784

Mnookin, R., & Szwed, E. (1983). The best interests syndrome as the allocation of power in child care. In H. Geach & E. Szwed (Eds.), *Providing civil justice for the child* (pp. 7–20). London: Edward Arnold.

Montt, G. (2011). Cross-national differences in educational achievement inequality. *Sociology of Education, 84*(1), 49–68. http://dx.doi.org/10.1177/0038040710392717

Moolenar, N.M., Sleegers, P.J.C., & Daly, A.J. (2012). Teaming up: Linking collaboration networks, collective efficacy, and student achievement. *Teaching and Teacher Education, 28*(2), 251–262. http://dx.doi.org/10.1016/j.tate.2011.10.001

Morgan, M., Ludlow, L., Kitching, K., O'Leary, M., & Clarke, A. (2010). What makes teachers tick? Sustaining events in new teachers' lives. *British Educational Research Journal, 36*(2), 191–208. http://dx.doi.org/10.1080/01411920902780972

Mortenson, G. (2009). *Stones into schools: Promoting peace through education in Afghanistan and Pakistan.* New York: Penguin.

Moss, P., & Petrie, P. (2002). *From children's services to children's spaces: Public policy, children and childhood.* London: Routledge-Falmer.

Murphy, L.W., Vagins, D.J., & Parker, A. (2010). Statement before the house education and labor subcommittee on healthy families and communities. Hearing on "Corporal punishment in schools and its effect on academic success." www.hrw.org Retrieved 4 Feb. 2010.

Murray, A., & Straus, M. (2003). Corporal punishment and academic achievement. Scores of young children: A longitudinal study. http://pubpages.unh.edu Retrieved 18 Oct. 2009.

Murray, C. (2009). Parent and teacher relationships as predictors of school engagement and functioning among low-income urban youth. *Journal of Early Adolescence, 29*(3), 376–404. http://dx.doi.org/10.1177/0272431608322940

Murray, C.S., Woodruff, A.L., & Vaughn, S. (2010). First-grade student retention within a 3-tier reading framework. *Reading and Writing Quarterly, 26*(1), 26–50. http://dx.doi.org/10.1080/10573560903396934

NCES. (2006). *National Center for Education Statistics. Base year to fourth follow-up data file user's manual.* Washington, D.C: Office of Educational Research and Improvement, U.S. Department of Education.

NCLB (2002). No Child Left Behind Act of 2001, Pub.L.No. 107–110, 114 Stat. 1425. http://www2.ed.gov/policy/elsec/leg/eseal02-110 Retrieved 13 June 2012.

Neuman, S.B. (2009). *Changing the odds for children at risk.* New York: Teachers College Press.

New, R.S. (2007). Reggio Emilia as cultural activity theory in practice. *Theory into Practice, 46*(1), 5–13. http://dx.doi.org/10.1080/00405840709336543

Newman, K., & Chin, M. (2003). High stakes, time in poverty, testing, and the children of the working poor. *Qualitative Sociology, 26*(1), 3–34. http://dx.doi.org/10.1023/A:1021487219440

Newman, M., & Thomas, P. (2008). Student participation in school design: One school's approach to student engagement in the BSF process. *CoDesign, 4*(4), 237–251. http://dx.doi.org/10.1080/15710880802524938

NICHD Early Child Care Research Network & Duncan, G. (2003) Modeling the impacts of child care quality on children's preschool cognitive development. *Child Development 74*, 1454–1475.

Niesyn, M.E. (2009). Strategies to success: Evidence-based instructional teaching practices for students with emotional and behavioral disorders. *Preventing School Failure, 53*(4), 227–234. http://dx.doi.org/10.3200/PSFL.53.4.227-234

Noble, K.G., Farah, M.J., & McCandliss, B.D. (2006a). Socioeconomic background modulates cognition-achievement relationships in reading. *Cognitive Development, 21*(3), 349–368. http://dx.doi.org/10.1016/j.cogdev.2006.01.007

Noble, K.G., McCandliss, B.D., & Farah, M.J. (2007). Socioeconomic gradients predict individual differences in neurocognitive abilities. *Developmental Science, 10*(4), 464–480. http://dx.doi.org/10.1111/j.1467-7687.2007.00600.x Medline:17552936

Noble, K.G., Norman, M.F., & Farah, M.J. (2005). Neurocognitive correlates of socioeconomic status in kindergarten children. *Developmental Science, 8*(1), 74–87. http://dx.doi.org/10.1111/j.1467-7687.2005.00394.x Medline:15647068

Noble, K.G., Wolmetz, M.E., Ochs, L.G., Farah, M.J., & McCandliss, B.D. (2006b). Brain-behavior relationships in reading acquisition are modulated by socioeconomic factors. *Developmental Science, 9*(6), 642–654. http://dx.doi.org/10.1111/j.1467-7687.2006.00542.x Medline:17059461

Nores, M., & Barnett, W.S. (2010). Benefits of early childhood interventions across the world: (Under)investing in the very young.

Economics of Education Review, 29(2), 271–282. http://dx.doi.org/10.1016/j.
econedurev.2009.09.001

OECD [Organization of Economic Cooperation and Development]. (2010a).
Education at a glance 2010. http://www.oecd.org/dataoecd/46/24/45925258.
pdf Retrieved 15 Oct. 2010.

OECD. (2010b). *Overcoming school failure: Policies that work.* Paris: OECD.

OECD. (2010c). *Family Database: Public spending on childcare and early education.*
http://www.oecd.org/ff/?404;http://www.oecd.org/els/social/family/data-
base Retrieved 13 June 2012.

OECD. (2008). *Growing unequal? Income distribution and poverty in OECD countries.* Paris: OECD.

OECD. (2006). *Starting strong II: Early childhood education and care – Final report
of the thematic review of early childhood education and care.* Paris: OECD.

OECD PISA (2011). Programme for International Student Assessment: PISA
2003 results, 2006 results, 2009 results. http://www.pisa.oecd.org has been
redirected to http://www.pisa.oecd.org/redirect/ Retrieved 13 June 2012.

Office of the Children's Commissioner of New Zealand. (2008). *A fair go for all
children.* Wellington: Office of the Children's Commissioner.

Office of the High Commissioner for Human Rights (2011). Treaty body database: Committee on the Rights of the Child. http://tb.ohchr.org/default.aspx
Retrieved 20 April 2011.

Olsen, G. (2002). *The politics of the welfare state: Canada, Sweden, and the United
States.* Oxford: Oxford University Press.

Olweus, D., & Limber, S.P. (2010). Bullying in school: Evaluation and dis-
semination of the Olweus Bullying Prevention Program. *American
Journal of Orthopsychiatry, 80*(1), 124–134. http://dx.doi.org/10.1111/j.1939-
0025.2010.01015.x Medline:20397997

Opfer, V.D., & Pedder, D. (2010). Access to continuous professional development by teachers in England. *Curriculum Journal, 21*(4), 453–471. http://
dx.doi.org/10.1080/09585176.2010.529680

Osler, A., & Starkey, H. (2010). *Teachers and human rights education.* Stoke on
Trent: Trentham Books.

Ou, S.R., & Reynolds, A.J. (2008). Predictors of educational attainment in the
Chicago longitudinal study. *School Psychology Quarterly, 23*(2), 199–229.
http://dx.doi.org/10.1037/1045-3830.23.2.199

Oyserman, D., Brickman, D., & Rhodes, M. (2007). School success, possible
selves and parent school involvement. *Family Relations, 56*(5), 479–489.
http://dx.doi.org/10.1111/j.1741-3729.2007.00475.x

Panayiotopoulos, C., & Kerfoot, M. (2007). Early intervention and prevention
for children excluded from primary schools. *International Journal of Inclusive
Education, 11*(1), 59–80. http://dx.doi.org/10.1080/13603110500392882

Pancer, S.M., Pratt, M., Hunsberger, B., & Alisar, S. (2007). Community and political involvement in adolescence: What distinguishes the activists from the uninvolved. *Journal of Community Psychology, 35*(6), 741–759. http://dx.doi.org/10.1002/jcop.20176

Passolunghi, M.C., Vercelloni, B., & Schadee, H. (2007). The precursors of mathematics learning: Working memory, phonological ability and numerical competence. *Cognitive Development, 22*(2), 165–184. http://dx.doi.org/10.1016/j.cogdev.2006.09.001

Patall, E.A., Cooper, H., & Robinson, J.C. (2008). Parent involvement in homework: A research synthesis. *Review of Educational Research, 78*(4), 1039–1101. http://dx.doi.org/10.3102/0034654308325185

Peck, S.C., Roeser, R.W., Zarrett, N., & Eccles, J.S. (2008). Exploring the roles of extracurricular activity quantity and quality in the educational resilience of vulnerable adolescents: Variable- and pattern-centered approaches. *Journal of Social Issues, 64*(1), 135–156. http://dx.doi.org/10.1111/j.1540-4560.2008.00552.x Medline:19543445

Peterson, K., & Deal, T. (2009). *The shaping school culture fieldbook.* San Francisco, CA: Jossey-Bass.

Petras, H., Masyn, K.E., Buckley, J.A., Ialongo, N.S., & Kellam, S. (2011). Who is most at risk for school removal? A multilevel discrete-time survival analysis of individual- and context-level influences. *Journal of Educational Psychology, 103*(1), 223–237. http://dx.doi.org/10.1037/a0021545

Pettit, G.S., Yu, T., Dodge, K.A., & Bates, J.E. (2009). A developmental process analysis of cross-generational continuity of educational attainment. *Merrill-Palmer Quarterly, 55*(3), 250–284.

Phillips, B.M., & Lonigan, J. (2009). Variations in the home literacy environment of preschool children: A cluster analytic approach. *Scientific Studies of Reading, 13*(2), 146–174. http://dx.doi.org/10.1080/10888430902769533

Pianta, R.C., La Paro, K.M., Payne, C., Cox, M.J., & Bradley, R. (2002). The relation of kindergarten classroom environment to teacher, family, and school characteristics and child outcomes. *Elementary School Journal, 102*(3), 225–238. http://dx.doi.org/10.1086/499701

Plunkett, S.W., Henry, C.S., Houltberg, B.J., Sands, T., & Abarca-Mortensen, S. (2008). Academic support by significant others and educational resilience in Mexican-origin ninth grade students from intact families. *Journal of Early Adolescence, 28*(3), 333–355. http://dx.doi.org/10.1177/0272431608314660

Pollak, S.D., & Tolley-Schell, S.A. (2003). Selective attention to facial emotion in physically abused children. *Journal of Abnormal Psychology, 112*(3), 323–338. http://dx.doi.org/10.1037/0021-843X.112.3.323 Medline:12943012

Pollak, S.D., Vardi, S., Putzer Bechner, A.M., & Curtin, J.J. (2005). Physically abused children's regulation of attention in response to hostility.

Child Development, 76(5), 968–977. http://dx.doi.org/10.1111/j.1467-8624.2005.00890.x Medline:16149995

Pong, S., Johnston, J., & Chen, V. (2010). Authoritarian parenting and Asian adolescent school performance: Insights from the U.S. and Taiwan. *International Journal of Behavioral Development, 34*(1), 62–72. http://dx.doi.org/10.1177/0165025409345073

Powell-Smith, K.A., Stoner, G., Shinn, M.R., & Good, R.H. (2000). Parent tutoring in reading using literature and curriculum materials: Impact on student reading achievement. *School Psychology Review, 29*, 5–27.

Prochner, L. (2004). Early childhood education programs for Indigenous children in Canada, Australia and New Zealand: An historical review. *Australian Journal of Early Childhood, 29*(4), 7–16.

Prosser, J. (1999). The evolution of school culture research. In J. Prosser (Ed.), *School culture* (pp. 1–14). London: Paul Chapman.

Public Health Agency of Canada (2010). Aboriginal Head Start. http://www.phac-aspc.gc.ca/hp-ps/dca-dea/index-eng.php Retrieved 13 June 2012.

Radel, R., Sarrazin, P., Legrain, P., & Wild, T.C. (2010). Social contagion of motivation between teacher and student: Analyzing underlying processes. *Journal of Education and Psychology, 102*(3), 577–587. http://dx.doi.org/10.1037/a0019051

Raffo, C., Dyson, A., Gunter, H., Hall, D., Jones, L., & Kalambouka, A. (2010). *Education and poverty in affluent countries*. New York: Routledge.

Ramey, S.L., & Ramey, C.T. (2006). Early educational interventions: Principles of effective and sustained benefits from targeted early education programs. In D. Dickinson & S. Neuman (Eds.), *Handbook of early literacy research* (Vol. 2, pp. 445–459). New York: Guilford Press.

Raskauskas, J., Gregory, J., Harvey, S.T., Rifshana, F., & Evans, I.M. (2010). Bullying among primary school children in New Zealand: Relationships with prosocial behavior and classroom climate. *Educational Research, 52*(1), 1–13. http://dx.doi.org/10.1080/00131881003588097

Ratcliff, N., & Hunt, G. (2009). Building teacher-family partnerships: The role of teacher preparation programs. *Education, 129*(3), 495–505.

Raver, C.C., Gershoff, E.T., & Aber, J.L. (2007). Testing equivalence of mediating models of income, parenting, and school readiness for white, black, and Hispanic children in a national sample. *Child Development, 78*(1), 96–115. http://dx.doi.org/10.1111/j.1467-8624.2007.00987.x Medline:17328695

Raver, C.C., Jones, S.M., Li-Grining, C.P., Metzger, M., Smallwood, K., & Sardin, L. (2008). Improving preschool classroom processes: Preliminary findings from a randomized trial implemented in Head Start settings. *Early Childhood Research Quarterly, 63*(3), 253–255. Medline:18364994

Ravitch, D. (2010). *The death and life of the great American school system: How testing and choice are undermining education*. New York: Basic Books.

Rebell, M., & Wolff, J. (2009). A viable and vital agenda for NCLB reauthorization. In M. Rebell & J. Wolff (Eds.), *NCLB at a crossroads: Reexamining the federal effort to close the achievement gap* (pp. 262–278). New York: Teachers College Press.

Reeves, D.B. (2003). High performance in high poverty schools: 90/90/90 and beyond. Center for Performance Assessment. www.sjboces.org.nisl/high%20performance%... Retrieved 15 Feb. 2011.

Reimer, J., Paolitto, D.P., & Hersh, R.H. (1983). *Promoting moral growth*. New York: Longman.

Rendleman, D.R. (1971). Parens patriae: From chancery to the juvenile court. *South Carolina Law Review, 23*, 205–259.

Repeal 43 Committee. (2012). School corporal punishment. www.repeal43org/schools.html Retrieved 5 Feb. 2012.

Reyes, O., Gillock, K.L., Kobus, K., & Sanchez, B. (2000). A longitudinal examination of the transition into senior high school for adolescents from urban, low-income status, and predominantly minority backgrounds. *American Journal of Community Psychology, 28*(4), 519–544. http://dx.doi.org/10.1023/A:1005140631988 Medline:10965389

Reynolds, A.J. (2000). *Success in early intervention: The Chicago Child-Parent Centers*. Lincoln, NB: University of Nebraska Press.

Ripley, A. (2010, Jan.-Feb.). What makes a great teacher? *The Atlantic*. www.theatlantic.com Retrieved 3 June 2010.

Rist, R.C. (1970). Student social class and teacher expectations: The self-fulfilling prophecy in ghetto education. *Harvard Educational Review, 40*, 411–451.

Roeser, R.W., Galloway, M., Casey-Cannon, S., Watson, C., Keller, L., & Tan, E. (2008). Identity representations in patterns of school achievement and well-being among early adolescent girls. *Journal of Early Adolescence, 28*(1), 115–152. http://dx.doi.org/10.1177/0272431607308676

Rogers, E., Moon, A.M., Mullee, M.A., Speller, V.M., & Roderick, P.J. (1998). Developing the "health-promoting school": A national survey of healthy schools awards. *Public Health, 112*(1), 37–40. Medline:9490887

Rogers, M.A., Theule, J., Ryan, B.A., Adams, G.R., & Keating, L. (2009). Parental involvement and children's school achievement. *Canadian Journal of School Psychology, 24*(1), 34–57. http://dx.doi.org/10.1177/0829573508328445

Romano, E., Babchishin, L., Pagani, L.S., & Kohen, D. (2010). School readiness and later achievement: Replication and extension using a nationwide Canadian survey. *Developmental Psychology, 46*(5), 995–1007. http://dx.doi.org/10.1037/a0018880 Medline:20822218

Rose, E. (2010). *The promise of preschool: From Head Start to universal pre-kinder-garten*. New York: Oxford University Press.

Rose, L., & Gallup, A. (2007). The 39th annual Phi Delta Kappa/Gallup Poll of the public's attitudes towards the public schools. *Phi Delta Kappan, 89*(1), 33–45.

Rosenberg, M., Sindelar, P., & Hardman, M. (2004). Preparing highly qualified teachers for students with emotional or behavioral disorders: The impact of NCLB and IDEA. *Behavioral Disorders, 29*, 266–278.

Rothstein, R. (2010). How to fix our schools. *EPI Issue Brief 286*. www.eddigest. com Retrieved 1 Feb. 2011.

Rowe, D. (2006). Taking responsibility: School behavior policies in England, moral development and implications for citizenship education. *Journal of Moral Education, 35*(4), 519–531. http://dx.doi. org/10.1080/03057240601026865

Rowles, L., McInnis, K., & Lowe, K. (2010). A reading revolution in classrooms: Focus on Reading 3–6 [online]. *Literacy learning: The middle years, 18*(2), 23–30.

Rubie-Davies, C.M., Peterson, E., Irving, E., Widdowson, D., & Dixon, R. (2010). Expectations of achievement: Student, teacher and parent perceptions. *Research in Education, 83*, 36–53.

Runswick-Cole, K., & Hodge, N. (2009). Needs or rights? A challenge to the discourse of special education. *British Journal of Education, 36*(4), 198–203.

Rutter, M. (2006). Is Sure Start an effective preventive intervention? *Child and Adolescent Mental Health, 11*(3), 135–141. http://dx.doi. org/10.1111/j.1475-3588.2006.00402.x

Ryan, J. (2005). *Inclusive leadership*. San Francisco, CA: Jossey-Bass.

Ryan, R.M., & Deci, E.L. (2000). Self-determination theory and the facilitation of intrinsic motivation, social development, and well-being. *American Psychologist, 55*(1), 68–78. http://dx.doi.org/10.1037/0003-066X.55.1.68 Medline:11392867

Saine, N.L., Lerkkanen, M.K., Ahonen, T., Tolvanen, A., & Lyytinen, H. (2011). Computer-assisted remedial reading intervention for school beginners at risk for reading disability. *Child Development, 82*(3), 1013–1028. http://dx.doi. org/10.1111/j.1467-8624.2011.01580.x Medline:21418055

Sanders, M., & Jordan, W. (2000). Student- teacher relations and academic achievement in high school. In M. Sanders (Ed.), *Schooling students placed at risk: Research, policy and practice in the education of poor and minority adolescents* (pp. 65–82). Mahwah, NJ: Lawrence Erlbaum.

Santavirta, N., Solovieva, S., & Theorell, T. (2007). The association between job strain and emotional exhaustion in a cohort of 1,028 Finnish teachers.

British Journal of Educational Psychology, 77(1), 213–228. http://dx.doi. org/10.1348/000709905X92045 Medline:17411496

Schaps, E., Battistich, V., & Solomon, D. (2004). Community in school as key to student growth: Findings from the Child Development Project. In J. Zins, R. Weissberg, M. Wang, & H. Walberg (Eds.), *Building academic success on social and emotional learning: What does the research say?* (pp. 189–205). New York: Teachers College Press.

Schlechter, M., & Milevsky, B. (2010). Parental level of education: Associations with psychological well-being, academic achievement and reasons for pursuing higher education in adolescence. *Educational Psychology, 30*(1), 1–10. http://dx.doi.org/10.1080/01443410903326084

Schoon, I., Parsons, S., & Sacker, A. (2004). Socioeconomic adversity, educational resilience, and subsequent levels of adult adaptation. *Journal of Adolescent Research, 19*(4), 383–404. http://dx.doi. org/10.1177/0743558403258856

Schroeder, V.M., & Kelley, M.L. (2010). Family environment and parent-child relationships as related to executive functioning in children. *Early Child Development and Care, 180*(10), 1285–1298. http://dx.doi. org/10.1080/03004430902981512

Scope, A., Empson, J., & McHale, S. (2010). Executive function in children with high and low attentional skills: Correspondences between behavioural and cognitive profiles. *British Journal of Developmental Psychology, 28*(2), 293–305. http://dx.doi.org/10.1348/026151009X410371 Medline:20481389

Shonkoff, J.P., & Philips, D.A. (2000). *From neurons to neighborhoods: The science of early childhood development.* Washington, DC: National Academy Press.

Seginer, R. (2006). Parents' educational involvement: A developmental ecological perspective. *Parenting, Science and Practice, 6*(1), 1–48. http://dx.doi. org/10.1207/s15327922par0601_1

Shaywitz, S. (2003). *Overcoming dyslexia: A new and complete science-based program for reading problems at any level.* New York: Knopf.

Sheldon, S.B. (2002). Parents' social networks and beliefs as predictors of parent involvement. *Elementary School Journal, 102*(4), 301–316. http://dx.doi. org/10.1086/499705

Sheldon, S.B., & Epstein, J.L. (2005). Involvement counts: Family and community partnerships and mathematics achievement. *Journal of Educational Research, 98*(4), 196–207. http://dx.doi.org/10.3200/JOER.98.4.196-207

Sheu, Y.-S., Polcari, A., Anderson, C.M., & Teicher, M.H. (2010). Harsh corporal punishment is associated with increased T2 relaxation time in dopamine-rich regions. *NeuroImage, 53*(2), 412–419. http://dx.doi.org/10.1016/j. neuroimage.2010.06.043 Medline:20600981

Silberglitt, B., Jimerson, S.R., Burns, M.K., & Appleton, J. (2006). Does the timing of grade retention make a difference? Examining the effects of early versus later retention. *School Psychology Review, 35*(1), 134–141.

Simons-Morton, B., & Chen, R. (2009). Peer and parent influences on school engagement among early adolescents. *Youth and Society, 41*(1), 3–25. http://dx.doi.org/10.1177/0044118X09334861 Medline:19888349

Sirvana, H. (2007). Effects of teacher communication with parents on students' mathematics achievement. *American Secondary Education, 36*, 31–46.

Small, M., & Limber, S. (2002). Advocacy for children's rights. In B. Bottoms, M. Kovera, & B. McAuliff (Eds.), *Children, social science and the law* (pp. 51–75). Cambridge: Cambridge University Press. http://dx.doi.org/10.1017/CBO9780511500114.003

Spera, C. (2005). A review of the relationship among parenting practices, parenting styles, and adolescent school achievement. *Educational Psychology Review, 17*(2), 125–146. http://dx.doi.org/10.1007/s10648-005-3950-1

Steifel, L., Berne, R., Iatarola, P., & Fruchter, N. (2000). High school size: Effects on budgets and performance in New York City. *Educational Evaluation and Policy Analysis, 22*(1), 27–39.

Stewart, E.A. (2003). School, social bonds, school climate and school misbehavior: A multilevel analysis. *Justice Quarterly, 20*(3), 575–604. http://dx.doi.org/10.1080/07418820300095621

Stewart, V. (2010/2011). Raising teacher quality. *Educational Leadership, 66*(2), 16–20.

Stone, L. (1977). *The family, sex and marriage in England*. New York: Harper and Row.

Stone, M.R., Barber, B.L., & Eccles, J.S. (2008). We knew them when: Sixth grade characteristics that predict adolescent high school social identities. *Journal of Early Adolescence, 28*(2), 304–328. http://dx.doi.org/10.1177/0272431607312743

Stormont, M., Reinke, W., & Herman, K. (2011). Teachers' knowledge of evidence-based interventions and available school resources for children with emotional and behavioral problems. *Journal of Behavioral Education, 20*(2), 138–147. http://dx.doi.org/10.1007/s10864-011-9122-0

Story, V. (2007). Can France give education action zones new life? *Florida Journal of Educational Administration and Policy, 1*(1), 34–47.

Sutherland, N. (2000). *Children in English Canadian society: Framing the twentieth-century consensus*. Waterloo, ON: Wilfrid Laurier University Press.

Symonds, W.C. (2006, 16 June). Meet the Met: A school success story. www.businessweek.com Retrieved 12 March 2011.

Talwar, V., Carlson, S.M., & Lee, K. (2011). Effects of a punitive environment on children's executive functioning: A natural experiment. *Social Development*, *20*(4), 805–824, 1–20.

Tavani, C.M., & Losh, S.C. (2003). Motivation, self-confidence, and expectations as predictors of the academic performances among our high school students. *Child Study Journal*, *33*(3), 141–151.

Tazouti, Y., Malarde, A., & Michea, A. (2010). Parental beliefs concerning development and education, family educational practices and children's intellectual and academic performances. *European Journal of Psychology of Education*, *25*(1), 19–35. http://dx.doi.org/10.1007/s10212-009-0002-0

Teaching for America. (2005). Equity within reach. http://eric.ed.gov/PDFS/ED495156.pdf Retrieved 13 June 2012.

Teemant, A., Wink, J., & Tyra, S. (2011). Effects of coaching on teacher use of sociocultural instructional practices. *Teaching and Teacher Education*, *27*(4), 683–693. http://dx.doi.org/10.1016/j.tate.2010.11.006

Terry, T.M. (2010). Blocking the bullies: Has South Carolina's Safe School Climate Act made public schools safer? *Clearing House (Menasha, Wis.)*, *83*(3), 96–100. http://dx.doi.org/10.1080/00098651003655902

Theriot, M.T., Craun, S.W., & Dupper, D.R. (2010). Multilevel evaluation of factors predicting school exclusion among middle and high school students. *Children and Youth Services Review*, *32*(1), 13–19. http://dx.doi.org/10.1016/j.childyouth.2009.06.009

Thomas, D.E., Bierman, K.L., & Conduct Problems Prevention Research Group. (2008). Double jeopardy: Child and school characteristics that predict aggressive-disruptive behavior in first grade. *School Psychology Review*, *37*(4), 516–532.

Thomas, D.E., Bierman, K.L., & Conduct Problems Prevention Research Group. (2006). The impact of classroom aggression on the development of aggressive behavior problems in children. *Development and Psychopathology*, *18*(2), 471–487. http://dx.doi.org/10.1017/S0954579406060251 Medline:16600064

Thomlison, R., & Foote, C. (1987). Children and the law in Canada: The shifting balance of children's, parents' and state's rights. *Journal of Comparative Family Studies*, *18*, 231–245.

Thompson, A., & Webber, K.C. (2010). Realigning student and teacher perceptions of school rules: A behavior management strategy for students with challenging behaviors. *Children and Schools*, *32*(2), 71–79. http://dx.doi.org/10.1093/cs/32.2.71

Thrupp, M., Mansell, H., Hawksworth, L., & Harold, B. (2003). Schools can made a difference – but do teachers, heads and governors really

agree? *Oxford Review of Education, 29*(4), 471–484. http://dx.doi.
org/10.1080/0305498032000153034

Tomoda, A., Suzuki, H., Rabi, K., Sheu, Y.-S., Polcari, A., & Teicher, M.H.
(2009). Reduced prefrontal cortical gray matter volume in young adults exposed to harsh corporal punishment. *NeuroImage, 47*(Suppl 2), T66–T71.
http://dx.doi.org/10.1016/j.neuroimage.2009.03.005 Medline:19285558

Ucar, S., & Sanalan, V.A. (2011). How has reform in science teacher education programs changed preservice teachers' views about science? *Journal
of Science Education and Technology, 20*(1), 87–94. http://dx.doi.org/10.1007/
s10956-010-9236-5

Ullucci, K. (2007). The myths that blind: The role of beliefs in school change.
Journal of Educational Controversy, 2(1). http://www.wce.wwu.edu/Re-
sources/CEP/eJournal/v002n001/a006.shtml Retrieved 16 Aug. 2011.

U.N. Committee. (2005). *Committee on the Rights of the Child. General Comment
No. 7. Implementing child rights in early childhood.* (UN/CRC/C/GC/7/Rev.1).
Geneva: United Nations.

U.N. Committee. (2001). *Committee on the Rights of the Child. General Comment
No.1. The aims of education.* (UN/CRC/GC/2001/1). Geneva: United Nations.

UNESCO Global Monitoring Team. (2003). *Gender and education for all: The leap
to equality, Summary Report.* Paris: UNESCO.

UNICEF. (2010). *The children left behind: A league table of inequality in child well-
being in the world's rich countries. Innocenti Report Card 9.* Florence: UNICEF
Innocenti Research Centre.

UNICEF. (2008). *The child care transition: A league table of early childhood education and care in economically advanced countries. Innocenti Report Card 8.* Florence: UNICEF Innocenti Research Centre.

UNICEF. (2007). *Child poverty in perspective: An overview of child well-being in
rich countries. Innocenti Report Card 7.* Florence: UNICEF Innocenti Research
Centre.

United Nations. (2009). *State of the world's Indigenous peoples.* New York: United
Nations.

United Nations Development Program. (2006). *Human development report.* New
York: Oxford University Press.

U.S. Department of Health and Human Services (2010). Early Head Start Research and Evaluation Project 1996-Current. http://www.acf.hhs.gov/pro-
grams/opre/ehs/ehs_resrch/index.html Retrieved 12 Nov. 2010.

Van Bueren, G. (1992). *The international law on the rights of the child.* Dordrecht:
Martinus Nijhoff.

Vandell, D. (2004). Early child care: The known and unknown. *Merrill-Palmer
Quarterly, 50*(3), 387–414. http://dx.doi.org/10.1353/mpq.2004.0027

Vandell, D.L., Belsky, J., Burchinal, M., Steinberg, L., Vandergrift, N., & NICHD Early Child Care Research Network. (2010). Do effects of early child care extend to age 15 years? Results from the NICHD study of early child care and youth development. *Child Development, 81*(3), 737–756. http://dx.doi.org/10.1111/j.1467-8624.2010.01431.x Medline:20573102

Van Houtte, M. (2005). Climate or culture? A plea for conceptual clarity in school effectiveness research. *School Effectiveness and School Improvement, 16*(1), 71–89. http://dx.doi.org/10.1080/09243450500113977

Vaughan, T., Harris, J., & Caldwell, B. (2011). *Bridging the gap in school achievement through the arts.* Abbotsford, AU: The Song Room.

Veland, J., Midthassel, U.V., & Idsoe, T. (2009). Perceived socioeconomic status and social inclusion in school: Interactions of disadvantages. *Scandinavian Journal of Educational Research, 53*(6), 515–531. http://dx.doi.org/10.1080/00313830903301994

Verhellen, E. (1994). *Convention on the Rights of the Child.* Kessel-Lo, Belgium: Garant.

Verhellen, E. (1993). Children's rights and education. *School Psychology International, 14*(3), 199–208. http://dx.doi.org/10.1177/0143034393143002

Wadsworth, M.E., Raviv, T., Reinhard, C., Wolff, B., Santiago, C.D.C., & Einhorn, L. (2008). An indirect effects model of the association between poverty and child functioning: The role of children's poverty-related stress. *Journal of Loss and Trauma, 13*(2–3), 156–185. http://dx.doi.org/10.1080/15325020701742185

Wagner, T. (2008). *The global achievement gap.* New York: Basic Books.

Walker, C.O., & Greene, B.A. (2009). The relations between student motivational beliefs and cognitive engagement in school. *Journal of Educational Research, 102*(6), 463–472. http://dx.doi.org/10.3200/JOER.102.6.463-472

Wallberg, P., & Kahn, M. (2011). The Rights Project: How rights education transformed a classroom. *Canadian Children, 36*(1), 31–35.

Wang, M., Selman, R.L., Dishion, T.J., & Stormshak, E.A. (2010). A Tobit regression analysis of the covariation between middle students' perceived school climate and behavioral problems. *Journal of Research on Adolescence, 20*(2), 274–286. http://dx.doi.org/10.1111/j.1532-7795.2010.00648.x Medline:20535244

Waters, T., Marzano, R., & McNulty, B. (2004). Developing a science of educational leadership. *ERS Spectrum, 22*(1), 4–13.

Webster-Stratton, C., Jamila Reid, M., & Stoolmiller, M. (2008). Preventing conduct problems and improving school readiness: Evaluation of the Incredible Years Teacher and Child Training Programs in high-risk schools. *Journal of Child Psychology and Psychiatry, and Allied Disciplines, 49*(5), 471–488. http://dx.doi.org/10.1111/j.1469-7610.2007.01861.x Medline:18221346

Wells, A. (2009). Our children's burden: A history of federal education policies that ask (now require) our public schools to solve societal inequality. In M. Rebell & J. Wolff (Eds.), *NCLB at a crossroads: Reexamining the federal effort to close the achievement gap* (pp. 1–42). New York: Teachers College Press.

Welsh, J.A., Nix, R.L., Blair, C., Bierman, K.L., & Nelson, K.E. (2010). The development of cognitive skills and gains in academic school readiness for children from low-income families. *Journal of Educational Psychology, 102*(1), 43–53. http://dx.doi.org/10.1037/a0016738 Medline:20411025

Wien, C.A. (Ed.). (2008). *Emergent curriculum in the primary classroom: Interpreting the Reggio Emilia approach in schools.* New York: Teachers College Press.

Wilkinson, R., & Pickett, K. (2010). *The spirit level: Why equality is better for everyone.* London: Penguin.

Willms, J.D. (2010). Social composition and contextual effects on student outcomes. *Teachers College Record, 112*(4), 1008–1037.

Willms, J.D. (2006). *Learning divides: Ten policy questions about the performance and equity of schools and schooling systems.* Montreal: UNESCO Institute for Statistics.

Witzel, B.S., Riccomini, P.S., & Schneider, E. (2008). Implementing CRA with secondary students with learning disabilities in mathematics. *Intervention in School and Clinic, 43*(5), 270–276. http://dx.doi.org/10.1177/1053451208314734

Wolf, J. (1992). The concept of the "best interest" in terms of the UN Convention on the Rights of the child. In M. Freeman & P. Veerman (Eds.), *The ideologies of children's rights* (pp. 125–133). Dordrecht: Martinus Nijhoff.

Woodhouse, B. (2006). The changing status of the child. In J. Todres, M. Wojcik, & C. Revaz (Eds.), *The U.N. Convention on the Rights of the Child: An analysis of treaty provisions and implications of U.S. ratification* (pp. 51–64). Ardsley, NY: Transnational Publishers. http://dx.doi.org/10.1163/ej.9781571053633.i-376.24

Woolley, M.E., & Bowen, G.L. (2007). In the context of risk: Supportive adults and the school engagement of middle school students. *Family Relations, 56*(1), 92–104. http://dx.doi.org/10.1111/j.1741-3729.2007.00442.x

Woolley, M.E., Grogan- Kaylor, A., Gilster, M., Karb, R.A., Gant, L., Reischl, T.M., & Alaimo, K. (2008). Neighborhood social capital, poor physical conditions, and school achievement. *Children and Schools, 30*(3), 133–145. http://dx.doi.org/10.1093/cs/30.3.133

Wu, J.Y., Hughes, J.N., & Kwok, O.M. (2010). Teacher-student relationship quality type in elementary grades: Effects on trajectories for achievement and engagement. *Journal of School Psychology, 48*(5), 357–387. http://dx.doi.org/10.1016/j.jsp.2010.06.004 Medline:20728688

Yeung, W.J., Linver, M.R., & Brooks-Gunn, J. (2002). How money matters for young children's development: Parental investment and family processes. *Child Development, 73*(6), 1861–1879. http://dx.doi.org/10.1111/1467-8624.t01-1-00511 Medline:12487499

Ylimaki, R., Jacobson, S., & Drysdale, L. (2007). Making a difference in challenging high-poverty schools: Successful principals in the USA, England, and Australia. *School Effectiveness and School Improvement, 18*(4), 361–381. http://dx.doi.org/10.1080/09243450701712486

Zimmer, R., Hamilton, L., & Christina, R. (2010). After-school tutoring in the context of No Child Left behind: Effectiveness of two programs in the Pittsburgh public schools. *Economics of Education Review, 29*(1), 18–28. http://dx.doi.org/10.1016/j.econedurev.2009.02.005

Zins, J., Bloodworth, M., Weissberg, R., & Walberg, H. (2004). The scientific base linking social and emotional learning to school success. In J. Zins, R. Weissberg, M. Wang, & H. Walberg (Eds.), *Building academic success on social and emotional learning: What does the research say?* (pp. 3–22). New York: Teachers College Press. http://dx.doi.org/10.1080/10474410701413145

Zullig, K., Huebner, E.S., & Patton, J.M. (2011). Relationships among school climate domains and school satisfaction. *Psychology in the Schools, 48*(2), 133–145. http://dx.doi.org/10.1002/pits.20532

Index